Lecture Notes in Artificial Intelligence 1409

Subseries of Lecture Notes in Comput
Edited by J. G. Carbonell and J. Siekm

Lecture Notes in Computer Science
Edited by G. Goos, J. Hartmanis and J. van Leeuwen

Springer
Berlin
Heidelberg
New York
Barcelona
Budapest
Hong Kong
London
Milan
Paris
Santa Clara
Singapore
Tokyo

Torsten Schaub

The Automation of Reasoning with Incomplete Information

From Semantic Foundations to Efficient Computation

 Springer

Series Editors

Jaime G. Carbonell, Carnegie Mellon University Pittsburgh, PA, USA
Jörg Siekmann, University of Saarland, Saarbrücken, Germany

Author

Torsten Schaub
Universität Potsdam, Institut für Informatik
Postfach 60 15 53, D-14415 Potsdam, Germany
E-mail: torsten@cs.uni-potsdam.de

Cataloging-in-Publication Data applied for

Die Deutsche Bibliothek - CIP-Einheitsaufnahme

Schaub, Torsten:
The automation of reasoning with incomplete information : from
semantic foundations to efficient computation / Torsten Schaub. -
Berlin ; Heidelberg ; New York ; Barcelona ; Budapest ; Hong Kong ;
London ; Milan ; Paris ; Santa Clara ; Singapore ; Tokyo : Springer,
1998
  (Lecture notes in computer science ; Vol. 1409 : Lecture notes in
  artificial intelligence)
  ISBN 3-540-64515-2

CR Subject Classification (1991): I.2.3, I.2, F.4.1

ISBN 3-540-64515-2 Springer-Verlag Berlin Heidelberg New York

Typesetting: Camera ready by author
SPIN 10639039   06/3142 – 5 4 3 2 1 0   Printed on acid-free paper

Preface

*"Almost no plan is guaranteed, no utterance utterly un-
ambiguous, no rule without exception — there's no such
thing as a sure thing."*   *David W. Etherington, 1986*

Reasoning with incomplete information constitutes a major challenge for any intelligent system. In fact, we expect from such systems that they are not paralyzed
by missing information but rather arrive at plausible results by bridging the gaps in
the available information. There are moreover situations in which it is necessary to
act despite incomplete information. In a word, intelligent systems have to provide
means for reasoning in the absence of total information. The automation of this form
of reasoning is the subject of this book.

A versatile way of reasoning in the absence of information is to reason *by default*. In this manner, we overcome a lack of information by making default assumptions about a situation at hand. Default reasoning puts faith in standard situations
that are free from strangeness and unexpectedness; it relies on general rules expressing anticipated states of affairs. A formalization of this form of reasoning is
furnished by *default logic* — a logical system developed by Raymond Reiter in
[Rei80].

This book aims at providing formal and practical means for automating reasoning with incomplete information by starting from the approach taken by default
logic. For this endeavor, we span a bridge between formal semantics, over logical
systems for default reasoning, to efficient implementations.

Acknowledgments

The act of expressing gratitude constitutes a privilege and a pleasure for everybody finishing a long piece of work. It is then a great source of satisfaction to lean back and think about all the little victories and defeats one was able to share with other people. However, such an account becomes longer and longer over the years and it bears the danger of overlooking many people that merit an acknowledgment but are not explicitly honored. Thanks to all of you! Nonetheless, I would like to express particular gratitude to those that are on the top of my mind:

First of all, I would like to thank my family and my friends. They never appear on the acknowledgments of a research paper but nonetheless bear many resulting moods. Thank you, Susanne and Larissa. You make all this worthwhile! A big hug is also due to my parents and grandparents who were always there when I needed them and who provided me with more than I deserved. I miss them all the more these days.

I am indebted to Philippe Besnard, Wolfgang Bibel, James Delgrande, and Josef Schneeberger, who supported me with advice, friendship, and encouragement. They have all enriched my scientific and personal career in a very lasting way: I would like to thank Philippe for the patience he had when clarifying my early (and even later) ideas, for his hospitality, and the fun we had, have, and will have! Philippe is not only an excellent researcher, he is also excellent in teaching how to research. I am indebted to Wolfgang Bibel for his encouragement, his constant support, and the time he spent on improving the presentation of many manuscripts. I would like to thank Jim for his support and hospitality, for all the intuitions he shared with me, his patience in office-sharing and correcting my English, and finally all the hugs he allowed me to hand over the ocean. I would like to thank Josef for his friendship and his lasting support from the very early days. Without them, I would be someone else somewhere else.

I gratefully acknowledge the significant contributions of all people with whom I had the pleasure of working together, in particular the co-authors of my research papers, namely Antje Beringer, Philippe Besnard, Wolfgang Bibel, Gerd Brewka, Stefan Brüning, James Delgrande, Christine Froidevaux, Steffen Hölldobler, Thomas Linke, Ken Jackson, Gerd Neugebauer, Pascal Nicolas, Aaron Rothschild, and Michael Thielscher. Thanks for your time, your ideas, and your inspiration!

In fact, this monograph describes the outcome of a research program that I have been able to pursue since 1990. As a matter of fact, a salient part of this book stems from material taken from my dissertation thesis [Sch92a] carried out at the Technical University of Darmstadt, Germany, and my habilitation thesis [Sch95a] accomplished at IRISA, Rennes, France. Therefore, I would like to take this opportunity to express my great appreciation to the members of the my dissertation committee: Peter Kammerer, Wolfgang Bibel, Alejandro Buchmann, James Delgrande, José Encarnação, and Rüdiger Reischuk, and to those of my habilitation committee: Jean-Pierre Banâtre, Wolfgang Bibel, Patrice Enjalbert, Christine Froidevaux, Philippe Besnard, Jean-Paul Delahaye, and Jean-Claude Raoult. I thank all of you for sharing with me and supporting me on the occasion of these decisive events of my scientific career!

I would like to thank all my friends within the Intellectics group at Darmstadt for many fruitful and not so fruitful discussions, for many Hütli sessions and lots of fun. Among them, a big hug goes to Maria, who always lent a helping hand. Thanks for the great time, Gene, Matthias, Sepp, Stebr, and, of course, Uwe! Thank you Steffen for kicking me at the right time. My Darmstadt days are inseparably connected with the TASSO project, providing a great research environment that was particularly stimulating due to many fruitful discussions, in particular those on nonmonotonic reasoning with Gerd Brewka and Ulrich Junker. In fact, it was Gerd who introduced me to many problems I have been working on in the last few years.

In the same way, I would like to express my warmest thanks to my friends in the REPCO group at IRISA, Rennes, who moreover had to endure my (early) French along with many "petits cafés dans des grandes tasses". M'enfin! Merci pour votre aide, Evelyne, MaO, Pascale, René, ſylvie et Σric!

Last, but not least at all, I'm indebted to my friends and colleagues at the University of Angers, in particular, the members of my group for their constant support and encouragement! Merci Beatrice, Gilles et Pascal de m'avoir toujours débroullié.

Saint Barthélémy d'Anjou, Spring 1996   Torsten Schaub

This research was partially supported by the German Federal Ministry for Research and Technology within project TASSO under grant number ITW 8900 C2 and by the Commission of the European Communities within the program "Human Capital and Mobility" under grant number ERB4001GT922433.

The author moved to the University of Potsdam during the printing phase of this monograph.

Table of Contents

1. Introduction

Since Gutenberg's epochal invention of the art of printing, we have seen a tremendous increase of communication and reception of information. Another such change of magnitude was the proliferation of electronic media, starting with radios, over television up to today's world-wide electronic information highways. As a result, each of us is faced with an overwhelming amount of information that becomes more complex every day. However, despite this enormity of information, it is still extremely difficult to access the information one wants. How can we cope with this problem?

Among the electronic devices that caused the second change of magnitude of information flow, an exposed position is clearly taken by *computer systems*. So, on the one hand, computers contribute to the progressive growth of information in size, amount, and intensity. On the other hand, however, computer systems are already one of the most important instruments for assisting human beings in information processing. What we thus need to solve our problem are intelligent computer systems that do not merely produce and multiply information but rather help us to manage the increasingly complex proliferation of information. Among other qualities, such a system needs strong capacities for reasoning. In addition, it has to overcome gaps in the available information without being paralyzed by missing information. In a word, such systems have to provide means for reasoning in the absence of complete information. The automation of this form of reasoning is the objection of this treatise.

For making reasoners out of computers, we need formal means that allow for expressing reasoning as bit manipulations. In the field of artificial intelligence, this problem is addressed on a symbolic level by modeling reasoning in terms of symbol manipulations. The corresponding mechanisms are in turn executable by bit manipulations. Hence, the problem rests on two issues: An adequate symbolic representation of information and a suitable formalization of corresponding reasoning capacities in terms of symbol manipulations. In other words, such a codification has to provide symbolic means for *knowledge representation and reasoning*.

A prime candidate for solving this fundamental problem is given by *formal logic*. The benefits of a logical approach to our problem in particular and computer science in general are manifold: The use of logic provides a formal language with a well-defined syntax along with a syntactical relation describing formal consequences.[1] This comes with a well-defined semantics that ascribes meaning to syntactic entities. Hence, any—given or derived—logical expression can be evaluated in terms of the underlying semantics. This clearly extends to entire logical formalizations which can thus be analyzed and subsequently justified or invalidated by semantical means. All this renders formal logic more than a mere system for symbol manipulations.

An exposed position among formal logics is clearly taken by first-order predicate logic (see [End72, Gal86]). Predicate logic, however, was mainly conceived to formalize mathematical reasoning. Hence, one should not expect it to address all other facets of reasoning (for instance, dealing with resource-oriented or even commonsense reasoning) in the same fully satisfactory manner. This problematic has given rise to so-called *non-classical logics*, like linear logic [Gir87] or modal logics [Bow79]. Often, as in the case of many modal logics, the resulting logical systems still comprise in one way or another classical predicate logic.

Also, it turns out that mere predicate logic cannot deal with incomplete information in an adequate way. This observation has motivated the introduction of so-called *nonmonotonic logics* in order to formalize reasoning in the absence of information (see [Bob80]). These systems are nonmonotonic in the sense that increasing the amount of available information may lead to an invalidation and so a loss of formerly drawn conclusions. This is in contrast to classical logical approaches where the addition of further information can never invalidate previous conclusions.

In every-day life, we frequently bridge a lack of information by making default assumptions or simply by *default reasoning*. This form of reasoning allows for inferences which turn out to be correct apart from a few exceptional cases. Hence, a conclusion may have to be withdrawn in the case of a later discovery of such an exceptional case. These inferences are often expressed as rules of thumb or *default rules*, that is, general rules admitting unforeseeable exceptions. In fact, almost all nonmonotonic logics aim at providing a formal framework that extends predicate logic by means for representing and reasoning with such default rules. In this way, they retain many desirable features of predicate logic while reasoning from incomplete information.

The standard example for default reasoning in the field of artificial intelligence deals with flying birds. Consider the statement *"birds fly"*. In fact, this sentence is not synonymous to *"all birds fly"* since it bears numerous exceptions. For example, penguins and ostriches do not fly; the same applies to newborn birds. It may be too that a bird simply does not fly, with no known attendant reason. Nevertheless, we would like to conclude that a particular bird, say Tweety, flies provided that there is no evidence to the contrary. In this way, we treat Tweety as being *typical* or *normal*. Accordingly, we interpret the statement *"birds fly"* as *"typical birds fly"* or *"normal birds fly"*. In default reasoning, this is formalized as a rule of the form *"if x is a bird, then assume by default that x flies"*. Note that this default rule comprises the reasoning pattern *"in the absence of information to the contrary, assume"*, which

---

[1] The combination of a logical language with a syntactical relation describing formal consequences is also called a *calculus*.

is embodied by *"assume by default"*. Hence, if we subsequently learn information to the contrary, for instance that Tweety is a penguin, we have to retract our former conclusion and conclude instead that Tweety cannot fly. This renders default reasoning nonmonotonic in the sense described above. Also, it shows us that monotonic logics, like predicate logic, cannot account for this form of reasoning.[2] (We discuss a formalization of this example in Chapter 2.)

Indeed, *default logic* was conceived by Raymond Reiter in [Rei80] as a formal account of reasoning in the absence of complete information. It has since proved to be one of the most widely-used formalizations of default reasoning. This is, among other reasons, due to its natural way to incorporate default reasoning into the framework of standard logic. Default logic addresses the problem of incomplete information by supplementing classical first-order logic with domain-dependent rules that can be triggered by the presence as well as the absence of certain items of information.

Consider for instance the phrase:[3]

"Someone is a suspect if he has a motive and no alibi".

Clearly, an investigator has to prove a person's motive in order to hold the person in suspicion, but is he also obliged[4] to furnish a proof assuring that the person has no alibi? This is arguably not a very practicable approach, because such a proof may not be obtainable at the time being. In such a case, we may have no information at all whether the person has an alibi or not. On the other hand, it is often advisable to delineate the group of suspects in order to move the investigation ahead. The usual proceeding is to "weaken" the necessity of proving the non-existence of an alibi by supposing that the person has no alibi unless there is evidence to the contrary. In this way, the investigation does not get stuck despite the absence of complete information about the person's alibi. That is, the conclusion that the person is a suspect is drawable on the basis of given and absent information, namely a proven motive and an unprovable alibi.

This type of reasoning is formalized in default logic by extending standard logic with nonstandard inference rules. The preceding example could be formalized by means of the "default rule" (see Chapter 2 for a formal introduction)

$$\frac{motive(x) \ : \ \neg alibi(x)}{suspect(x)}. \tag{1.1}$$

This inference rule may be read as *"If we can prove motive(x) and it can be consistently assumed that ¬alibi(x) holds, then we can infer suspect(x) for some individual x."*[5] Now, given an individual, say *Philippe*, for which we can prove *motive(Philippe)* while there is no proof for *alibi(Philippe)*, we can infer the

---

[2] A more detailed discussion showing that predicate logic is inadequate for formalizing reasoning in the absence of information can be found in [Min75, Rei87a, Bes89].

[3] This example is derived from the one discussed in [Eth88].

[4] This question is of course more delicate when talking about guiltiness.

[5] The variable x is taken to range over all such individuals (see Chapter 2 for details).

proposition $suspect(Philippe)$ by means of Rule (1.1). Observe that the treatment of $\neg alibi(Philippe)$ corresponds to the paradigm of *"negation as failure to prove"*.

In fact, if we subsequently learn that *Philippe* has indeed an alibi, that is, if we can actually derive that $alibi(Philippe)$ holds, then we have to retract our former conclusion $suspect(Philippe)$ and conclude nothing about him being a suspect. This is what renders default logic nonmonotonic.

Since its introduction, default logic has proven to be extremely valuable for formalizing default reasoning in various domains. This great expressiveness is one of the reasons why we have chosen default logic as our formal starting point. In fact, among others, default logic has been applied to

– diagnosis [PGA87, Rei87b],
– natural language [Per87, Mer88],
– inheritance networks and terminological logics [ER83, Fro90, BH92],
– mathematical domains [MNR90],
– rule-based systems [Fro92],
– configuration and design [JP92, BS95b],
– database systems [CEG94],
– formal disputation theory [Bre94b],
– reasoning about action [Tur97],
– information retrieval [Hun95, Hun96] and
– paraconsistent reasoning [BS96a].

Moreover, default logic provides semantics for

– truth maintenance systems [Bre91c] and
– diverse forms of logic programming [BF91, GL90].

As a matter of fact, this treatise aims at providing means for automating reasoning in the absence of information (mainly) on the basis of default logic. For this endeavor, we furnish several analytic and synthetic methods along with alternative approaches to default logic; this ranges from semantic foundations to practical implementations of systems for processing incomplete information.

1.1 The plan of the book

The overall objection of this book is the automation of reasoning with incomplete information. For this undertaking, we have chosen default logic as our formal point of departure. **Chapter 2** lays the basic foundations for the overall endeavor; it introduces Reiter's original approach to default logic and discusses its most important properties and difficulties.

Chapter 3 introduces an alternative approach to default logic which is further developed in subsequent chapters. The resulting system, called constrained default logic, addresses situations not dealt with in the original system by formalizing differing intuitions of default reasoning. As a result, it rectifies various difficulties in the original system and subsequent variants.

Chapter 4 contains an extensive study of the relationships between the various derivatives of default logic and discusses their differences wrt some basic properties, while benefiting from constrained default logic as an instrument for comparing the diverse approaches. In fact, default logic's evolution has resulted in diverse variants enjoying many interesting properties. This has sometimes led to default logics that are difficult to compare due to different formal characterizations—sometimes even dealing with different objects of discourse.

Chapter 5 furnishes a context-based framework for default logics. The resulting system generalizes existing variants of default logic and provides a unified framework for default logics. In fact, it allows for embedding existing variants of default logic along with more traditional approaches like the closed world assumption. A key advantage of this approach is that it provides a syntactical instrument for comparing existing default logics in a unified setting. In particular, the approach reveals that existing default logics mainly differ in the way they deal with an explicit or implicit underlying context.

Chapter 6 describes a general semantical framework for default logics. This semantics allows for comparing existing default logics in a simple but very substantial and meaningful manner. No other semantics for any default logic offers this generality. Moreover, the approach remedies several difficulties encountered in former proposals aiming at individual default logics.

Chapter 7 describes an approach addressing the failure of default logics to prefer more specific default rules over less specific conflicting default rules. This is accomplished by means of a two-phase system: First, we determine specificity information by appeal to techniques found in conditional logics. Then, we enrich the original default theory with its intrinsic specificity information and obtain a default theory in which specificity is appropriately handled.

Chapter 8 describes an approach addressing the failure of default logics to account for lemma handling. The idea is to change the status of a default conclusion whenever it is added to a world-description by turning it into a new default rule. This default rule contains information about the default proof of the original conclusion and so tells us when this proof valid or not.

Chapter 9 presents a new methodology to query-answering in default logics. The basic idea is to treat default rules as classical implications along with some qualifying conditions restricting the use of such rules while query-answering. We accomplish this by taking advantage of the conception of structure-oriented theorem proving provided by Bibel's connection method [Bib87]. The structure-sensitive nature of the connection method allows for an elegant characterization of proofs in default logic. In turn, we give various refinements of the basic approach that lead to conceptionally different algorithms and implementations.

Chapter 10 attains the ultimate goal of this book: By building on the approach to query-answering introduced in the previous chapter, we show how Prolog technology can be used for efficient implementation of query answering in default logics. The idea is to translate a default theory along with query into a Prolog program and a Prolog query such that the original query belongs to an extension of the default theory iff the Prolog query is derivable from the Prolog program.

1.2 The book in context

The study of diverse forms of *reasoning* has become one of the major research topics in the field of artificial intelligence. This stems from one of the fundamental principles in artificial intelligence saying that intelligent systems must be capable of drawing conclusions about the domain they deal with. In fact, there is a large spectrum in which the faculty of reason can be used to draw conclusions: The classical form of reasoning is certainly *deductive reasoning*, which has led to the conception of mathematical logic long before the raise of artificial intelligence. The resulting formal systems like first-order logic are symbolic systems in which representation and reasoning are accomplished by pure symbolic means.

For a complement, let us briefly consider two other important forms of reasoning that are orthogonal to deductive reasoning due to their appeal to numerical means: *probabilistic reasoning* [Nil86, Pea88] and *fuzzy reasoning* [Zad75, Zad83]. Both approaches use in general numerical techniques for reasoning from items of information, which are themselves usually associated with some numerical information. In the case of probabilistic reasoning the numerical information often represents statistical information expressed by means of probabilities. Reasoning is then usually concerned with propagation and combination of probabilities towards inferred information. Briefly, probabilistic reasoning provides means for dealing with uncertain information. In fuzzy reasoning the numerical information is meant to express vague concepts like "small" and "tall". For this purpose, items of information consist sometimes even of numerical functions. On the whole, fuzzy reasoning is thus concerned with inferences involving vague concepts. There are many other essential reasoning modes, like *approximate, epistemic, inductive, limited ... , etc. reasoning*, whose discussion would lead us far beyond the scope of this treatise.

Our focus, namely *nonmonotonic reasoning*[6], is a particular form of plausible reasoning that relies on extensions and modifications to deductive reasoning. Hence, it refrains from using numerical techniques and rather aims at providing pure symbolic systems. The objective of nonmonotonic reasoning is to provide formal systems for drawing plausible (but not necessarily infallible) conclusions. Any such conclusion has a tentative nature; it is subject to revision and may have to be withdrawn in the light of new information. In this way, the addition of premises may decrease the set of conclusions. This is why this kind of reasoning is referred to as being nonmonotonic.

On the one hand, nonmonotonic reasoning constitutes an important facet of commonsense reasoning. We often expect things to happen in a usual way. So, if we are asked whether something is going to happen, we normally apply general rules for prediction. Usually, these rules allow for exceptions. Hence, if we get to know

---

[6] This term was originally proposed by Minsky in [Min75].

more specific information, a former conclusion has sometimes to be withdrawn. For instance, it happens that we expect something to hold in a certain situation. However, we might have to retract this expectation if we find out that things happened under abnormal circumstances. This renders our reasoning nonmonotonic. Such a situation is described in the introductory section in our flying birds as well as our criminological example.

On the other hand, nonmonotonic reasoning techniques are also encountered in traditional areas of computer science. For instance, in database theory, one usually refrains from explicitly representing negative information and rather deals with this information implicitly. This is accomplished by appeal to the so-called *closed world assumption* [Rei78], which is a particular form of nonmonotonic reasoning. The closed world assumption formalizes the hypothesis that all relevant information has been represented and that each missing proposition is false. This approach is an extremely versatile approach to nonmonotonic reasoning in many restricted settings, such as standard databases or deductive Horn-databases (cf. [Rei78]); it also constitutes a restricted fragment of default logic (see [Rei80] along with Chapter 5). A procedural variant of the closed world assumption and thus another pattern of nonmonotonic reasoning is found in the programming language Prolog in form of the *negation as failure* [Cla78] operator not. The *negation as failure rule* in Prolog allows for inferring $not(A)$, if A is not finitely provable from the program at hand. This form of nonmonotonic reasoning was first studied by [Cla78] and is detailed in [Llo87]. In general, logic programming can be seen as a restricted form of default logic [BF91, GL90]. Another nonmonotonic operator, namely THNOT, is found in the programming languages PLANNER [Hew72] and Micro-PLANNER [SWC71]. A further area of computer science integrating nonmonotonic reasoning techniques concerns systems involving property inheritance over exceptional subclasses. This variety includes systems modeling terminological or frame-based systems such as NETL [Fah79]. In these systems one has to provide intrinsic means to resolve conflicts, as given in our birds example, where penguins constitute an exception to the class of birds wrt the property of flying. Other applications of nonmonotonic reasoning were mentioned in the context of default logic on Page 4.

An early collection of work in the field of nonmonotonic reasoning is given in [Bob80]. This special issue of the *"Journal of Artificial Intelligence"* contains three major approaches to nonmonotonic reasoning: *circumscription* [McC80], *default logic* [Rei80], and a *nonmonotonic logic* [MD80]. These classical approaches along with their succeeding variants are still omnipresent and constitute nowadays the most widely-used formalisms of nonmonotonic reasoning. All of these approaches extend or modify classical first-order logic in a certain way.

Circumscription was introduced by John McCarthy in [McC80, McC86] as an approach to formalizing diverse nonmonotonic aspects of commonsense reasoning. This is accomplished by "logical minimization". That is, a formula α follows from a theory W by circumscription, if α is true in all models of W that are minimal in a certain sense. For this purpose, one has to add either a second-order axiom or a possibly infinite set of first-order sentences (expressed as a schema) to the world-description W. Circumscription was developed further mainly by Vladimir Lifschitz [Lif84, Lif85a, Lif85b, Lif86, Lif87, Lif89]. The development of circumscription along with its relation to default logic is summarized in [Eth86]. Lifschitz shows that circumscription is strictly subsumed by a variant of default logic proposed in [Lif90]. Implementation issues of this approach are addressed in [GL88, Gin89, IH89].

Circumscription has moreover initiated the development of a variety of semantical approaches to nonmonotonic reasoning, which are usually referred to as *preferential models* approaches. These systems impose a preference relation on the models of a given world-description and then distinguish certain minimal models, which are regarded as the preferred models of the given theory. This general approach was initiated by [BS85, Sho86] and was pursued further, among others, in [BS88, KLM90]. The relationship between the various forms of circumscription and preferential models approaches have been studied in [MR94].

Nonmonotonic logic was proposed by McDermott and Doyle in [MD80]. In this approach, a standard first-order language is augmented with a unary modal operator M, where a formula Mα is to be read as "α is consistent". In turned out that the notion of consistency used in [MD80] is too weak and thus leads to a couple of technical problems. These problems have been addressed in two ways: First, the system has been strengthened by substituting first-order logic by certain modal logics. This approach is pursued in [McD82] and [MST91]. The latter gives moreover a systematic analysis of the various obtainable systems along with their properties. Second, the approach of [MD80] has been turned into logics for knowledge and belief. This has in particular led to *autoepistemic logic* [Moo85], which is nowadays the most prominent descendant of nonmonotonic logic. Autoepistemic logic itself has produced a number of variants, among them [Kon88a, Shv90]. Other modal approaches to nonmonotonic reasoning can be found in [Tru91b, SS93]. Implementation issues of autoepistemic logic are addressed in [Nie88, JK90, Nie94]. This line of research along with its relation to default logic is discussed in detail in [MT93a]. The relationship between autoepistemic and default logic was first investigated in [Kon88b] and then pursued further in [MT89, Tru91b, Tru91a]. Notably, [Tru91a] argues that default logic is superior to autoepistemic logic in formalizing logic programs with negation.

Since the publication of the aforementioned three formalisms, other promising research avenues in nonmonotonic reasoning have come up. First, a subsystem of default logic, given by so-called *prerequisite-free normal default theories*, has been isolated and turned into a practically appealing system for default reasoning [Poo88]. This has resulted in the implementation of the Theorist system [PGA87, Poo91]. A formal analysis of the underlying formal system can be found in [Poo88, Dix92, Thi93]. A prioritized version of this approach is described in [Bre89b]. Second, logics of knowledge and belief have emerged from autoepistemic logic. In these approaches the phenomena of nonmonotonicity is addressed in terms of self-knowledge. The idea is that certain assumptions are based on a lack of other beliefs. This has led to appealing approaches, among which we find the "only knowing" approach of Levesque [Lev90] and Lifschitz' approach in [Lif91] to "minimal belief and negation as failure" Third, there is a variety of approaches to nonmonotonic reasoning based on conditional logics. This idea is due to [Del87, Del88] and has meanwhile been taken up by many other researchers. Apart from Delgrande's system N [Del87], there is Pearl's System $\mathbf{Z}$ [Pea90] (see Chapter 7) inducing 0- and 1-entailment, Boutilier's CO^* [Bou91], and *rational closure* by [KLM90]. Even though these systems are based on distinct semantic intuitions, they are however closely related: [GP90] has shown that 1-entailment is equivalent to rational closure; [Bou91] has shown that CO^* is equivalent to 1-entailment and that N is equivalent to the more basic notion of 0-entailment, proposed in [Pea89] as a "conservative core" for conditional default reasoning. Gaining in popularity is an attempt to understand nonmonotonic reasoning in terms of structural properties of nonmonotonic consequence relations. This line of research has been initiated in [Gab85] and pursued by many other others like [Bes88, Mak89, KLM90]. We take up these inquiries in Section 2.1, where we discuss the structural properties of default logic's consequence relations. For a more detailed introduction to the diverse formal systems to nonmonotonic reasoning, we have to refer the reader to the following surveys: [Bre89a, Som90, Łuk90, BHS93].

As regards default logic, in fact, Reiter's original paper [Rei80], which is reprinted in [Gin87], remains one of the most comprehensive descriptions of the original approach. A complete treatment of classical default logic can be found in [Eth88, Bes89, Bre91c, MT93a]. This literature describes also alternative approaches to default reasoning, like autoepistemic logic [Moo85] and circumscription [McC80], and their relationship to default logic. An excellent overview of approaches for nonmonotonic reasoning is given in [Rei87a].

1.3 Preliminaries

We assume the reader to be familiar with the basic concepts of first-order logic (cf. [End72, Bib87]) as well as some acquaintance with modal logics (cf. [Bow79, Che80]). We shall be dealing with a standard first-order language $\mathcal{L}$.[7] That is, $\mathcal{L}$ is the set of all first-order formulas which can be formed using an alphabet consisting of countably many variables $x, y, z, \ldots$; countably many function symbols $a, b, c, \ldots, f, g, h, \ldots$; countably many predicate symbols $P, Q, \ldots$; the usual punctuation signs, the symbols $\top$ (for verum) and $\bot$ (for falsum), and the standard logical connectives $\neg$ (for negation), $\wedge$ (for conjunction), $\vee$ (for disjunction), $\rightarrow$ (for implication), $\leftrightarrow$ (for equivalence), and quantifiers $\forall$ (for universal quantification) and $\exists$ (for existential quantification). Letters $\mathsf{A}, \mathsf{B}, \mathsf{C}, \ldots$ denote propositional variables or simply atoms; Greek letters $\alpha, \beta, \gamma, \eta, \ldots$ are variables for arbitrary formulas; letters $S, T, U, V, \ldots$ denote sets of formulas.

We denote first-order derivability by $\vdash$ and the corresponding consequence operator by $Th(\cdot)$, that is $Th(S) = \{\alpha \mid S \vdash \alpha\}$. We denote first-order interpre-

---

[7] Restrictions to a propositional language are indicated in the text.

tations by $\mathfrak{i}$ and first-order entailment by $\models$. Accordingly, we write models as $\mathfrak{m}$. Classes of interpretations and models, respectively, are denoted by $\mathfrak{J}$ and $\mathfrak{M}$. The class of all models of a set of formulas S is written as $\mathfrak{Mod}(S)$. That is, $\mathfrak{Mod}(S) = \{\mathfrak{m} \mid \mathfrak{m} \models S\}$. For Kripke-models, we use $\mathfrak{k}$ and for classes of them, $\mathfrak{K}$.

Further definitions and conventions will be introduced when they occur for the first time.

2. The original approach: Classical default logic

In default logic, default knowledge is added to standard first-order logic by means of so-called default rules as nonstandard rules of inference. These rules differ from standard inference rules in sanctioning inferences that rely upon given as well as absent information. Such inferences therefore could not be made in a standard framework. Hence, default rules can be seen as rules of conjecture whose role it is to augment an underlying incomplete first-order theory. For the sake of clarity, we will often refer to Reiter's original default logic as *classical* default logic.

In formal terms, a default rule is any expression of the form

$$\frac{\alpha(x) \ : \ \beta_1(x), \ldots, \beta_m(x)}{\gamma(x)} \ ,$$

where $\alpha(x), \beta_1(x), \ldots, \beta_m(x)$ and $\gamma(x)$ are first-order formulas whose free variables are among $x = (x_1, \ldots, x_n)$ for[1] $m \geq 1$ and $n \geq 0$. $\alpha(x)$ is called the *prerequisite*, $\beta_i(x)$ a *justification*, and $\gamma(x)$ the *consequent* of the default rule. If none of these contain free variables, the default rule is said to be *closed*. Usually, open default rules are regarded as schemata and represent all instantiations of the considered default rule.[2] Almost all default rules discussed in the literature fall into the class of *singular* default rules having one justification only. In the sequel, we shall consider mainly closed singular default rules while omitting such attributes whenever possible.[3] For convenience, we denote the prerequisite of a (singular) default rule δ by $Prereq(\delta)$, its justification by $Justif(\delta)$ and its consequent by $Conseq(\delta)$.[4] Also, we hereafter refer to sentences of first-order logic simply as formulas (instead of closed formulas).

The basic idea behind default logic is to start with a set of formulas, W, representing a logically valid, but generally incomplete, description of the world. This description is supplemented with a set of default rules, D, in order to provide means for filling in the gaps in our initial world knowledge. For this, default rules sanction plausible but not necessarily true conclusions. In this way, we obtain a more

---

[1] This definition stipulates the existence of at least one justification.

[2] In [Rei80], skolemization is used to generate all ground instances of an open default rule. In contrast to this, [Lif90] treats free variables in open default rules as genuine objects.

[3] As shown in [MT93b], any default theory comprising default rules with multiple justifications can be transfered into one consisting of singular default rules only (see Section 2.2).

[4] These projections extend to sets D of default rules in the obvious way, for instance $Justif(D) = \bigcup_{\delta \in D} \{Justif(\delta)\}$.

complete *extension* of our initial world description. For instance, if our initial theory contains *motive(Philippe)* and we can consistently assume that *alibi(Philippe)* does not belong to our resulting theory, then we can apply Default rule (1.1) and extend our initial theory with *suspect(Philippe)*.

Now, let us make this more precise. A *default theory* (D, W) consists of a set of consistent[5] formulas W and a set of default rules D. A *classical extension* of a default theory is defined as follows.

Definition 2.0.1. [Rei80] *Let (D, W) be a default theory. For any set of formulas S, let $\Gamma(S)$ be the smallest set of formulas S' such that*

1. $W \subseteq S'$,
2. $Th(S') = S'$,
3. *For any $\frac{\alpha : \beta}{\gamma} \in D$, if $\alpha \in S'$ and $\neg\beta \notin S$ then $\gamma \in S'$.*

A set of formulas E is a classical extension of (D, W) iff $\Gamma(E) = E$.

This definition is clearly a difficult one due to its fixed point construction. A more comprehensive yet pseudo-iterative construction is the following one.

Theorem 2.0.1. [Rei80] *Let (D, W) be a default theory and let E be a set of formulas. Define*

$$E_0 = W$$

and for $i \geq 0$

$$E_{i+1} = Th(E_i) \cup \left\{ \gamma \mid \frac{\alpha : \beta}{\gamma} \in D, \alpha \in E_i, \neg\beta \notin E \right\}.$$

Then, E is a classical extension of (D, W) iff $E = \bigcup_{i=0}^{\infty} E_i$.

The above procedure is not strictly iterative since E appears in the specification of E_{i+1}.

Given an extension E, its set of *generating default rules* is defined as

$$GD_{(D,W)}^{E} = \left\{ \frac{\alpha : \beta}{\gamma} \in D \mid \alpha \in E, \neg\beta \notin E \right\}. \tag{2.1}$$

This terminology is justified by the fact that any extension E of a default theory (D, W) satisfies $E = Th\left(W \cup Conseq\left(GD_{(D,W)}^{E}\right)\right)$, as shown in [Rei80].

For more illustration, let us consider the example given in the introductory section, where *"birds fly"*, *"birds have wings"*, *"penguins are birds"*, and *"penguins don't fly"*. We can express these statements by means of three simple default rules[6] along with a standard implication. Given P, for penguins, we can represent this by means of the following default theory:

---

[5] The restriction to consistent set of facts is not really necessary, but it simplifies matters, in particular, when dealing with consistency checking in subsequent sections.

[6] This sort of default rules is called *normal* and discussed in detail Section 2.2.

$$\left(\left\{\ \frac{\mathsf{B}\ :\ \mathsf{F}}{\mathsf{F}},\ \frac{\mathsf{B}\ :\ \mathsf{W}}{\mathsf{W}},\ \frac{\mathsf{P}\ :\ \neg\mathsf{F}}{\neg\mathsf{F}}\ \right\},\{\mathsf{P},\ \mathsf{P}\to\mathsf{B}\}\right) \qquad (2.2)$$

For example, the first rule aims at formalizing the statement *"birds fly"* via the inference schema roughly saying that *"if we can prove* B *(for "birds") and there is no information contradicting F (for "fly"), then conclude F by default"*. On the other hand, we used a standard implication for formalizing *"penguins are birds"* since this item of information embodies (more or less) strict knowledge. As a result, the above theory has two extensions: one in which P, B, W, and F are true and another one in which P, B, W, and ¬F are true, or formally $Th(\{\mathsf{P},\mathsf{B},\mathsf{W},\mathsf{F}\})$ and $Th(\{\mathsf{P},\mathsf{B},\mathsf{W},\neg\mathsf{F}\})$, respectively. While the first extension is generated by the two first default rules in (2.2), the latter has generating default rules $\left\{\frac{\mathsf{B}\,:\,\mathsf{W}}{\mathsf{W}},\frac{\mathsf{P}\,:\,\neg\mathsf{F}}{\neg\mathsf{F}}\right\}$.

This example brings the following issues about: Multiple extensions are possible. Any such extension represents a possible set of beliefs about the world at hand. This leaves room for two principal reasoning modes. Accepting each extension as a possible set of beliefs is referred to as being *credulous reasoning*. Complementary to this, accepting only the intersection of all extensions as the set of consequences, is called *skeptical reasoning*. Accordingly, a formula is a credulous conclusion of a given default theory if it belongs to one of its extensions, while it is a skeptical conclusion if it belongs to all extensions. In the sequel, we primarily deal with the more basic notion of credulous default reasoning. Note that both modes of reasoning are not semi-decidable in the full first-order case due to the involved satisfiability test (see [Rei80]). These problems are however decidable if the underlying logic is decidable, as for instance in propositional logic.[7]

The example illustrates yet some other features of default logic: On the one hand, default logic supports full *inheritance* reasoning (see [ER83, Tou86]). That is, in both extensions of (2.2) we conclude that W is true, and so penguins have wings by virtue of being birds. On the other hand, default logic does not respect the principle of *specificity*. Arguably, we would want to conclude ¬F from Theory (2.2) and therefore prefer the second extension over the first one. This is so because, intuitively, being a penguin is a more specific notion than that of being a bird, and, in the case of a conflict, we would want to use the more specific default. (This issue is addressed in Chapter 7.)

2.1 Formal properties

Let us now turn to the formal properties of classical default logic. First, we deal with classical extensions. As shown in [Rei80], a default theory (D,W) has an inconsistent extension iff W is inconsistent.[8] [9] Then, such an extension is the only one. This shows that classical default logic is *consistency preserving*.[10] Moreover,

---

[7] Problems due to skolemization are discussed in [BH92].

[8] As discussed in [Mak94], this is not the case when dealing with default rules that may have no justification, such as $\frac{\;:\;}{\mathsf{A}\wedge\neg\mathsf{A}}$.

[9] Recall from Page 12 that we restrict our attention to consistent sets of formulas W.

[10] Observe that this does not apply to the induced skeptical inference relation (see below).

classical extensions are *maximal* in that no extension is a subset of another one. On the other hand, however, default theories do not always have classical extensions. To see this, consider the simple default theory:

$$\left(\left\{\frac{:\,\neg A}{A}\right\},\emptyset\right) \qquad (2.3)$$

This default theory has no classical extension. This drawback is overcome in most of the variants of default logic described in Section 4.1. Section 2.2 gives restricted default theories guaranteeing the existence of classical extensions.

Another, more or less "cognitive shortcoming" is that distinct classical extensions need not to be mutually contradictory, or according to [Rei80] *orthogonal* to each other. Since extensions are intended to represent maximal consistent sets of beliefs, one would expect that distinct extensions would be inconsistent. The next example shows that this is indeed not the case.

$$\left(\left\{\frac{:\,\neg B}{C},\frac{:\,\neg C}{B}\right\},\emptyset\right) \qquad (2.4)$$

This theory has two classical extensions: $Th(\{C\})$ and $Th(\{B\})$. Obviously, both set of beliefs are compatible with each other. [11]

Another way to access the formal behavior of default logic is to investigate the inference relations induced by the extensions of a default theory. This amounts to studying structural properties of logical systems which can be traced back to Gentzen [Gen35] and Tarski [Tar36]. This line of inquiry was initiated by Gabbay in [Gab85] for nonmonotonic logics and then mainly pursued by Makinson in [Mak89, Mak94] and in [Bes88, KLM90]. Similar examinations focusing on certain default logics can be found in [Dix92, FM94, Bra93]. Hence let us discuss in what follows exemplarily some of these structural properties and refer to [Mak94] for a complete treatment. One of the simplest among these properties is *reflexivity* or *inclusion*. Intuitively, this property stipulates that the initial set of facts belongs to the set of its consequences. Formally, it is expressible as $S \subseteq C(S)$ for some consequence operation C and a set of formulas S.[12] This property is only enjoyed by the consequence operation induced by the skeptical inference relation in classical default logic, since the existence of extensions is not guaranteed in the general case. This renders the credulous consequence relation irreflexive.

Another basic structural property is that of *monotonicity*, which is clearly neither satisfied by the credulous nor the skeptical inference relation. Formally, monotonicity stipulates that $S \subseteq T$ implies $C(S) \subseteq C(T)$. The failure of monotonicity has led to the separation of weaker properties that "ought" to be satisfied by nonmonotonic

---

[11] We discuss in Section 4.1.3 a related property, called *weak orthogonality* that incorporates also the underlying consistency assumptions given by the set of justifications of applied defaults.

[12] Eg. $Th(\cdot)$ is the consequence operation induced by the classical inference relation $\vdash$ (cf. Section 1.3).

inference relations. A central role in this context is played by the property of *cumu-lativity*[13] indicating a certain stability of inference relations. Formally, cumulativity stipulates that $S \subseteq T \subseteq C(S)$ implies $C(S) = C(T)$. Intuitively, cumulativity demands that the addition of a conclusion to the set of facts should not change the entire set of conclusions. The next example, taken from [Mak89], demonstrates that classical default logic does not enjoy cumulativity. Consider the following default theory.

$$\left(\left\{ \frac{: A}{A}, \frac{A \vee B : \neg A}{\neg A} \right\}, \emptyset \right) \tag{2.5}$$

This theory has one classical extension, $Th(\{A\})$, containing $A \vee B$. Adding the latter conclusion to the set of facts yields default theory

$$\left(\left\{ \frac{: A}{A}, \frac{A \vee B : \neg A}{\neg A} \right\}, \{A \vee B\} \right) \tag{2.6}$$

whose classical extensions are $Th(\{A\})$ and $Th(\{\neg A, B\})$. Thus, regardless of whether or not we employ a skeptical or a credulous inference relation, in both cases we change the set of conclusions when turning Default theory (2.5) into (2.6). Accordingly, neither of the inference relations enjoys cumulativity.[14] This lack has led to a number of variants of default logic enjoying the property of cumulativity. These variants are discussed in Section 4.2.

As a final structural property let us mention *reasoning by cases*, also called *or* or *distribution* [Mak94]. One way to capture this is to stipulate that $C(S \cup \{\alpha\}) \cap C(S \cup \{\beta\}) \subseteq C(S \cup \{\alpha \vee \beta\})$. Consider the next default theory.

$$\left(\left\{ \frac{A : B}{B}, \frac{\neg A : B}{B} \right\}, \emptyset \right) \tag{2.7}$$

This theory has one classical extension, $Th(\emptyset)$, which does not contain B despite the presence of $A \vee \neg A$. This shows that neither the skeptical nor the credulous inference relation of default logic allows for reasoning by cases. Arguably, this is no severe drawback of default logic since it can be avoided by different encodings of defaults, as described in Section 2.2.

The inability to reason by cases is a characteristic feature emerging from default logic's philosophy to encode defaults as inference rules rather than propositions in the object language. This leads us to a property distinguishing default logics from other approaches, like autoepistemic logic (cf. [Kon88b]), namely the property of *groundedness*. In fact, the character of an inference rule can be captured by the notion of groundedness. A set of default rules D is *grounded* in a set of facts W iff there exists an enumeration $\langle \delta_i \rangle_{i \in I}$ of D such that for all $i \in I$, we have

---

[13] In fact, cumulativity comprises the properties of *cautious monotony* and *cut* (see [Mak89, Mak94]).

[14] However, the skeptical inference relation satisfies cut (see below and [Rei80, Mak89] for details).

$$W \cup Conseq(\{\delta_0, \ldots, \delta_{i-1}\}) \vdash Prereq(\delta_i).$$ (2.8)

Any set of default rules generating an extension is grounded in the initial set of facts. This distinguishes default logic from other approaches, in particular autoepistemic logic [Moo85]. Although groundedness was already implicit in [Rei80], this property was first explicated for default logic in [Sch90b]. Note that the concept of groundedness is common to (almost) all existing variants of default logics.[15] This issue is detailed in [FM94, DSJ94]. [Kon88b] contains a discussion on different forms of groundedness encountered in default and autoepistemic logic.

Let us now regard the dynamic behavior of classical default logic. We have already seen that default logic is nonmonotonic and that therefore the addition of new premises may invalidate previously drawn conclusions. Also, we have observed that the addition of derived consequences may change the set of conclusions (in particular, by inducing new extensions) due to the failure of cumulativity. At least, Reiter shows in [Rei80] that an extension at hand remains unchanged, if we add parts of it to the facts of the underlying default theory. That is, if E is an extension of (D, W) and $S \subseteq E$, then E is also an extension of $(D, W \cup S)$. Makinson extends this result in [Mak89] and shows that the skeptical inference relation of default logic satisfies one half of the above cumulativity condition, also referred to as *cut*, namely $S \subseteq T \subseteq C(S)$ implies $C(S) \subseteq C(T)$.

In this context, it is natural to ask what happens if default rules are added to a theory at hand. The formal counterpart to this is given by the property of *semi-monotonicity*. This stands for monotonicity wrt default rules and stipulates intuitively that adding a set of default rules to a default theory should at least preserve or only enlarge existing extensions. This can be expressed formally as follows. A default logic is *semi-monotonic* iff for any default theory (D, W) and any set of default rules $D' \subseteq D$, we have that if E' is an extension of (D', W) then there is an extension E of (D, W) where $E' \subseteq E$. As already noted by [Rei80], classical default logic does not enjoy semi-monotonicity. Consider the following default theory.

$$\left(\left\{ \frac{:\mathsf{B}}{\mathsf{C}} \right\}, \emptyset \right)$$ (2.9)

This theory has one classical extension, $Th(\{\mathsf{C}\})$. Adding default rule $\frac{:\mathsf{D}}{\neg\mathsf{B}}$ yields default theory

$$\left(\left\{ \frac{:\mathsf{B}}{\mathsf{C}}, \frac{:\mathsf{D}}{\neg\mathsf{B}} \right\}, \emptyset \right)$$ (2.10)

whose only classical extension is $Th(\{\neg\mathsf{B}\})$. This shows that the set of conclusions may change when adding default rules.

Semi-monotonicity has several advantages. First, semi-monotonicity guarantees the existence of extensions and thus implies reflexivity. Second, it is indispensable

---

[15] The system described in [ZM90] dealing with so-called *minimal extensions* allows for "ungrounded" conclusions.

from a computational point of view. This is so because semi-monotonicity allows for a proof-theory that is local wrt the default rules entering a proof. In this way, irrelevant default rules can be ignored. Note that in the absence of semi-monotonicity a proof procedure must necessarily consider all default rules in the given default theory. Third, semi-monotonicity implies that extensions are constructible in a truly iterative way by applying one applicable default rule after another. This allows in particular for non-fixed point definitions of extensions. On the other hand, semi-monotonicity influences the interaction of default rules. As raised in [Bre91b], semi-monotonicity may cause certain representational problems. In fact, its presence may restrict the representation of certain priorities between default rules (see [Bre91b, DSJ94] for details). Semi-monotonicity holds only for a restricted fragment of classical default logic, whereas it is enjoyed by many variants discussed in Section 4.1 and 4.2 in their full generality.

Next, we examine the interpretation of justifications and so the underlying notion of consistency employed in classical default logic. Justifications deal with absent information. That is, a default rule is applicable if its justification is consistent with the final extension, or, in other words, if the negation of the justification does not belong to the final extension. This is the notion of consistency employed in classical default logic. Observe that justifications need only be individually consistent with an extension. This conception of consistency is called *weak regularity* [L91, FM94], or *individual consistency* [DSJ94]. More formally, weak regularity can be captured as follows. A set of default rules D is *weakly regular* wrt a set of facts W iff $W \cup Conseq(D) \cup Justif(\{\delta\})$ is consistent for each $\delta \in D$. We call a default logic weakly regular according to its treatment of the generating default rules of extensions. A consequence of this conception of consistency is that classical extensions may be justified by contradictory consistency assumptions. Consider the next default theory.

$$\left(\left\{ \frac{:\mathsf{B}}{\mathsf{C}}, \frac{:\neg\mathsf{B}}{\mathsf{D}} \right\}, \emptyset \right) \tag{2.11}$$

This theory has one classical extension, $Th(\{\mathsf{C}, \mathsf{D}\})$. Both default rules contribute to the formation of this extension even though their justifications are contradictory to each other. Thus, classical default logic enjoys weak regularity. This property causes the phenomenon of *non-commitment to assumptions*, as discovered in [Poo89b]. As further discussed in [Poo89b, Sch92b, Bre91b, DSJ94], this phenomenon may lead to counterintuitive results. We discuss this issue in more detail in Section 4.1.1 and 5.1.

The notion complementary to weak regularity is called *strong regularity* [FM94], or *joint consistency* [Bre91b, DSJ94]. This leads to *commitment to assumptions*, as discussed in [Bre91b, Sch92b, DSJ94]. This notion of consistency views justifications more as providing "implicit assumptions" or "unverifiable working hypotheses". Accordingly, strong regularity suggests that the *set* of justifications used in the specification of an extension should be consistent, rather than each individual justification. A set of default rules D is *strongly regular* wrt a set of facts W iff

$W \cup Conseq(D) \cup Justif(D)$ is consistent. We call a default logic strongly regular according to its treatment of the default rules generating extensions. This is one of the salient principles underlying the variants discussed in Chapter 3, Section 4.1.4, and 4.2.1. Section 2.2 provides subclasses of classical default logic enjoying strong regularity. Chapter 5 describes a more general approach encompassing both notions of regularity.

Finally, let us deal with the computational complexity and the related issue of expressiveness of default logics. As shown in [Got92], credulous reasoning in propositional default logic is Σ_2^P-complete, while skeptical reasoning is Π_2^P-complete. This reflects the intuition that default reasoning in default logic (in the propositional case) is computationally harder than classical reasoning, unless $NP = \Sigma_2^P$. Now, there are two ways to interpret this. One is simply to argue that default logic is intractable. On the other hand, complexity is always related to expressiveness. So one might argue that the high complexity of default logic offers a much larger expressive power. It has been shown in [CEG94] that a default logic query language is strictly more expressive than other approaches. In fact, default logic allows for more compact representations of knowledge than for instance obtainable in standard logic. The size of the propositional theory obtained as an encoding of a given propositional default theory may be exponential in the size of the original default theory (cf. [BED92]). Hence there is a trade-off between compactness of representation and computational complexity. That is, as argued in [CDS94], the intractability of default reasoning is the price we have to pay for extra-compact knowledge representation.

2.2 Restricted default theories

One way to overcome some of the shortcomings described in the previous section is to restrict oneself to certain fragments of default logic, provided by particular restricted default theories.

The most prominent such class of default theories is certainly the class of *normal default theories*. In fact, many default theories discussed in the literature fall into the class of normal default theories [Rei87a]. These theories consist of *normal default rules* of the form

$$\frac{\alpha : \beta}{\beta} \, .$$

That is, normal default rules are default rules whose single justification is equivalent to the consequent (by substitution of equivalent formulas). Normal default rules guarantee that once they have been applied, their justification remains consistent. Because of this, normal default theories possess numerous desirable properties which do not hold in the general case. Normal default theories guarantee the existence of extensions, they provide orthogonality, semi-monotonicity and strong regularity. In addition, normal default theories capture many common patterns of reasoning (see [Rei80]). Originally, Reiter even stated in [Rei80] that he " ... *know*[s] *of no naturally occurring default which cannot be represented in this form*".

However, together with Criscuolo, he introduced in [RC81] *semi-normal default theories* in order to avoid several shortcomings induced by interacting normal default rules. In analogy to normal default theories, semi-normal default theories consist of *semi-normal default rules* which are of the form

$$\frac{\alpha \; : \; \gamma \wedge \beta}{\gamma}.$$

That is, in general semi-normal default rules are default rules whose single justification implies the consequent. An application of semi-normal default rules is given in our previous birds example. In fact, if we turn the normal default rule $\frac{B:F}{F}$ into the semi-normal one $\frac{B:F \wedge \neg P}{F}$ by adding $\neg P$ to the justification, we can eliminate the conclusion that penguins fly by virtue of being birds.[16]

Semi-normal default rules allow for more expressiveness and are usually regarded as being sufficiently expressive for formalizing default reasoning. In fact, Marek and Truszczyński [MT93b] show that any default theory (including those with default rules having multiple justifications) can be represented as a seminormal default theory. This is accomplished by extending the underlying language and by introducing new default rules. Thus, the new semi-normal default theory may be much larger than the original one (see [MT93b, MT93a]). As a consequence, semi-normal default theories have the same properties as general default theories and so lack the desirable properties possessed by normal default theories.

However, there remain a couple of properties not even enjoyed by normal default theories, like reasoning by cases or cumulativity. The failure of these properties in the case of normal default theories is due to default logic's treatment of defaults as inference rules.

For reasoning by cases, it was suggested in [DSJ94] to transform default theories into prerequisite-free default theories, since they allow us to retain the properties of standard implications (unless explicitly blocked):

$$\frac{\alpha \; : \; \beta}{\gamma} \qquad \mapsto \qquad \frac{: \; (\alpha \to \gamma) \wedge \beta}{\alpha \to \gamma} \qquad\qquad (2.12)$$

With this transformation, the emphasis shifts to the implication itself, rather than a rule involving a prerequisite and a justification for a conclusion. Independently, the same transformation has been proposed in [Bes89] for normal default theories. Other transformations can be found in [Kon88b, Bre91c].

Now, let us apply Transformation (2.12) to Default theory (2.7):

$$\left(\left\{ \frac{: \; A \to B}{A \to B}, \frac{: \; \neg A \to B}{\neg A \to B} \right\}, \emptyset \right)$$

---

[16] The reader is referred to [Poo94, Rei87a] for further knowledge representation issues in default logic.

The transformed theory has the classical extension, $Th(\{B\})$. In contrast to Default theory (2.7), from which we got $Th(\emptyset)$ as the only classical extension, we now obtain B by reasoning by cases. [DSJ94] shows that Transformation (2.12) yields more general theories than the original ones. First, extensions of the original default theories may form subsets of extensions of the transformed, prerequisite-free default theories. Also, we may get more classical extensions from default theories transformed by (2.12) (see [DSJ94] for details).

For obtaining cumulativity, we have to restrict ourselves to prerequisite-free normal default theories in classical default logic. This has been independently shown in [Dix92] and [Sch92a, DSJ94]:[17] That is, for a prerequisite-free normal default theory (D, W) all of whose classical extensions contain α, we have that E is a classical extension of (D, W) iff E is a classical extension of $(D, W \cup \{\alpha\})$. This shows that cumulativity is enjoyed by the skeptical inference relation in the case of prerequisite-free normal default theories in classical default logic. This result does not extend to prerequisite-free default theories in classical default logic, as is the case in other variants described in Section 4.1.

We refer the reader for a general discussion on the properties of various subclasses of classical default logic to [Bes89, DSJ94].

2.3 A semantics for classical default logic

Although classical default logic has intuitively been well understood, it took several years until a model-theoretic semantics was given. As a first step, Łukaszewicz [Łuk85] provides a semantical characterization of normal default theories. The general idea is that every normal default rule can be regarded as a transition from classes of models to classes of models. In other words, "*default logic's semantics can be viewed in terms of restrictions of the set of models of the underlying theory. The first-order theory partially specifies a world, which is further specified by the defaults . Each default can be viewed as extending the world-description by restricting the set of possible worlds assumed to contain the "real" world, at the same time constraining how other defaults may further extend the world-description.*" [Eth87, p 496].

In order to account for general default theories and their behavior, Etherington introduced in [Eth87] a *preference relation* $\geq_\delta$ between classes of models of W.[18] Intuitively, this relation captures a default rule's preference for more specialized world descriptions. Unlike other approaches, such as for instance circumscription, that impose a preference relation on classes of models, here the same is done on the power class.

Formally, the preference relation $\geq_\delta$ is defined as follows.

---

[17] This result is obtained as an easy corollary to the cumulativity result for constrained default logic, given in Theorem 3.3.6.

[18] If it is clear from the context, we simply speak about models rather than models of W.

Definition 2.3.1. *Let* (D, W) *be a default theory. Let* $\delta = \frac{\alpha : \beta}{\gamma} \in D$ *and let* $\mathfrak{M} \subseteq$ $\mathfrak{Mod}(W)$ *be a class of models. The order* $\geq_\delta$ *on* $2^{\mathfrak{M}}$ *is defined as follows. For all* $\mathfrak{M}_1, \mathfrak{M}_2 \in 2^{\mathfrak{M}}$ *we have that*

$$\mathfrak{M}_1 \geq_\delta \mathfrak{M}_2$$

holds iff the following conditions hold:

1. *for every* $\mathfrak{m} \in \mathfrak{M}_2$ *we have* $\mathfrak{m} \models \alpha$,
2. *there exists* $\mathfrak{m} \in \mathfrak{M}_2$ *such that* $\mathfrak{m} \models \beta$,
3. $\mathfrak{M}_1 = \{\mathfrak{m} \in \mathfrak{M}_2 \mid \mathfrak{m} \models \gamma\}$.

According to this definition, a default rule $\frac{\alpha : \beta}{\gamma}$ prefers a class of models $\mathfrak{M}_1$ in which its consequent γ holds over a superclass of models $\mathfrak{M}_2$ where the prerequisite α is true and the justification β is consistent but the consequent is not necessarily satisfied.

The induced order $\geq_D$ is defined as the transitive closure of all orders $\geq_\delta$ such that $\delta \in D$.

Definition 2.3.2. *Let* (D, W) *be a default theory and let* $\mathfrak{M} \subseteq \mathfrak{Mod}(W)$ *be a class of models. The order* $\geq_D$ *on* $2^{\mathfrak{M}}$ *is defined as follows. For all* $\mathfrak{M}_1, \mathfrak{M}_2 \in 2^{\mathfrak{M}}$ *we have*

$$\mathfrak{M}_1 \geq_D \mathfrak{M}_2$$

iff one of the following two conditions holds:

1. *there exists* $\delta \in D$ *such that* $\mathfrak{M}_1 \geq_\delta \mathfrak{M}_2$ *or else*
2. *there exists some* $\mathfrak{M}_3 \in 2^{\mathfrak{M}}$ *such that* $\mathfrak{M}_1 \geq_D \mathfrak{M}_3$ *and* $\mathfrak{M}_3 \geq_D \mathfrak{M}_2$.

For normal default theories it is sufficient to take into account the $\geq_D$-maximal elements of $2^{\mathfrak{Mod}(W)}$. However, an additional so-called *stability* condition is necessary in order to capture general default theories. The reason is that we have to ensure the satisfiability of each justification of the applied default rules by the resulting class of models.

Definition 2.3.3. *Let* (D, W) *be a default theory and let* $\mathfrak{M}$ *be a* $\geq_D$-*maximal class of models in* $2^{\mathfrak{Mod}(W)}$. $\mathfrak{M}$ *is called stable for* (D, W) *iff there is a set of default rules* $D' \subseteq D$ *such that*

1. $\mathfrak{M} \geq_{D'} \mathfrak{Mod}(W)$,
2. *for each* $\delta = \frac{\alpha : \beta}{\gamma} \in D'$ *there exists some* $\mathfrak{m} \in \mathfrak{M}$ *such that* $\mathfrak{m} \models \beta$.

Etherington gives in [Eth87] correctness and completeness results relating classical extensions and stable $\geq_D$-maximal classes of models.

Regarding the semantics, we now see why classical default logic does not commit to assumptions. Together, the second condition of Definition 2.3.1 and 2.3.3 require only one model to satisfy the justification of a considered default rule. But it is not required that there has to be one model satisfying all of the justifications of the default rules used during a derivation. Hence, concerning the justifications, classical default logic preserves only a kind of "distributed consistency".

3. An alternative approach: Constrained default logic

A distinguishing feature of default logics is their appeal to *consistency* for handling absent information. To this end, one identifies reasoning patterns of the form *"in the absence of information to the contrary of"* with patterns like *"it is consistent to assume that"*. Yet this gives no hint which notion of consistency is the most appropriate for being associated with a default. In fact, Reiter writes in [Rei80, p. 83] that *"providing an appropriate formal definition of this consistency requirement is perhaps the thorniest issue in defining a logic for default reasoning"*.

This chapter describes an alternative approach to default logic that relies on a more "global" notion of consistency: Constrained default logic. This approach was introduced in [Sch91a, Sch91b] and further developed in [Sch92b, DSJ94, Sch93]. Due to its strong semantical foundations, this approach remedies several problems encountered in default logic in an arguably simpler way than other proposals. The resulting default logic guarantees the existence of extensions and enjoys, among others, the formal properties of semi-monotonicity and strong regularity. This is achieved by a coherent treatment of implicit consistency assumptions suggested by the underlying semantics.

3.1 Motivation

The primary motivation for the development of constrained default logic was to change the interpretation of justifications towards unverifiable working hypotheses. Looking at commonsense reasoning, we observe that people do not arbitrarily assume things, rather they keep track of their assumptions and at least verify that they do not contradict each other. No one would justify a conclusion by an assumption as well as its opposite. The original formulation of default logic however takes justifications as straightforward consistency conditions. In classical default logic this yields an interpretation of justifications that is closer to "is possible".

This conception of dealing with absent information leads sometimes to counterintuitive results in classical default logic. A first, pretty technical, example was given in (2.11) on Page 17, where we concluded $C \wedge D$ based on the assumption that B as well as $\neg B$ is possible.

This phenomenon shows up more subtly in the "broken arms" example, given in [Poo89b]. Our variant of this example involves a robot. Among other rules, we have a default rule saying that a robot's arm is usable unless it is broken. Now, suppose we are told that one of the robot's arms, the left one or the right one, is broken. And we are given no other detail. [Poo89b][1] gives the following formalization for this example:

$$\left(\left\{\frac{:\ \neg Bl}{Ul},\ \frac{:\ \neg Br}{Ur}\right\},\{Bl \lor Br\}\right).\tag{3.1}$$

The set of facts asserts that the left arm, Bl, or the right arm, Br, is broken. The default rules express that an arm is usable, Ul or Ur, unless it is broken, ie. if we can consistently assume that it is not broken, $\neg Bl$ or $\neg Br$, respectively. We observe that the facts and the justifications of the two default rules are jointly inconsistent.

In classical default logic, Default theory (3.1) has one extension containing Ul and Ur along with the fact $Bl \lor Br$. That is, classical default logic directs us to conclude that both arms are usable even though one of them is known to be broken. In fact, both default rules apply, although they have contradictory justifications according to the set of facts. This is so because each justification, $\neg Bl$ and $\neg Br$, is separately consistent with the extension.

According to [Poo89b], the solution to the "broken-arms" example obtained in classical default logic is rather unintuitive.[2] Poole writes in [Poo89b]: "*The problem is we have implicitly made an assumption, but have been prevented from considering what other assumption we made as a side effect of this assumption.*" The reason for this is that classical default logic does not commit to its assumptions (or is weakly regular). Technically, the problem arises since in Definition 2.0.1 the mere possibility (or consistency) of a justification allows for the application of a default rule. In fact, the consistency of each justification is only checked separately (due to weak regularity). Thus, there is no way to avoid incompatible sets of justifications.

Arguably, the failure of classical default logic to commit to assumptions may be seen not as a "bug", but rather as reflecting an alternative intuition concerning default reasoning. In what follows, however, we explore an alternative formulation that commits to assumptions.

3.2 Constrained default logic

The "broken arms" example illustrates that, depending on one's intuitions, classical default logic may produce conclusions that are stronger than desired. In fact, the example suggests that the *set* of justifications used in the specification of an extension should be consistent, rather than each individual justification. This indicates that, for certain patterns of commonsense reasoning, the property of strong regularity is preferable over that of weak regularity. In this section we develop and explore this intuition.

---

[1] The original formulation given in [Poo89b] uses semi-normal default rules, like $(: Ul \land \neg Bl/Ul)$. For presentation, we have simplified the justifications. This leaves the default theory's formal behavior unaffected.

[2] We have to refer the reader to the literature [Poo89b, Bre91b, GLPT91, DSJ94] for a more detailed analysis why this is an unintuitive solution.

We introduce the notion of a *constrained extension* and call the resulting system *constrained default logic*. A constrained extension is composed of two sets of formulas E and C, where $E \subseteq C$. The *extension E* contains all formulas which are assumed to be true and the set of *constraints C* consists of E and the justifications of all applied default rules. In this approach, we regard the consistency assumptions (given by the justifications of the applied default rules) as constraints on a given extension.

For a default rule $\frac{\alpha:\beta}{\gamma}$ to apply in classical default logic its prerequisite α must be in E and its justification β must be consistent with E. In constrained default logic, however, the prerequisite α must be in extension E whereas the consistency of the justification β is checked with respect to the set of constraints C. While this slightly complicates the definition of an extension, it also means that rules and extensions are now represented uniformly, in that both consist of a consistency condition along with conclusions based on the consistency conditions.

Even though, constrained default logic was originally defined by appeal to a fixed-point-operator in the style of Definition 2.0.1, we give below the more comprehensive, pseudo-iterative specification:

Definition 3.2.1. [DSJ94] *Let (D, W) be a default theory and let E and C be sets of formulas. Define*

$$E_0 = W \qquad and \qquad C_0 = W$$

and for $i \geq 0$

$$E_{i+1} = Th(E_i) \cup \left\{ \gamma \;\middle|\; \frac{\alpha:\beta}{\gamma} \in D, \alpha \in E_i, C \cup \{\beta\} \cup \{\gamma\} \not\vdash \bot \right\}$$

$$C_{i+1} = Th(C_i) \cup \left\{ \beta \wedge \gamma \;\middle|\; \frac{\alpha:\beta}{\gamma} \in D, \alpha \in E_i, C \cup \{\beta\} \cup \{\gamma\} \not\vdash \bot \right\}$$

Then, (E, C) is a constrained extension of (D, W) if $(E, C) = (\bigcup_{i=0}^{\infty} E_i, \bigcup_{i=0}^{\infty} C_i)$.

The set of constraints C is generated by accumulating the justifications from the applied default rules along with the conclusions. Thus, each justification is jointly consistent with the extension and all other justifications of applied defaults. Compared with Theorem 2.0.1, the fixed-point condition relies now only on the constraints C. Intuitively, this means that our context of reasoning has to coincide with our set of accumulated constraints.[3]

A different solution to the "broken-arms" example is offered by constrained default logic. In fact, Default theory (3.1) yields two constrained extensions.

$$\begin{aligned}(\, Th(\{\mathsf{Bl} \vee \mathsf{Br}, \mathsf{Ul}\}) \, , \; Th(\{\neg \mathsf{Bl}, \mathsf{Br}, \mathsf{Ul}\}) \,), \\ (\, Th(\{\mathsf{Bl} \vee \mathsf{Br}, \mathsf{Ur}\}) \, , \; Th(\{\mathsf{Bl}, \neg \mathsf{Br}, \mathsf{Ur}\}) \,)\end{aligned} \tag{3.2}$$

That is, we obtain one extension containing Ul and another one containing Ur from Default theory (3.1). In the first constrained extension, the constraints consist of the

---

[3] Definition 3.2.1 gives a non-fixed point characterisation of constrained extensions which even allows for discarding the set C.

justification of the default rule $\frac{:\,\neg Bl}{Ul}$ along with the default rule's consequent and the world knowledge. In the second constrained extension, the constraints contain the justification of the default rule $\frac{:\,\neg Br}{Ur}$, its consequent, and the set of facts. Intuitively, this amounts to two alternative world-descriptions: One asserting that the left arm is usable by relying on the assumption that it is not broken and another one asserting that the right arm is usable based on the assumption that this arm is not broken.

In both cases, the constraints consist of the respective extension along with the justification of the applying default rule. While forming both extensions one of the two default rules is inapplicable since its justification is inconsistent with the justification of the other default rule that has "already" established a certain "context" of reasoning. In this way, each extension is embedded in a context given by the set of constraints (cf. Chapter 5). This context provides an extended world-description enriched by implicit assumptions given by the justifications of the applying default rules.

Reconciling the views expressed by the two extensions by intersecting them yields conclusion Ul ∨ Ur, saying that the left arm or the right arm is usable. According to [Poo89b], this corresponds to the preferred solution to the "broken-arms" example.

3.3 Formal properties

Let us now turn to the formal properties of constrained default logic. First of all, it is clear that constrained default logic shares with classical default logic the philosophy of encoding defaults as inference rules and thus also all resulting properties. Hence, for instance, constrained default logic respects groundedness but does not allow for reasoning by cases (in its full generality). Also, both default logics are consistency preserving.

However, constrained default logic extends several properties, only found in restricted subclasses in classical default logic, to the general case. These properties are summarized in the following theorems and can be found in [Sch92b, DSJ94].

Theorem 3.3.1. *Existence. Every default theory has a constrained extension.*
Semi-monotonicity. Constrained default logic is semi-monotonic.
Strong regularity. Constrained default logic is strongly regular.

Observe that the existence of extensions in constrained default logic renders the credulous inference relation reflexive.

Another consequence of this conceptualization is that extensions are characterizable without fixed-point definitions. For constrained default logic, this yields the following alternative specification of a constrained extension:

Theorem 3.3.2. [Sch95b] *Let (D, W) be a default theory and let E and C be sets of formulas. Then, (E, C) is a constrained extension of (D, W) iff*

$$E = Th(W \cup Conseq(D'))$$
$$C = Th(W \cup Justif(D') \cup Conseq(D'))$$

for a maximal $D' \subseteq D$ such that D' is grounded in W and $W \cup Justif(D') \cup Conseq(D')$ is consistent.

Note that C can be eliminated in the above definition, which then allows to characterize the actual extension, E, in a constrained extension (E, C) without any appeal to the set of constraints C.

In addition, semi-monotonicity and compactness imply that constrained extensions are constructible in a truly iterative way by applying one applicable default rule after another. Such characterizations are of great importance for computational purposes, as we see in Chapter 9.

A common way of characterizing extensions in default logics uses the set of *generating default rules*:

Definition 3.3.1. *Let (D, W) be a default theory and S and T sets of formulas. The set of generating default rules for (S, T) wrt D is defined as*

$$GD_D^{(S,T)} = \left\{ \frac{\alpha : \beta}{\gamma} \in D \ \Big| \ \alpha \in S, \ T \cup \{\beta\} \cup \{\gamma\} \not\vdash \bot \right\}.$$

Then, constrained extensions are characterized unambiguously by their set of generating default rules as is shown next.

Theorem 3.3.3. *Let (E, C) be a constrained extension of a default theory (D, W). We have*

$$E = Th\left(W \cup Conseq\left(GD_D^{(E,C)}\right)\right),$$

$$C = Th\left(W \cup Conseq\left(GD_D^{(E,C)}\right) \cup Justif\left(GD_D^{(E,C)}\right)\right).$$

Next, we discuss properties specific to constrained default logic due to the explication of the underlying consistency assumptions. First of all, extensions are uniquely determined by their underlying set of constraints. Second, constrained extensions are pairwisely maximal, even though the extensions alone is not necessarily maximal.

Theorem 3.3.4. [Sch91b, MT95] *Let (D, W) be a default theory and (E, C) and (E', C') constrained extensions of (D, W).*

Uniqueness. If $C = C'$ then $E = E'$.
Maximality. If $C \subseteq C'$ then $E = E'$ and $C = C'$.

Another property which holds for constrained extensions, we refer to as *weak orthogonality*. This is analogous to the property of orthogonality in default logic, which holds for normal default theories, and states that distinct extensions are mutually contradictory.

Theorem 3.3.5. *Let (D, W) be a default theory.*

Weak orthogonality. If (E, C) and (E', C') are distinct constrained extensions of (D, W) then $C \cup C'$ is inconsistent.

That is, given two different constrained extensions the *constraints* of the extensions are mutually contradictory. Note that weak orthogonality is not applicable to classical default logic, since no mention is made of the *set* of constraints used in constructing an extension. (In anticipation of Section 4.1.2, we mention that it is inapplicable to justified default logic, too, because the set of formulas attached to extensions in justified default logic may be inconsistent.)

Finally, let us turn to properties possessed by certain exclusive default theories in constrained default logic: An immediate consequence of Definition 3.2.1 is that semi-normal and general default theories are equivalent. This is seen by noting that the definition coincides for defaults of the form $\frac{\alpha\,:\,\beta}{\gamma}$ and $\frac{\alpha\,:\,\beta\wedge\gamma}{\gamma}$. On the other hand, we observe that the important role of normal default theories in classical default logic vanishes in constrained default logic since the properties of normal default theories in classical default logic are extended to the general case in constrained default logic. So let us focus on prerequisite-free default theories, as another distinguished subclass in classical default logic. For instance, prerequisite-free default theories allow for reasoning by cases due to translations like (2.12). Clearly, this carries over to constrained default logic.

Notably, the cumulative fragment is extended in constrained default logic to prerequisite-free default theories [Sch92a, DSJ94]:

Theorem 3.3.6. *Let (D, W) be a prerequisite-free default theory and let $\alpha \in E'$ for all constrained extension (E', C') of (D, W).*

Cumulativity. (E, C) is a constrained extension of (D, W) iff (E, C) is a constrained extension of $(D, W \cup \{\alpha\})$.

This theorem shows that cumulativity is enjoyed by the skeptical inference relation in the case of prerequisite-free default theories in constrained default logic.

Another appealing feature of prerequisite-free default theories in constrained default logic is that they allow for reasoning about default rules. As shown in [DSJ94], this is accomplishable with techniques borrowed from modal logic KT [Che80]. See [DSJ94] for details.

Clearly, the worst-case complexity of default logic carries over to constrained default logic. However, it has been shown in [Dim93], that in certain disjunction-free default theories reasoning is significantly easier than in classical default logic. See [Dim93] for details.

3.4 The focused models semantics

Another argument in favor of strengthening the role of justifications towards unverifiable working hypotheses is that people quite often verify their reasoning by means of examples. Such an example then provides a model of the underlying theory.

This behavior is reflected by the *focused models semantics* that was introduced in [Sch91a]. This semantics is based on a notion of preference between world-descriptions induced by some set of default rules. The underlying approach is due to Etherington who uses in [Eth87] classes of models $\mathfrak{M}$ for characterizing classical extensions (cf. Section 2.3). In our context, a world-description is given by a pair $(\mathfrak{M}, \breve{\mathfrak{m}})$ of classes of models such that $\breve{\mathfrak{m}} \subseteq \mathfrak{M}$. Such pairs are called *focused models structures*. The reason for considering such structures is the following one. In addition to the models of our extension given by $\mathfrak{M}$, we also need to consider those models satisfying our implicit assumptions, given in the totality of the justifications of the applied defaults. Since we do not require that the justifications be valid, there may exist models that falsify them. Consequently, we impose more structure on the classes of models under consideration, viewing the second component $\breve{\mathfrak{m}}$, which is a subclass of $\mathfrak{M}$, as our focused class of models.

A default rule $\frac{\alpha:\beta}{\gamma}$ prefers a focused models structure $(\mathfrak{M}_1, \breve{\mathfrak{m}}_1)$ to another $(\mathfrak{M}_2, \breve{\mathfrak{m}}_2)$ if its prerequisite α is valid in $\mathfrak{M}_2$ and the conjunction of its justification and consequent $\beta \wedge \gamma$ is satisfiable in some focused model in $\breve{\mathfrak{m}}_2$, and lastly if $\mathfrak{M}_1$ and $\breve{\mathfrak{m}}_1$ entail the consequent γ (in addition to the previous requirements). Formally, we achieve all this by defining an order relating the consistency of the justifications with their satisfiability in the focused models:

Definition 3.4.1. *Let (D, W) be a default theory. Let $\delta = \frac{\alpha:\beta}{\gamma} \in D$ and let $\mathfrak{M} \subseteq \mathfrak{Mod}(W)$ be a class of models. The order $\succeq_\delta$ on $2^{\mathfrak{M}} \times 2^{\mathfrak{M}}$ is defined as follows. For all focused models structures $(\mathfrak{M}_1, \breve{\mathfrak{m}}_1), (\mathfrak{M}_2, \breve{\mathfrak{m}}_2) \in 2^{\mathfrak{M}} \times 2^{\mathfrak{M}}$ we have that*

$$(\mathfrak{M}_1, \breve{\mathfrak{m}}_1) \succeq_\delta (\mathfrak{M}_2, \breve{\mathfrak{m}}_2)$$

holds iff the following conditions hold:

1. *for every $\mathfrak{m} \in \mathfrak{M}_2$ we have $\mathfrak{m} \models \alpha$,*
2. *there exists $\mathfrak{m} \in \breve{\mathfrak{m}}_2$ such that $\mathfrak{m} \models \beta \wedge \gamma$,*
3. *$\mathfrak{M}_1 = \{\mathfrak{m} \in \mathfrak{M}_2 \mid \mathfrak{m} \models \gamma\}$,*
4. *$\breve{\mathfrak{m}}_1 = \{\mathfrak{m} \in \breve{\mathfrak{m}}_2 \mid \mathfrak{m} \models \beta \wedge \gamma\}$.*

The induced order $\succeq_D$ is defined as the transitive closure of all orders $\succeq_\delta$ such that $\delta \in D$:

Definition 3.4.2. *Let (D, W) be a default theory and let $\mathfrak{M} \subseteq \mathfrak{Mod}(W)$ be a class of models. The order $\succeq_D$ on $2^{\mathfrak{M}} \times 2^{\mathfrak{M}}$ is defined as follows. For all focused models structures $(\mathfrak{M}_1, \breve{\mathfrak{m}}_1), (\mathfrak{M}_2, \breve{\mathfrak{m}}_2) \in 2^{\mathfrak{M}} \times 2^{\mathfrak{M}}$ we have*

$$(\mathfrak{M}_1, \breve{\mathfrak{m}}_1) \succeq_D (\mathfrak{M}_2, \breve{\mathfrak{m}}_2)$$

iff one of the following two conditions holds:

1. *there exists $\delta \in D$ such that $(\mathfrak{M}_1, \breve{\mathfrak{m}}_1) \succeq_\delta (\mathfrak{M}_2, \breve{\mathfrak{m}}_2)$ or else*
2. *there exists some $(\mathfrak{M}_3, \breve{\mathfrak{m}}_3) \in 2^{\mathfrak{M}} \times 2^{\mathfrak{M}}$ such that $(\mathfrak{M}_1, \breve{\mathfrak{m}}_1) \succeq_D (\mathfrak{M}_3, \breve{\mathfrak{m}}_3)$ and $(\mathfrak{M}_3, \breve{\mathfrak{m}}_3) \succeq_D (\mathfrak{M}_2, \breve{\mathfrak{m}}_2)$.*

The order $\succeq_D$ is thus the transitive closure of the union of the relations $\succeq_\delta$ for every $\delta \in D$. We refer to the $\succeq_D$-maximal classes above $(\mathfrak{Mod}(W), \mathfrak{Mod}(W))$ as the *preferred focused models structures* for a default theory (D, W).

Given a preferred focused models structure $(\mathfrak{M}, \breve{\mathfrak{M}})$, an extension is formed by all formulas that are valid in $\mathfrak{M}$, whereas the focused models $\breve{\mathfrak{M}}$ express the constraints surrounding the extension. According to [Sch92b, DSJ94], we have the following correctness and completeness theorem establishing the correspondence between constrained extensions and preferred focused models structures.

Theorem 3.4.1. *Let* (D, W) *be a default theory. Let* $(\mathfrak{M}, \breve{\mathfrak{M}})$ *be a pair of classes of models and* E, C *deductively closed sets of formulas such that* $\mathfrak{M} = \{\mathfrak{m} \mid \mathfrak{m} \models E\}$ *and* $\breve{\mathfrak{M}} = \{\mathfrak{m} \mid \mathfrak{m} \models C\}$. *Then,* (E, C) *is a constrained extension of* (D, W) *iff* $(\mathfrak{M}, \breve{\mathfrak{M}})$ *is a* $\succcurlyeq_D$-*maximal element above* $(\mathfrak{Mod}(W), \mathfrak{Mod}(W))$.

Compared with the semantics for classical default logic described in Section 2.3, we have strengthened the notion of consistency in extensions, by requiring that all justifications and consequents be jointly satisfiable by the focused models. In particular, we do not require an posterior stability condition, as expressed in Definition 2.3.3.

An alternative semantics for constrained default logic is given as a part of the general semantical framework for default logics developed in Chapter 6.

3.5 Variations of constrained default logic

Two simple yet powerful extensions of constrained default logic are discussed in this section. The first extension is called *pre-constrained default logic*. The basic idea is to supplement the constraints found in a constrained extension with some sort of initial consistency constraints, called *pre-constraints*. The purpose of pre-constraints is to direct the reasoning process by enforcing their consistency. This is a well-known technique, also used in the Theorist-system [Poo88], in which the "context of reasoning" is predetermined and subsequently dominated by some initial consistency requirements.

A *pre-constrained default theory* (D, W, C_P) consists of a set of formulas W, a set of default rules D, and a set of formulas C_P representing the pre-constraints. In order to ensure that pre-constraints do not introduce any inconsistencies, we require that $W \cup C_P$ being inconsistent implies W being inconsistent.

Definition 3.5.1. *Let* (D, W, C_P) *be a pre-constrained default theory and let* E *and* C *be sets of formulas. Define* $E_0 = W$ *and* $C_0 = W \cup C_P$ *and for* $i \geq 0$

$$E_{i+1} = Th(E_i) \cup \{ \ \gamma \ \mid \tfrac{\alpha \,:\, \beta}{\gamma} \in D, \alpha \in E_i, C \cup \{\beta\} \cup \{\gamma\} \nvdash \bot\}$$
$$C_{i+1} = Th(C_i) \cup \{\beta \wedge \gamma \mid \tfrac{\alpha \,:\, \beta}{\gamma} \in D, \alpha \in E_i, C \cup \{\beta\} \cup \{\gamma\} \nvdash \bot\}$$

Then, (E, C) *is a pre-constrained extension of* (D, W) *if* $(E, C) = (\bigcup_{i=0}^{\infty} E_i, \bigcup_{i=0}^{\infty} C_i)$.

Observe that the pre-constraints C_P enter merely the constraints C, namely at C_0, and not the extension E. Thus, pre-constraints direct the reasoning process without actually becoming a part of it. Notice furthermore that adding pre-constraints never increases the number of applying default rules. Moreover, the step from constrained default logic to pre-constrained default logic is so small that all of the properties of constrained default logic carry over to its pre-constrained counterpart.

This becomes even more apparent by the fact that a pre-constrained extension can be computed by appeal to constrained default logic [Sch93]:

Theorem 3.5.1. *Let* (D, W, C_P) *be a pre-constrained default theory and let*

$$D' = \left\{ \frac{\alpha : \beta \wedge \widehat{C}_P}{\gamma} \;\middle|\; \frac{\alpha : \beta}{\gamma} \in D \right\} \cup \left\{ \frac{: \widehat{C}_P}{\top} \right\},$$

where $\widehat{C}_P$ *is the conjunction of all formulas contained in a finite set of pre-constraints* C_P. *Let* E *and* C *be sets of formulas. Then,* (E, C) *is a pre-constrained extension of* (D, W, C_P) *iff* (E, C) *is a constrained extension of* (D', W).

The purpose of the synthetic default rule $\frac{: \widehat{C}_P}{\top}$ (where $\top$ is any tautology) is to add the pre-constraints C_P to the resulting constraints C if no other default rule applies.

The approach taken by pre-constraints provides means for controlling the inference process in constrained default logic. In fact, pre-constrained default logic allows for several enhancements of the original approach: Apart from the incorporation of heuristic control information, the approach provides a simple way of handling default lemmas (see Section 8.1); it also allows for an elegant way of incorporating priorities into constrained default logic, as described below. Moreover, pre-constraints are exploited in the approach to skeptical reasoning that is summarized in Section 9.8.3. Finally, pre-constrained default logic yields more precise relationships to other approaches, like Theorist [Poo88] and cumulative default logic [Bre91b], than obtainable in the original approach. For brevity, these relationships are not given here; see [Sch93] for details.

A second extension is the incorporation of priorities: A *prioritized default theory* $(\tilde{D}, W)$ consists of a set of formulas W and a *sequence* of finite sets of default rules $\tilde{D} = \langle D_0, \ldots, D_m \rangle$ representing a hierarchy of sets of default rules. The default rules in a layer D_i are meant to have a higher priority than those in a layer D_j provided that $j > i$. A *prioritized constrained extension* is defined as follows (where $GD_D^{(E,C)}$ is the set of generating default rules defined in Definition 3.3.1).

Definition 3.5.2. *Let* $(\langle D_0, \ldots, D_m \rangle, W)$ *be a prioritized default theory. Define* (E_0, C_0) *to be a constrained extension of* (D_0, W) *and for* $i \geq 0$ (E_{i+1}, C_{i+1}) *to be a pre-constrained extension of*

$$\left(\bigcup_{j=0}^{i+1} D_j, W \cup Conseq\left(GD_{\bigcup_{j=0}^{i} D_j}^{(E_i, C_i)} \right), Justif\left(GD_{\bigcup_{j=0}^{i} D_j}^{(E_i, C_i)} \right) \right)$$

Then, we define $(\bigcup_{i=0}^{m} E_i, \bigcup_{i=0}^{m} C_i)$ *as a prioritized constrained extension of* $(\langle D_0, \ldots, D_m \rangle, W)$.

Notice that each "layer" admits several extensions which themselves may produce multiple extensions. Observe also that by semi-monotonicity every prioritized constrained extension is also a constrained extension but not vice versa:

Theorem 3.5.2. [Sch91b] *Let* $(\tilde{D}, W)$ *be a prioritized default theory such that* $\tilde{D} = \langle D_0, \ldots, D_m \rangle$ *and let* E *and* C *be sets of formulas. If* (E,C) *is a prioritized constrained extension of* $(\tilde{D}, W)$, *then* (E,C) *is a constrained extension of the default theory* $(D_1 \cup \ldots \cup D_m, W)$.

Note that this result does not hold for the prioritized variant of classical default logic proposed in [Bre91c], since classical default logic does not enjoy semi-monotonicity. Another interesting point in Definition 3.5.2 is that a default rule in D_i may contribute to all partial constrained extensions (E_j, C_j) where $j > i$. Again, this is different from [Bre91c], where the application of default rules whose prerequisite is derived in a "higher" layer is impossible.

On the other hand, [Sch93] shows that prioritized constrained default logic subsumes Brewka's preferred subtheory approach [Bre89b]. For brevity, this relationship is not given here; see [Sch93] for details.

3.6 Conclusion

We have described an alternative approach to default logic, called constrained default logic, that addresses situations not dealt with in the original system, that formalizes differing intuitions in approaches to default reasoning, and that rectifies difficulties in the original system. This approach was introduced in [Sch91a, Sch91b] and further developed in [Sch92b, DSJ94, Sch93].

In classical default logic a default rule is applicable when the prerequisite is provable and the justification is consistent with the final extension. In constrained default logic the justification must be consistent with the final extension together with the set of justifications of all the other applied rules. Consequently, the set of justifications forms a context of which the default conclusions are a subset. While slightly more complex than the original formulation, constrained default logic arguably better conforms to intuitions regarding assumption-based default reasoning. This variant is strongly regular, and possesses among others the properties of semi-monotonicity and weak orthogonality; as well it guarantees the existence of extensions.

We discuss the relationship to Reiter's default logic and other variants in Chapter 4, like those of Łukaszewicz [Łuk88] and Brewka [Bre91b]. [FM94] extends this investigation to other variants of default logic. [DSJ94] shows also that constrained default logic is closely related to the Theorist system of [Poo88] and so provides a link between Theorist and default logics.

4. Putting default logics into perspective

The evolution of Reiter's default logic has resulted in diverse variants enjoying many interesting properties. This process however seems to be diverging because it has led to default logics that are difficult to compare due to different formal characterizations—sometimes even dealing with different objects of discourse. This problem is addressed in this chapter by elaborating on the relationships between different types of default logics and discussing their differences wrt some basic properties.

4.1 Variants modifying the notion of consistency

A salient feature of default logics is their appeal to consistency. For addressing absent information, they propose to identify reasoning patterns of the form *"in the absence of information to the contrary of"* with patterns like *"it is consistent to assume that"*. However, this leaves room for numerous interpretations; it gives no hint which notion of consistency is the most appropriate for being associated with a default. This section describes alternative approaches to default logic that rely on different notions of consistency.

4.1.1 A guiding example

In order to facilitate the treatment of the various approaches, we concentrate in this section on how far each of the approaches "commits to assumptions", a notion indicating in how far underlying consistency assumptions (provided by the justifications of the applying default rules) influence the formation of extensions. For this purpose, we consider the following default theory, emerging from the one in (2.11).

$$\left(\left\{ \frac{: B}{C}, \frac{: \neg B}{D}, \frac{: \neg C \wedge \neg D}{E} \right\}, \emptyset \right) \tag{4.1}$$

This default theory serves as an indicator of how far each variant of default logic commits to assumptions, where the latter is understood in a broader sense dealing with the properties of regularity and semi-monotonicity. Technically, the above default theory combines several potential conflicts which reveal the degree of commitment to assumptions for each considered default logic. As we have observed in

Example (2.11), the first two default rules indicate whether a given system detects inconsistencies among the set of justifications during the formation of an extension; or in other words whether it, say, "strongly commits to assumptions" by maintaining the joint consistency of already applied default rules. The fact of whether or not the third default rule applies (in the presence of one of the first two rules) indicates whether or not the considered variant is semi-monotonic; or in other words whether it, say, "weakly commits to assumptions" by maintaining the individual consistency of already applied default rules.

Our usage of the term "commitment to assumptions" should not be confused with the property of (strong) regularity, since the former appeals to the dynamics involved in forming an extension (in particular the preservation of consistency conditions), while the latter is more or less a static property on resulting extensions (and their generating default rules). For instance, strong commitment implies strong regularity (and semi-monotonicity) but not necessarily vice versa.

As we have already seen in Section 2.1 on Theory (2.11), classical default logic does not commit to assumptions. Obviously, this extends to Default theory (4.1). Namely, classical default logic ignores the inconsistency between the justifications of the first two default rules, which results in a single classical extension, $Th(\{C, D\})$. As in (2.11), the first two default rules apply, although they have contradicting justifications. On the other hand, default rule $\frac{: \neg C \wedge \neg D}{E}$ is blocked since $\neg C \wedge \neg D$ cannot be consistently assumed in the presence of C and D. Notice that, due to the lack of semi-monotonicity in classical default logic, the last default rule cannot contribute to any classical extension, provided that one of the first two rules is applicable. Therefore, classical default logic does not even weakly commit to assumptions.

4.1.2 Justified default logic

Łukaszewicz [Łuk88] modified default logic in order to guarantee the existence of extensions and semi-monotonicity for general default theories. For this purpose, he attaches sets of formulas to extensions in order to strengthen the applicability condition of default rules. Formally, a *justified extension*[1] is composed of two sets of formulas E and J; it is defined as follows.[2]

Definition 4.1.1. [Łuk88] *Let* (D, W) *be a default theory and let* E *and* J *be sets of formulas. Define*

$$E_0 = W \qquad and \qquad J_0 = \emptyset$$

and for $i \geq 0$

$$E_{i+1} = Th(E_i) \cup \left\{ \gamma \ \middle| \ \frac{\alpha : \beta}{\gamma} \in D, \alpha \in E_i, \forall \eta \in J \cup \{\beta\}. \ E \cup \{\gamma\} \cup \{\eta\} \not\vdash \bot \right\}$$

$$J_{i+1} = J_i \ \cup \left\{ \beta \ \middle| \ \frac{\alpha : \beta}{\gamma} \in D, \alpha \in E_i, \forall \eta \in J \cup \{\beta\}. \ E \cup \{\gamma\} \cup \{\eta\} \not\vdash \bot \right\}$$

---

[1] Originally, Łukaszewicz called his extensions *modified* extensions.

[2] As above, we give only the pseudo-iterative characterization of extensions and refer to [Łuk88] for a definition based on an explicit fixed-point operator.

Then, (E, J) is a justified extension of (D, W) if $(E, J) = (\bigcup_{i=0}^{\infty} E_i, \bigcup_{i=0}^{\infty} J_i)$.

Roughly speaking, the components E and J of a justified extension form a set of beliefs and justifications supporting these beliefs. In these terms, a default applies if *"its prerequisite is believed and adding its consequent to the set of beliefs neither leads to inconsistency nor contradicts the justifications of this or some other already applied default"* [Łuk90, p. 204].

First, we notice that justified default logic employs a different consistency check than classical or constrained default logic: A default rule $\frac{\alpha : \beta}{\gamma}$ applies if all justifications of other applying default rules are consistent with the considered extension E and γ; and if additionally γ and β are consistent with E.[3] Second, we observe that the set of constraints J merely consists of the justifications of applied default rules. This set has to be neither deductively closed nor consistent. All this prevents justified default logic from strongly committing to assumptions, as is shown below. That is, even though justified default logic detects inconsistencies between consequents and justifications, it ignores inconsistencies among the justifications of the applying default rules.

In fact, Default theory (4.1) has two justified extensions:

- $(\mathit{Th}(\{C, D\}), \{B, \neg B\})$,
- $(\mathit{Th}(\{E\}), \{\neg C \wedge \neg D\})$.

As in classical default logic, the first justified extension is generated by the default rules $\frac{:B}{C}$ and $\frac{:\neg B}{D}$, which have contradicting justifications. Thus, the extension is justified by an inconsistent set of constraints. The second justified extension stems from the fact that justified default logic is semi-monotonic: Assume we have applied default rule $\frac{:\neg C \wedge \neg D}{E}$. In order to apply default rule $\frac{:B}{C}$, its consequent C must be consistent with $\neg C \wedge \neg D$. Obviously, this is not the case and the default rule is inapplicable. For the same reason, default rule $\frac{:\neg B}{D}$ is not applied.

Formal properties. Let us now turn to the formal properties of justified default logic. First of all, it is clear that justified default logic shares with classical default logic all properties due to the philosophy of encoding defaults as inference rules. Hence, for instance, justified default logic respects groundedness but does not allow for reasoning by cases (in its full generality). Also, both default logics are consistency preserving.

However, justified default logic extends several properties, only found in restricted subclasses in classical default logic, to the general case. These properties are summarized in the following theorems.

Theorem 4.1.1. [Łuk88, FM94]

Existence. Every default theory has a justified extension.
Semi-monotonicity. Justified default logic is semi-monotonic.
Weak regularity. Justified default logic is weakly regular.

---

[3] Observe that omitting γ in the last part of the condition meets exactly the consistency requirement of classical default logic.

Actually, semi-monotonicity implies the existence of justified extensions. Observe that the latter property renders the credulous inference relation in justified default logic reflexive.

Another, even more important, consequence of semi-monotonicity is that extensions are characterizable without fixed-point definitions. In fact, semi-monotonicity and compactness imply that justified extensions are constructible in a truly iterative way by applying one applicable default rule after another. Such characterizations are of great importance for computational purposes.

Another difference to classical default logic manifests itself by *non-maximality* of extensions. Consider the following default theory, taken from [Łuk90]:

$$\left(\left\{ \frac{: B}{C}, \frac{: D}{\neg B} \right\}, \{C\} \right) \tag{4.2}$$

It has two justified extensions: $(Th(\{C\}), \{B\})$ and $(Th(\{C, \neg B\}), \{\neg D\})$. Hence, the actual extensions of justified extensions are not necessarily maximal wrt set-inclusion. This is somehow a consequence of semi-monotonicity, or in other words the resulting phenomenon of weak-commitment. That is, once a default rule has been applied, its justifications' consistency are preserved. This is, for instance, how the first, non-maximal extension is formed.

As regards the property of cumulativity, it was conjectured[4] in [DSJ94] that this property holds in justified default logic for prerequisite-free default theories (as opposed to classical default logic, where it holds for normal prerequisite-free default theories only); this conjecture was recently shown by [Ris95a].

Clearly, the worst-case complexity of default logic carries over to justified default logic, since it has been established for prerequisite-free normal default theories (see [Got92]) on which classical and justified default logic coincide, as shown in Theorem 4.1.2.

We elaborate more on justified default logic in Section 4.1.3.

Relationship to other approaches. In the remainder, we give some results characterizing the relationship among classical and justified default logic. In fact, classical and justified default logic coincide on the class of normal default theories:

Theorem 4.1.2. [Łuk88] *Let (D, W) be a normal default theory and E a set of formulas. Then, E is a classical extension of (D, W) iff (E, J) is a justified extension of (D, W), where $J = \{\beta \mid \frac{\alpha : \beta}{\beta} \in D, \alpha \in E, \neg\beta \notin E\}$.*

This correspondence extends to the general case only in one direction:

Theorem 4.1.3. [Łuk88] *Let (D, W) be a default theory and E a set of formulas. If E is a classical extension of (D, W) then (E, J) is a justified extension of (D, W), where $J = \{\beta \mid \frac{\alpha : \beta}{\gamma} \in D, \alpha \in E, \neg\beta \notin E\}$.*

In other words, the set of justified extensions of a default theory forms a superset of its classical extensions.

---

[4] That is, it was conjectured that the proof for constrained default logic is adaptable for justified default logic.

4.1.3 Constrained default logic: Revisited

This section aims at putting constrained default logic into perspective. We recall that this approach guarantees the existence of extensions and enjoys, among others, the formal properties of semi-monotonicity and strong regularity. In fact, the primary motivation for the development of constrained default logic was to change the interpretation of justifications towards unverifiable working hypotheses. Unlike this, the two previously described formulations, classical and justified default logic, take justifications as straightforward consistency conditions. In classical default logic this yields an interpretation of justifications that is closer to "is possible". A slightly stronger yet conceptually similar treatment is found in justified default logic.[5] As argued above, for certain patterns of commonsense reasoning, the property of strong regularity is preferable over that of weak regularity (and vice versa as discussed in Section 5.1).

As a result, a different solution to our running example in (4.1) is offered by constrained default logic. In fact, we obtain three constrained extensions:

- $(Th(\{C\}), Th(\{C, B\}))$,
- $(Th(\{D\}), Th(\{D, \neg B\}))$,
- $(Th(\{E\}), Th(\{E, \neg C \wedge \neg D\}))$.

While the first two extensions are formed in the same way as those obtained in the "broken-arms" example on Page 25, the third one is formed in analogy to the second justified extension obtained from Theory (4.1). This relationship is due to the fact that both, justified and constrained default logic, enjoy the property of semi-monotonicity which makes them weakly commit to assumptions.

As with justified default logic, the actual extensions need not be maximal wrt set-inclusion. In fact, we obtain from Default theory (4.2) two constrained extensions $(Th(\{C\}), Th(\{C, B\}))$ and $(Th(\{C, \neg B\}), Th(\{C, \neg B, D\}))$.

Relationship to other approaches. In the remainder, we give some results characterizing the relationship among classical and justified default logic on one side and constrained default logic on the other side.

First of all, classical and constrained default logic coincide on the class of normal default theories:

Theorem 4.1.4. [DSJ94] *Let* (D, W) *be a normal default theory and* E *a set of formulas. Then,* E *is a classical extension of* (D, W) *iff* (E, E) *is a constrained extension of* (D, W).

When looking at the extensions of our running example, it might seem that constrained default logic is strictly weaker than its classical counterpart and that every constrained extension is "subsumed" by a standard one. To see that this is not the case, consider the following default theory.

$$\left(\left\{ \frac{: B}{C}, \frac{: \neg B}{D}, \frac{: \neg C}{E}, \frac{: \neg D}{F} \right\}, \emptyset \right) \tag{4.3}$$

---

[5] Recall that classical as well as justified default logic enjoy weak regularity.

This theory has one classical extension, $Th(\{C, D\})$, but three constrained extensions:

- $(Th(\{C, F\}), Th(\{B, C, \neg D, F\}))$,
- $(Th(\{D, E\}), Th(\{\neg B, \neg C, D, E\}))$,
- $(Th(\{E, F\}), Th(\{\neg C, \neg D, E, F\}))$.

The only classical extension is neither a superset nor a subset of the extensions obtained in constrained default logic. Hence, constrained default logic is neither stronger nor weaker than its classical counterpart.

We can describe the relationship between classical and constrained default logic by using the justifications of the generating default rules, that is, for a classical extension E,

$$C_E = \left\{ \beta \;\middle|\; \frac{\alpha : \beta}{\gamma} \in D,\; \alpha \in E,\; \neg\beta \notin E \right\}.$$

Theorem 4.1.5. [DSJ94] *Let (D, W) be a default theory and let E be a classical extension of (D, W). If $E \cup C_E$ is consistent, then $(E, Th(E \cup C_E))$ is a constrained extension of (D, W).*

Observe that the converse of the above theorem does not hold since classical default logic does not guarantee the existence of extensions. However, if the extensions coincide we have:

Theorem 4.1.6. [DSJ94] *Let (D, W) be a default theory. If (E, C) is a constrained extension of (D, W) and E is a classical extension of (D, W), then $C \subseteq Th(E \cup C_E)$.*

Also, it is interesting to observe how the specification of a problem in constrained default logic can be represented in classical default logic. This is done by using the set of generating default rules[6] $GD_D^{(E,C)}$ of a constrained extension:

Theorem 4.1.7. [DSJ94] *Let (D, W) be a default theory and E and C sets of formulas. Let $\hat{C} = \bigwedge_{\delta \in GD_{(D,W)}^{(E,C)}} Conseq(\delta) \wedge Justif(\delta)$ with finite $GD_{(D,W)}^{(E,C)}$ and*

$$D' = \left\{ \frac{\alpha : \beta \wedge \gamma \wedge \hat{C}}{\gamma} \;\middle|\; \frac{\alpha : \beta}{\gamma} \in D \right\}$$

Then, if (E, C) is a constrained extension of (D, W) then E is a classical extension of (D', W).

Now, let us detail the relationship to justified default logic: Since Łukaszewicz is primarily interested in avoiding inconsistencies between justifications and consequents of individual default rules, he neglects inconsistencies among the constraints. So, even though the set of constraints, J, is consistent, it might be inconsistent together with the extension, E, or even the set of premises, W. As an example, consider Default theory

---

[6] See Definition 3.3.1 for a formal definition of the set of generating default rules.

$$\left(\left\{\frac{:B}{A}, \frac{:D}{C}\right\}, \{\neg B \vee \neg D\}\right)$$

having one justified extension: $(\mathit{Th}(\{\neg B \vee \neg D, A, C\}), \{B, D\})$. Obviously, the set of constraints $\{B, D\}$ is inconsistent with the set of facts $\{\neg B \vee \neg D\}$.

Nevertheless, we have the following relationship between the two approaches in the case of no such inconsistencies.

Theorem 4.1.8. *[DSJ94] Let (D, W) be a default theory and (E, J) a justified extension of (D, W). If $E \cup J$ is consistent then $(E, \mathit{Th}(E \cup J))$ is a constrained extension of (D, W).*

Thus, provided that the set of justifications, J, is consistent with the extension, E, we obtain the same extension in justified and constrained default logic.

At first sight, the set of examples given by means of Default theory (4.1) suggests that the stronger the consistency check of a default logic the more extensions are obtained. Indeed, Default theory (4.1) has one classical, two justified, and three constrained extensions. However, this increasing number of extensions is not a universal principle. In fact, we have just illustrated above via default Theory (4.3) that constrained default logic is neither stronger nor weaker than its classical counterpart. While we obtained above one classical and three constrained extensions, we obtain actually four justified extensions of Default theory (4.3), namely

- $(\mathit{Th}(\{C, D\}), \{B, \neg B\})$,
- $(\mathit{Th}(\{C, F\}), \{B, \neg D\})$,
- $(\mathit{Th}(\{D, E\}), \{\neg B, \neg C\})$,
- $(\mathit{Th}(\{E, F\}), \{\neg C, \neg D\})$.

The reason for this phenomenon is as follows. Since justified default logic is semi-monotonic (or "weakly commits to assumptions"), it allows for the application of each default rule. However, since it discards inconsistencies among the justifications of applying default rules it does not exclude the combination of the default rules $\frac{:B}{C}$ and $\frac{:\neg B}{D}$. In other words, although "weak commitment" guarantees the individual consistency of each justification, it does not prevent inconsistent sets of justifications.

On the whole, justified default logic allows for the application of more default rules than constrained default logic as is shown next.

Theorem 4.1.9. *[DSJ94] Let (D, W) be a default theory and (E, C) be a constrained extension of (D, W). Then, there is a justified extension (E', J') of (D, W) such that $E \subseteq E'$ and $C \subseteq \mathit{Th}(E' \cup J')$.*

Whenever the actual extensions coincide we have the following relationship.

Theorem 4.1.10. *[Sch92b] Let (D, W) be a default theory and let E, C, and J be sets of formulas. If (E, C) is a constrained extension of (D, W) and (E, J) is a justified extension of (D, W) then $C \subseteq \mathit{Th}(E \cup J)$.*

4.1.4 Rational default logic

Another variant based on the property of strong regularity was proposed independently in [MT93c]; the system is referred to as *rational default logic* and its extensions are called *rational extensions*. For the sake of a uniform representation, we give here an alternative characterization in the style of constrained default logic. The original definition of rational extensions is given in Appendix A.1.

Definition 4.1.2. *Let* (D, W) *be a default theory and let* E *and* C *be sets of formulas. Define*

$$E_0 = W \qquad and \qquad C_0 = W$$

and for $i \geq 0$

$$E_{i+1} = Th(E_i) \cup \left\{ \gamma \;\middle|\; \frac{\alpha : \beta}{\gamma} \in D, \alpha \in E_i, C \cup \{\beta\} \not\vdash \bot \right\}$$

$$C_{i+1} = Th(C_i) \cup \left\{ \beta \wedge \gamma \;\middle|\; \frac{\alpha : \beta}{\gamma} \in D, \alpha \in E_i, C \cup \{\beta\} \not\vdash \bot \right\}$$

Then, (E, C) *is a rational extension of* (D, W) *if* $(E, C) = (\bigcup_{i=0}^{\infty} E_i, \bigcup_{i=0}^{\infty} C_i)$.

The correspondence of this characterization with the original one is described in Appendix A.1. Nonetheless we note that the original definition does deal explicitly with a set of constraints.

The only difference between the above definition and the one of a constrained extension is that the former does not integrate the consequent of a default rule into the consistency check. Even though, this does not affect the requirement of jointly consistent justifications of applying default rules, it affects however many other properties, as we will see in the next section.

Formal properties. Rational default logic's key property is obviously that of strong regularity:

Theorem 4.1.11. *Strong regularity. Rational default logic is strongly regular.*

Unlike all previously discussed variants, however, rational default logic yields two rational extensions from our guiding example in (4.1), namely:

- $(Th(\{C\}), Th(\{C, B\}))$,
- $(Th(\{D\}), Th(\{D, \neg B\}))$.

That is, as opposed to justified and constrained default logic, rational default logic does not yield an extension containing E.

Actually, this phenomenon reveals that rational default logic does not even weakly commit to assumptions even though it enjoys strong regularity. In other words, rational default logic is not semi-monotonic. To see this, consider the following default theory.

$$\left(\left\{ \frac{: \neg C \wedge \neg D}{E} \right\}, \emptyset \right)$$

This theory has clearly a single rational extension, $(Th(\{E\}), Th(\{E, \neg C \wedge \neg D\}))$. Now, observe that adding the default rules $\frac{:B}{C}$ and $\frac{:\neg B}{D}$ results in Default theory (4.1), none of whose extensions contains or even coincides with the previous one. This shows that rational default logic is not semi-monotonic. Also, it does not guarantee the existence of extensions, as one may verify by means of Default theory (2.3). Other properties, like non-maximality of actual extensions, pairwise maximality, or complexity results, carry over from constrained to rational default logic.

Relationship to other approaches. At this point, the key question is clearly that on the relationship between constrained and rational default logic. Due to the alternative characterization of rational extensions given in Definition 4.1.2, it should be obvious that both default logics coincide on the class of semi-normal default theories:

Theorem 4.1.12. [MT95] *Let (D, W) be a semi-normal default theory and E and C be sets of formulas. Then, (E, C) is a rational extension of (D, W) iff (E, C) is a constrained extension of (D, W).*

This theorem was proved first by other methods in [MT95].

In fact, from the perspective of constrained default logic, one obtains rational default logic simply by replacing condition $C \cup \{\beta\} \cup \{\gamma\} \not\vdash \perp$ by $C \cup \{\beta\} \not\vdash \perp$ in Definition 3.2.1. Conversely, rational default logic can be seen as a generalization of constrained default logic.

In fact, we have in the general case that each rational extension is also a constrained extension:

Theorem 4.1.13. [MT95] *Let (D, W) be a default theory and E and C be sets of formulas. If (E, C) is a rational extension of (D, W) then (E, C) is a constrained extension of (D, W),*

In other words, the set of constrained extensions of a default theory forms a superset of its rational extensions.

This tight relationship is clearly mutually beneficial to both approaches. While rational default logic can utilize the body of knowledge already gathered since the introduction of constrained default logic in 1991, the latter is now faced with new perspectives beyond properties like semi-monotonicity.

4.2 Variants recording consistency assumptions

An interesting role among the formal properties discussed in Section 2.1 is played by cumulativity. From a theoretical point of view, this is due to the following considerations, initiated by Gabbay in [Gab85]: A monotonic consequence relation, like that of standard first-order logic, enjoys the structural properties of reflexivity, idempotence,[7] and monotonicity. While the first two properties can arguably be stipulated for nonmonotonic consequence relations, too, the question arises how mono-

---

[7] Idempotence amounts to the property: $C(S) = C(C(S))$.

tonicity can be weakened in order to obtain a similar property for nonmonotonic consequence relations. This made [Gab85] propose the property of cumulativity.

In fact, despite its theoretical importance, the property of cumulativity is moreover of practical relevance. For instance, in automated theorem proving, one often caches so-called lemmas, ie. auxiliary propositions used in the demonstration of another proposition, in order to reduce computational efforts. Such a technique is however not applicable in the previously introduced default logics, since the addition of derived propositions may change the entire set of conclusions due to the lack of cumulativity.

As detailed in [Bre91b], cumulativity fails in default logics because the implicit consistency assumptions are lost, whenever a conclusion is added to the set of premises. Therefore, we can trace back the failure of cumulativity to default logics' inability to be aware of the consistency assumptions underlying a default conclusion. This problem has been addressed in [Bre91b] by labeling formulas for recording their consistency assumptions.

The idea of labeling formulas instead of, for instance, meta-theoretic fixes is governed by the theoretical demand that cumulativity is a condition on consequence relations dealing with formulas as the objects of discourse. We have seen in Section 2.1, how the addition of the formula $A \vee B$ changed the set of extensions of Theory (2.5). The reason for this is that adding simply $A \vee B$ ignores the fact that $A \vee B$ has been derived under the consistency assumption A. As opposed to adding strictly classically derived formula, however, the addition of default conclusions to an initial world description may have two interpretations: First, while sticking to the objects of discourse, one may trace default inferences by accumulating the consistency assumptions underlying a derived formula by attaching them to the formulas themselves. This has led to labeled formulas. In this way, one does not simply add a formula to the premises but rather a formula along with its underlying consistency assumptions. This approach is taken by the default logics described in this section; it is definitely the one closer to the formal side of cumulativity since it strictly manipulates the objects of discourse.

In the second approach, a default conclusion is transformed into a default rule whenever it is added to the premises. The resulting default rule is considered as a compact representation of the default inferences made for deriving the conclusion. The default rule is then added to the set of default rules initially supplied by a given default theory. The underlying consistency assumptions form the justification of this default rule. This alternative approach is described in Chapter 8; it is non-logical in the sense that the formation of new default rules steps outside the logical machinery.

Risch nicely distinguishes in [Ris95b] these two principled approaches via the terms $W-$ and $D-cumulativity$; thus indicating to which part of the premises a default conclusion is added.

4.2.1 Cumulative default logic

Brewka adds in [Bre91b] cumulativity *and* strong regularity to default logic by strengthening the applicability condition for default rules and making the reasons for believing something explicit.[8] In order to keep track of implicit assumptions, he introduces so-called *assertions*, ie. formulas labeled with the set of justifications and consequents of the default rules which were used for deriving them. Intuitively, assertions represent formulas together with the reasons for believing them.

Definition 4.2.1. [Bre91b] *Let* $\alpha, \gamma_1, \ldots, \gamma_m$ *be formulas. An assertion* ξ *is any expression of the form* $\langle \alpha, \{\gamma_1, \ldots, \gamma_m\}\rangle$, *where* $\alpha = Form(\xi)$ *is called the asserted formula and the set* $\{\gamma_1, \ldots, \gamma_m\} = Supp(\xi)$ *is called the support of* α.[9]

To guarantee the proper propagation of supports, Brewka extends the standard inference relation. This leads to the notion of the set of *supported theorems* $\widehat{Th}(S)$ of a set of assertions S:

Definition 4.2.2. [Bre91b] *Let* S *be a set of assertions and let* $\widehat{Th}$ *denote the assertional consequence operator. Then,* $\widehat{Th}(S)$ *is the smallest set of assertions such that*

1. $S \subseteq \widehat{Th}(S)$,
2. if $\xi_1, \ldots, \xi_n \in \widehat{Th}(S)$ *and* $Form(\xi_1), \ldots, Form(\xi_n) \vdash \gamma$, *then*
   $\langle \gamma, Supp(\xi_1) \cup \cdots \cup Supp(\xi_n)\rangle \in \widehat{Th}(S)$.

An *assertional default theory* becomes a pair (D, W), where D is a set of (standard) default rules and W is a set of assertions. In what follows, we deal with *well-based* assertional default theories (D, W) guaranteeing that $Form(W) \cup Supp(W)$ is consistent. Then, an *assertional extension* is defined as follows.

Definition 4.2.3. [Bre91b] *Let* (D, W) *be an assertional default theory and let* $\mathcal{E}$ *be a set of assertions. Define*

$$\mathcal{E}_0 = W$$

and for each $i \geq 0$

$$\mathcal{E}_{i+1} = \widehat{Th}(\mathcal{E}_i) \cup \{\langle \gamma, Supp(\alpha) \cup \{\beta\} \cup \{\gamma\}\rangle \mid \frac{\alpha : \beta}{\gamma} \in D,$$
$$\langle \alpha, Supp(\alpha)\rangle \in \mathcal{E}_i, Form(\mathcal{E}) \cup Supp(\mathcal{E}) \cup \{\beta\} \cup \{\gamma\} \nvdash \bot\}$$

Then, $\mathcal{E}$ *is an assertional extension of* (D, W) *if* $\mathcal{E} = \bigcup_{i=0}^{\infty} \mathcal{E}_i$.

Comparing this definition with that of justified or constrained extensions, we see that the justifications and consequents of applied default rules are recorded locally to the default conclusions. In order to illustrate this briefly, we consider the simple assertional default theory $\left(\left\{\frac{A : B}{C}\right\}, \{\langle A, \emptyset\rangle\}\right)$. This assertional default theory yields the assertional extension $\widehat{Th}(\{\langle A, \emptyset\rangle, \langle C, \{B, C\}\rangle\})$. We see that the default conclusion C is labeled with a certain set of constraints.

---

[8] Cumulative default logic was actually the first strongly regular default logic.
[9] The two projections extend to sets of assertions in the obvious way. The projection *Supp* is also used to denote the support of an asserted formula, eg. $\langle \alpha, Supp(\alpha)\rangle$.

In fact, a closer look reveals that the applicability conditions for a default rule $\frac{\alpha:\beta}{\gamma}$ in both constrained and cumulative default logic require the joint consistency of its justification β and its consequent γ with the set of justifications and consequents of all other applying default rules. Therefore, assertional extensions share the notion of joint consistency (or strong regularity) with constrained extensions—but in a distributed way. That is, while cumulative default logic deals with "formulas with constraints", constrained default logic deals with constrained extensions.

As with constrained default logic, semi-normal and general assertional default theories are equivalent. Also, cumulative default logic strongly commits to assumptions and it therefore enjoys strong regularity: The assertional counterpart of Default theory (4.1) has three assertional extensions:

- $\widehat{Th}(\{\langle C, \{B, C\}\rangle\})$,
- $\widehat{Th}(\{\langle D, \{\neg B, D\}\rangle\})$,
- $\widehat{Th}(\{\langle E, \{\neg C \wedge \neg D, E\}\rangle\})$.

Let us examine the assertional extension containing $\langle D, \{\neg B, D\}\rangle$. This assertion is derived by applying default rule $\frac{:\neg B}{D}$. In order to apply another default rule the corresponding justification and consequent have to be consistent with $\{D\} \cup \{\neg B, D\}$, ie. the asserted formula and the support of the assertion $\langle D, \{\neg B, D\}\rangle$. As can be easily verified, none of the two other default rules is applicable. So, once we have derived a conclusion, we are aware of its underlying assumptions. Therefore, cumulative default logic prevents the derivation of conclusions which contradict previously derived conclusions or their underlying consistency assumption.

In all, cumulative and constrained default logic are very close to each other. In order to characterize this relation directly, we give kind of an equivalence result between the two formulations:

Theorem 4.2.1. [DSJ94] *Let (D, W) be a default theory and $(D, \mathcal{W})$ the assertional default theory, where $\mathcal{W} = \{\langle \alpha, \emptyset \rangle \mid \alpha \in W\}$. Then, if (E, C) is a constrained extension of (D, W) then there is an assertional extension $\mathcal{E}$ of $(D, \mathcal{W})$ such that $E = Form(\mathcal{E})$ and $C = Th(Form(\mathcal{E}) \cup Supp(\mathcal{E}))$; and, conversely if $\mathcal{E}$ is an assertional extension of $(D, \mathcal{W})$ then $(Form(\mathcal{E}), Th(Form(\mathcal{E}) \cup Supp(\mathcal{E})))$ is a constrained extension of (D, W).*

Observe that we get a one-to-one correspondence between the "real" extensions, namely $E = Form(\mathcal{E})$. However, the constraints of a constrained extension correspond to the deductive closure of the supports and the asserted formulas of the extension. Thus, we can map assertional extensions onto constrained extensions only modulo equivalent sets of supports.

Also, notice that Theorem 4.2.1 establishes a relationship between constrained extensions and assertional extensions of assertional default theories $(D, \mathcal{W})$ which have a non-supported set of assertional facts, ie. $Supp(\mathcal{W}) = \emptyset$. A corresponding relationship in the case of supported sets of assertional facts between assertional extensions and pre-constrained extensions is given in [Sch93].

Because of this closeness, cumulative default logic shares several properties with constrained default logic: the existence of assertional extensions is guaranteed, cumulative default logic is semi-monotonic and all assertional extensions of a given assertional default theory are weakly orthogonal to each other (ie. the supports of two distinct assertional extensions are always contradictory to each other). In particular, cumulative default logic is cumulative in the following sense:

Theorem 4.2.2. [Bre91b] *Let (D, W) be an assertional default theory. If (D, W) has an assertional extension containing $\langle \alpha, Supp(\alpha) \rangle$, then $\mathcal{E}$ is an assertional extension of (D, W) containing $\langle \alpha, Supp(\alpha) \rangle$ iff $\mathcal{E}$ is an assertional extension of $(D, W \cup \{\langle \alpha, Supp(\alpha) \rangle\})$.*

This is illustrated by means of the following example (cf. default theories (2.5/2.6)). The assertional default theory

$$\left(\left\{ \frac{: A}{A}, \frac{A \vee B : \neg A}{\neg A} \right\}, \emptyset \right) \tag{4.4}$$

has one assertional extension: $\widehat{Th}(\{\langle A, \{A\} \rangle\})$.

Adding assertion $\langle A \vee B, \{A\} \rangle \in \widehat{Th}(\{\langle A, \{A\} \rangle\})$ to the set of assertional facts yields assertional default theory

$$\left(\left\{ \frac{: A}{A}, \frac{A \vee B : \neg A}{\neg A} \right\}, \{\langle A \vee B, \{A\} \rangle\} \right) \tag{4.5}$$

which has the same assertional extension: $\widehat{Th}(\{\langle A, \{A\} \rangle\})$. As opposed to conventional default logics, we thus obtain no extension containing $\neg A$.

The case of the assertional extension of (4.4) is analogous to that of the first classical extension obtained from (2.5). There, classical default logic allows for the derivation of A and A $\vee$ B. In contrast to this, cumulative default logic allows us to derive assertions $\langle A, \{A\} \rangle$ and $\langle A \vee B, \{A\} \rangle$.

Let us detail the case of the assertional extension obtained from (4.5). We observe that changing Assertional default theory (4.4) into (4.5) by adding assertion $\langle A \vee B, \{A\} \rangle$ amounts to the addition of a nonmonotonic theorem together with its underlying consistency assumptions. Although the prerequisite of default rule $\frac{A \vee B : \neg A}{\neg A}$ is derivable from the assertional facts (compare with (2.5)) the default rule remains inapplicable, since its justification $\neg A$ is inconsistent with the support of the assertion $\langle A \vee B, \{A\} \rangle$. Notice that this is similar to the case of Assertional default theory (4.4) where the justification $\neg A$ is denied by the consequent of default rule $\frac{: A}{A}$ (which has to be applied in order to derive the prerequisite of default rule $\frac{A \vee B : \neg A}{\neg A}$).

The following Theorem summarizes the previously mentioned properties of cumulative default logic.

Theorem 4.2.3. [Bre91b]

Existence. Every default theory has an assertional extension.

Semi-monotonicity. Cumulative default logic is semi-monotonic.
Strong regularity. Cumulative default logic is strongly regular.
Cumulativity. Cumulative default logic is cumulative.[10]

We have seen by means of Theorem 4.2.1 that constrained and cumulative default logic are very close to each other. However, since constrained extensions consist of standard formulas they do not run into the *"floating conclusions"* problem [BMS91] that arises whenever we want to reason skeptically by intersecting several extensions. Hence, let us reconsider an adaptation of Theory (2.4):

$$\left(\left\{ \frac{:\neg B}{A}, \frac{:\neg A}{B} \right\}, \{\langle A \to C, \emptyset \rangle, \langle B \to C, \emptyset \rangle\} \right)$$

This theory has two assertional extensions:

- $\widehat{Th}(\{\langle A, \{\neg B, A\}\rangle, \langle C, \{\neg B, A\}\rangle\})$
- $\widehat{Th}(\{\langle B, \{\neg A, B\}\rangle, \langle C, \{\neg A, B\}\rangle\})$.

Reasoning skeptically, we cannot draw any conclusion about C. Although C is asserted in both extensions the corresponding supports differ and, hence, also the assertions as such are different and do not belong to the intersection.[11]

Let us take a look at the corresponding default theory

$$\left(\left\{ \frac{:\neg B}{A}, \frac{:\neg A}{B} \right\}, \{A \to C, B \to C\} \right)$$

and its two constrained extensions:

- $(Th(\{A, C\}), Th(\{A, C, \neg B\}))$
- $(Th(\{B, C\}), Th(\{B, C, \neg A\}))$.

Reasoning skeptically by intersecting the above extensions and set of constraints yields the following set of skeptical conclusions: $Th(\{A \lor B, C\})$ in the context of $Th(\{C, \neg(A \leftrightarrow B)\})$. Hence, we obtain C as a skeptical conclusion.[12]

The crux in the two previous examples lies in the possibility of introducing the exclusive disjunction $\neg(A \leftrightarrow B)$ as a constraint on the skeptical theorem C. Using assertions we cannot apply any kind of deduction to the supports — apart from considering them when checking consistency. But, by encoding the underlying consistency assumptions as a context guiding our beliefs, we have the whole deductive machinery of standard logic at hand. Consequently, both of the above sets of constraints contain the proposition $\neg(A \leftrightarrow B)$.

---

[10] In the sense of Theorem 4.2.2.
[11] The "floating conclusions" problem has been attacked in [Bre91a] by computing first one set of assertions containing all assertional extensions and then filtering out the respective assertional extensions.
[12] Observe that constrained extensions are not closed under intersection.

4.2.2 Variants of cumulative default logic

The original approach to cumulative default logic kills two birds with a single stone. Brewka's proposal addresses simultaneously the properties of cumulativity and strong regularity. Also, cumulative default logic is semi-monotonic and thus guarantees the existence of extensions. In Section 4.1.3 and 4.1.4, we have already seen that strong regularity is obtainable without imposing cumulativity. An obvious question is now, whether one can add cumulativity in the absence of strong regularity and/or semi-monotonicity. This question has been addressed in [GM94], where it is shown that the two previous properties are not required for cumulativity. Giordano and Martelli define in [GM94] two cumulative variants of default logic that do not enjoy the property of semi-monotonicity. While the first one is strongly regular, the second one is weakly regular.

First of all, [GM94] show that cumulativity is obtainable in presence of strong regularity and absence of semi-monotonicity. To achieve this, only the justifications of the applying default rules are recorded and thus integrated into the consistency check. This yields a default logic, to which we refer to as *rational cumulative default logic*[13] and whose extensions are defined in the following way.

Definition 4.2.4. [GM94] *Let* $(D, \mathcal{W})$ *be an assertional default theory and let* $\mathcal{E}$ *be a set of assertions. Define*

$$\mathcal{E}_0 = \mathcal{W}$$

and for each $i \geq 0$

$$\mathcal{E}_{i+1} = \widehat{Th}(\mathcal{E}_i) \cup \{\langle \gamma, Supp(\alpha) \cup \{\beta\}\rangle \mid \tfrac{\alpha \,:\, \beta}{\gamma} \in D,$$
$$\langle \alpha, Supp(\alpha)\rangle \in \mathcal{E}_i, Form(\mathcal{E}) \cup Supp(\mathcal{E}) \cup \{\beta\} \not\vdash \bot\}$$

Then, $\mathcal{E}$ *is a rational assertional extension for* $(D, \mathcal{W})$ *if* $\mathcal{E} = \bigcup_{i=0}^{\infty} \mathcal{E}_i$.

Note that in the above definition only the justifications of the applying default rules are tested for consistency. In this way, default rules are not implicitly treated as semi-normal, as it is the case in cumulative default logic. In fact, the previous variant is equivalent to Brewka's cumulative default logic on the broad class of semi-normal default theories:

Theorem 4.2.4. [GM94] *Let* $(D, \mathcal{W})$ *be a semi-normal assertional default theory and let* $\mathcal{E}$ *be a set of assertions. Then,* $\mathcal{E}$ *is an assertional extension of* $(D, \mathcal{W})$ *iff* $\mathcal{E}$ *is a rational assertional extension of* $(D, \mathcal{W})$.

Moreover, one can show that the set of assertional extensions of an assertional default theory forms a superset of its rational assertional extensions:

---

[13] This default logic was originally baptized CA-default logic for *commitment to assumptions* default logic. Observe that our terminology distinguishes between strong regularity and commitment to assumptions, as opposed to the usage in [GM94].

   The reason for choosing the name *rational cumulative default logic* will become obvious when regarding Theorem 4.2.7.

Theorem 4.2.5. [LS96] *Let* (D, W) *be an assertional default theory and* $\mathcal{E}$ *be a set of assertions. If* $\mathcal{E}$ *is a rational assertional extension of* (D, W) *then there is an assertional extension* $\mathcal{F}$ *of* (D, W), *with* $Form(\mathcal{E}) = Form(\mathcal{F})$ *and* $Supp(\mathcal{E}) \subseteq Supp(\mathcal{F})$.

The following theorem summarizes the essential properties of this variant of cumulative default logic:

Theorem 4.2.6. [GM94]

Strong regularity. Rational cumulative default logic is strongly regular.
Cumulativity. Rational cumulative default logic is cumulative.[14]

It is easy to see that our default logic at hand does not enjoy semi-monotonicity by working through default theories (2.9) and (2.10). Also, rational cumulative default logic does not guarantee the existence of extensions, as can be seen by regarding Theory (2.3).

Actually, apart from cumulativity, this variant of cumulative default logic shares all properties with rational default logic, such as strong regularity, non-semi-monotonicity, and non-existence of extensions. In fact, both variants turn out to be equivalent modulo representational issues:

Theorem 4.2.7. [LS96] *Let* (D, W) *be a default theory and* $(D, \mathcal{W})$ *the assertional default theory, where* $\mathcal{W} = \{\langle \alpha, \emptyset \rangle \mid \alpha \in W\}$. *Then, if* (E, C) *is a rational extension of* (D, W) *then there is a rational assertional extension* $\mathcal{E}$ *of* $(D, \mathcal{W})$ *such that* $E = Form(\mathcal{E})$ *and* $C = Th(Form(\mathcal{E}) \cup Supp(\mathcal{E}))$; *and, conversely if* $\mathcal{E}$ *is a rational assertional extension of* $(D, \mathcal{W})$ *then* $(Form(\mathcal{E}), Th(Form(\mathcal{E}) \cup Supp(\mathcal{E})))$ *is a rational extension of* (D, W).

The theorem shows that rational default logic and its assertional counterpart are related in the same way as constrained and cumulative default logic. This is actually why we refer to the variant in focus as rational cumulative default logic.[15]

The second cumulative default logic proposed in [GM94] is closer to classical default logic, since it enjoys weak regularity and it is not semi-monotonic.[16] Due to its closeness to classical default logic, we refer to this variant as *classical cumulative default logic* and call its extensions *classical assertional extensions*.[17]

Definition 4.2.5. [GM94] *Let* (D, W) *be an assertional default theory and let* $\mathcal{E}$ *be a set of assertions such that there is no formula* α *such that* $\alpha \in Supp(\mathcal{E})$ *and* $\neg \alpha \in Form(\mathcal{E})$. *Define*

---

[14] In the sense of Theorem 4.2.2.

[15] Apart from the fact that our notion of commitment to assumptions is not the one that led to the name CA-default logic. Because [GM94] use the former notion rather in the spirit of strong regularity.

[16] Historically, it was David Makinson who proposed the first cumulative default logic without strong regularity. This is described in [Bre91b]. This approach requires however an even more complicated format of assertions, since justifications and consequents of applying default rules must be kept separately.

[17] In [GM94], this default logic was originally baptized Q-default logic for *quasi* default logic.

$$\mathcal{E}_0 = \mathcal{W}$$

and for each $i \geq 0$

$$\mathcal{E}_{i+1} = \widehat{Th}(\mathcal{E}_i) \cup \{\langle \gamma, Supp(\alpha) \cup \{\beta\}\rangle \mid \tfrac{\alpha : \beta}{\gamma} \in D,$$
$$\langle \alpha, Supp(\alpha)\rangle \in \mathcal{E}_i, Form(\mathcal{E}) \cup \{\beta\} \not\vdash \perp\}$$

Then, $\mathcal{E}$ is a classical assertional extension for $(D, \mathcal{W})$ if $\mathcal{E} = \bigcup_{i=0}^{\infty} \mathcal{E}_i$.

As opposed to the two previous cumulative default logics, the above definition does not take into account the recorded supports for testing consistency. There is only a condition imposed in the preamble of Definition 4.2.5, assuring that the resulting extension is "well-defined". Actually, Giordano and Martelli note in [GM94] that without this condition their variant would coincide with Reiter's classical default logic. On the other hand, this condition is essential for obtaining cumulativity. To see this, consider Assertional default theory (4.5). This theory has a single classical assertional extension, $\widehat{Th}(\{\langle A, \{A\}\rangle\})$. Actually, there is a second candidate for this, namely

$$\widehat{Th}(\{\langle A \vee B, \{A\}\rangle, \langle \neg A, \{A, \neg A\}\rangle\}),$$

which is however ruled out by the "well-definedness" condition given in the preamble of Definition 4.2.5.

Nonetheless, we have the following relation between Reiter's and Giordano and Martelli's approach:

Theorem 4.2.8. [GM94] *Let (D, W) be a default theory and let $(D, \mathcal{W})$ be the assertional default theory, where $\mathcal{W} = \{\langle \alpha, \emptyset\rangle \mid \alpha \in W\}$. Then, $\mathcal{E}$ is a classical assertional extension of $(D, \mathcal{W})$ iff $Form(\mathcal{E})$ is a classical extension of (D, W).*

That is, classical default logic and its assertional counterpart are equivalent whenever all formulas in an assertional default theory have empty supports. In this case, the aforementioned condition is obsolete.

The next theorem summarizes the essential properties of this variant of cumulative default logic:

Theorem 4.2.9. [GM94]

Weak regularity. Classical cumulative default logic is weakly regular.
Cumulativity. Classical cumulative default logic is cumulative.[18]

Interestingly, there is no assertional counterpart of justified default logic that enjoys cumulativity. In fact, the more complex consistency check in justified default logic necessitates a more complex structure than provided by assertions. As shown in [LS97], one may use *affirmations* as proposed by Makinson [Bre91b, p. 192][19] for obtaining a cumulative counterpart of justified default logic.

---

[18] In the sense of Theorem 4.2.2.
[19] That is, [Bre91b] cites a private communication between Brewka and Makinson.

4.3 Other Variants

A couple of other variants of default logic have been conceived since the introduction in [Rei80]. All of them addressed some purportedly counterintuitive or technical shortcomings of the original approach. A detailed exposition of this variety is unfortunately beyond the scope of this chapter, so that we have to restrict ourselves to mentioning only few of them, while relating them to the approaches discussed so far.

Historically, one of the first such variant was proposed by Łukaszewicz in [Łuk88]. This variant, discussed in Section 4.1.2, adds semi-monotonicity to default logic and consequently also guarantees the existence of extensions. Also, extensions need not be maximal anymore. This shortcoming has been addressed by Rychlik in [Ryc91], where justified default logic is modified in order to eliminate default rules redundant to the formation of extensions. Guerrerio, Casanova, and Hermerly have proposed in [dGCH90] a proof theory that turns out to be identical to Łukaszewicz' proof theory in the finite case.

A couple of other variants address the failure of cumulativity in default logic. A first such variant was proposed by Brewka in [Bre91b]: Cumulative default logic deals with labeled formulas; it is strongly regular, semi-monotonic and thus guarantees the existence of extensions. Moreover, cumulative default logic enjoys cumulativity. Other variants addressing the latter property can be found in [GM94, PP92].

Delgrande and Jackson propose in [DJ91] a strongly regular variant of default logic that is also semi-monotonic and guarantees the existence of extensions. This variant is subsumed by the one introduced in Section 4.1.3 (cf. [Sch92b, DSJ94]).

Tan and Treur introduce in [TT92] the concept of a selection function for selecting default rules applicable at each step in Definition 2.0.1. This allows for a great flexibility, in particular, for obtaining various properties, depending on the underlying selection function. [GLPT91] extends the notion of a default rule in order to allow for an additional disjunctive connective.

Froidevaux and Grossetête extend default logic in [FG90] by attaching uncertainty grades to formulas in default logic. In this way, their resulting system, graded default logic, allows for handling incomplete and uncertain information. This approach is generalized and further developed in [CF91].

Other authors experiment with different underlying logics. Giordano describes in [Gio93] a modal approach to default logic based on the possible worlds semantics described in [BS94]. Pearce describes in [Pea94] a default logic based on a constructive logic, while Radzikowska substitutes in [Rad96] classical logic by a three-valued logic.

Other authors, like [JB91, Mac91, BH92, Bre94a], extend default logic by means for handling prioritization.

4.4 Conclusion

We have summarized the relationships presented in this chapter in Table 4.1, taken from [LS97]. The table gives the properties of the treated variants and indicates the

	Conventional Default Logic		Assertional/Affirmational Default Logic	
wR	Default Logic ⇓ Justified Default Logic	⇔ ⇔	Q-Default Logic ⇓ Affirmational Default Logic	S
sR	Constrained Default Logic ⇑ Rational Default Logic	⇔ ⇔	Cumulative Default Logic ⇑ CA-Default Logic	
			C	

Table 4.1. Default logics' interrelationships.

relationships that have been discovered so far. While the first two rows comprise all variants enjoying weak regularity, the last two rows account for strongly regular default logics. The first column lists all conventional default logics, while the second one gives their assertional counterparts. The properties of the respective variants are indicated by letters attached to the borders of Table 4.1: wR and sR stand for weak and strong regularity, respectively, S for semi-monotonicity, and C for cumulativity. For instance, cumulative default logic enjoys all of the three last properties, which is reflected by the fact that its name is in the intersection of the zones labeled with sR, S, and C. The relationships between the listed variants are symbolized by ⇓, ⇑, and ⇔, respectively. The latter indicates that two default logics are equivalent, while the former tell us that we find the same extensions (possibly among others) by following the arrow. For example, each extension in classical default logic is also an extension in justified default logic (but not vice versa).

5. A context-based framework for default logics

In the preface of Chapter 4, we have already emphasized the importance of the conceptualization of consistency in default logic. However, it turned out that there is no "right" and ever appropriate formalization of consistency. Rather there are subtle differences causing a need for a more flexible treatment of consistency. This problem has been addressed in [BS93, BS95a] by appeal to the notion of *context*. In fact, the variety of different notions of consistency encountered in several default logics can be captured by means of certain contexts. As a result, we present in this chapter a context-based approach to default logic. The resulting system generalizes existing variants of default logic and provides a unified framework for default logics. In fact, it allows for embedding existing variants of default logic along with more traditional approaches like the closed world assumption. Since this is accomplished in a homogeneous way, we gain additional expressiveness by combining the diverse approaches. A key advantage of this approach is that it provides a syntactical instrument for comparing existing default logics in a unified setting. In particular, the approach reveals that existing default logics mainly differ in the way they deal with an explicit or implicit underlying context.

5.1 Motivation

In the previous chapter, we have seen variants of default logic that commit more or less to previously drawn consistency assumptions. This was achieved in turn by changing the interpretation of justifications and with it the conception of a default rule. Apart from the restoration of several formal properties, the respective notions of defaults have often led to the intuitively expected solutions on a certain class of commonsense examples.

For instance, we have seen in Section 3.1 that the "broken-arms" example is treated most adequately in the presence of the property of strong regularity. There are however other classes of commonsense reasoning patterns that require the treatment of justifications found in classical default logic, formally captured by weak regularity. To see this, consider the so-called "holidays" example discussed in [DSJ94]. Assume we are set about packing our bag for a trip to Rennes. As usual, we do so by relying on rules of thumb, like if it is possible that it will be warm then take a T-shirt; if it is possible that it will be cold then take a sweater. Of course, if we know nothing about the weather, apart from the fact that warm and cold weather are mutually exclusive, we are willing to take both our T-shirt and our sweater. In this example, it makes sense to draw both conclusions simultaneously. We want to take a T-shirt if it is merely possible for the weather to be fine, and similarly for the sweater if there is a chance for cold weather. Of course, it is both possible that the weather will be warm and possible that the weather will be cold. Hence, we want to take both clothes with us to Rennes. The account of the underlying assumptions used in the "holidays" example is weaker than in the "broken-arms" example. Here, in the "holidays" example, our intended interpretation of the justifications in the rules is closer to "is possible".

[DSJ94] gives the following formalization for the "holidays" example:

$$\left(\left\{ \frac{: W}{T}, \frac{: C}{S} \right\}, \{\neg W \vee \neg C\} \right) \tag{5.1}$$

The set of facts reflect the common knowledge that warm, W, and cold weather, C, are mutually exclusive. The default rules represent the assertions: If it is possible that it will be warm then take a T-shirt; if it is possible that it will be cold then take a sweater. Observe that even though the "holidays" example relies on intuitions different from the ones behind the "broken-arms" example, both formalizations are similar.

As in the case of the "broken-arms" example, we obtain one extension in classical default logic and two extensions in constrained default logic. That is, from Default theory (5.1) we obtain a single classical extension containing $T \wedge S$ and two constrained extensions, one containing T and another one containing S. As opposed to Section 3.1, the intuitively more appealing result is obtained now in classical default logic since it directs us to take both a T-shirt and a sweater with us to Rennes.

So, classical and constrained default logic (and with them the properties of weak and strong regularity) have exchanged their roles: In the "broken-arms" example, constrained default logic produces the intuitive result. This has been with roles reversed in the "holidays" example, where classical default logic yields the more appealing solution. This indicates that none of them is able to account for the variety of commonsense reasoning patterns needed for an appropriate treatment of default reasoning.

In the field of default logic, such controversies were so far unfortunately the rule rather than an exception. Since its introduction in [Rei80], several variants of Reiter's original default logic have been proposed, eg. [Łuk88, Bre91b, DJ91, Sch91b, DSJ94]. Each such variant rectified purportedly counterintuitive features of the original approach. This development of default logic was however diverging. Although it has resulted in diverse variants sharing many interesting properties, it has altered the notion of a default rule. In particular, most of the aforementioned variants deal with a different notion of consistency. As we have seen in Chapter 2 and 3, Reiter's default logic employs some sort of local consistency, whereas others, like constrained default logic, employ some sort of global consistency. As a result, each variant deals with certain commonsense reasoning patterns very well, while it suffers from expressing others.

This problem is addressed in this chapter. We describe a default reasoning system proposed in [BS93] and further developed in [BS95a]. This system integrates the different variants of default logic in a more general but uniform system, which combines the expressiveness of the various default logics. The basic idea is twofold. First, we supply each default extension with an underlying context. Second, we extend the notion of a default rule in order to allow for a variety of different application conditions which arise naturally from the distinction between the initial set of facts, the default extension at hand, and its context.

A detailed examination of the aforementioned phenomena from the viewpoint of context-based reasoning is given in [BS95a]. There, it is argued that contexts provide an important and meaningful notion in default reasoning. In fact, we will see below that existing default logics differ mainly in the way they deal with an explicit or implicit underlying context. On the whole, however, we confine ourselves in what follows to an introduction of the relevant details and refer the reader to [BS95a] for a more deliberate discussion.

5.2 Contextual default logic

We introduce a uniform approach to default logic by extending the notions of default rules and extensions. The resulting system is called *contextual default logic*.

In order to combine the variants of default logic, we have to compromise different notions of consistency, like for instance individual and joint consistency as found in classical and constrained default logic, respectively. In particular, we have to deal with joint consistency requirements in the presence of inconsistent individual consistency requirements. Therefore, we allow for "contexts" containing contradictory formulas, like B and ¬B as in Example (2.11) on Page 17, without containing all possible formulas. Thus, we admit contexts which are not deductively closed. In Example (2.11), the extension $Th(\{C, D\})$ will then have the context $Th(\{C, D, B\}) \cup Th(\{C, D, \neg B\})$ being composed of two incompatible subcontexts. A useful notion is then that of *pointwise closure $Th_S(T)$*.

Definition 5.2.1. *Let T and S be sets of formulas. If T is non-empty, the pointwise closure of T under S is defined as*

$$Th_S(T) = \bigcup_{\phi \in T} Th(S \cup \{\phi\}).$$

In addition, $Th_S(\emptyset) = Th(S)$.

If S is a singleton set $\{\varphi\}$, we simply write $Th_\varphi(T)$ instead of $Th_{\{\varphi\}}(T)$. Given two sets of formulas T and S, we say that T is *pointwisely closed under S* iff $T = Th_S(T)$. In particular, we simply say that T is pointwisely closed whenever $T = Th_\top(T)$ for any tautology $\top$.

Observe that the aforementioned context can now be represented as the pointwise closure of $\{B, \neg B\}$ under $\{C, D\}$, namely $Th_{\{C,D\}}(\{B, \neg B\})$.

In our approach, we consider three sets of formulas: A set of facts W, an extension E, and a certain *context* C such that $W \subseteq E \subseteq C$. The set of formulas C is somehow established from the facts, the default conclusions (ie. the consequences of the applied default rules), as well as all underlying consistency assumptions (ie. the justifications of all applied default rules). In fact, this approach trivially captures the above application conditions for existing default rules, eg. $\alpha \in E$ and $\neg\beta \notin E$ in the case of classical default logic.

Yet our approach allows for even more ways of forming application conditions of default rules. Consider a formula φ and three consistent, deductively closed sets of formulas W, E, and C such that $W \subseteq E \subseteq C$. Six more or less strong application conditions are obtained which can be ordered from left to right by decreasing strength; whereby $>$ is read as "implies":

$$\varphi \in W > \varphi \in E > \varphi \in C > \neg\varphi \notin C > \neg\varphi \notin E > \neg\varphi \notin W \qquad (5.2)$$

We can think of W as a deductively closed set of facts, E as a default extension of W, and C as the above mentioned context for E. Then, the first condition $\varphi \in W$ stands for first-order derivability from the facts W. The second condition $\varphi \in E$ stands for derivability from W using standard logic and certain default rules. This is used in existing default logics as the test for the prerequisite of a default rule. The third condition, $\varphi \in C$, expresses "membership in a context of reasoning". The last three conditions are consistency conditions. The fourth condition $\neg\varphi \notin C$ corresponds to the consistency condition used in constrained default logic, the fifth one $\neg\varphi \notin E$ is used in classical default logic. Finally, the last condition $\neg\varphi \notin W$ is the one used for the closed world assumption [Rei77], where it is restricted to ground negative literals.

This variety of application conditions motivates an extended notion of a default rule.

Definition 5.2.2. *A contextual default rule δ is an expression of the form*[1]

$$\frac{\alpha_W \mid \alpha_E \mid \alpha_C \ : \ \beta_C \mid \beta_E \mid \beta_W}{\gamma}$$

where α_W, α_E, α_C, β_C, β_E, β_W, and γ are formulas.

α_W, α_E, α_C *are called the W-, E-, and C-prerequisites, also noted $Prereq_W(\delta)$, $Prereq_E(\delta)$, $Prereq_C(\delta)$, β_C, β_E, β_W are called the C-, E-, and W-justifications, also noted $Justif_C(\delta)$, $Justif_E(\delta)$, $Justif_W(\delta)$, and γ is called the consequent, also noted $Conseq(\delta)$.* [2]

The six antecedents of a contextual default rule are to be treated along the above intuitions. Whenever we omit one of the antecedents, we expect a tautology, like $\top$.

---

[1] For simplicity, we restrict ourselves to contextual default rules having only one justification of each type.

[2] These projections extend to sets of contextual default rules in the obvious way (eg. $Justif_E(\Delta) = \bigcup_{\delta \in \Delta}\{Justif_E(\delta)\}$).

A contextual default theory is a pair (D, W), where D is a set of contextual default rules and W is a deductively closed[3] set of formulas. A contextual extension is to be a pair (E, C), where E is a deductively closed set of formulas and C is a pointwisely closed set of formulas. This leads to the following definition [BS93].

Definition 5.2.3. *Let (D, W) be a contextual default theory and let E and C be sets of formulas. Define*

$$E_0 = W, \qquad C_0 = W$$

and for $i \geq 0$

$$\Delta_i \;=\; \left\{ \frac{\alpha_W \,|\, \alpha_E \,|\, \alpha_C \;:\; \beta_C \,|\, \beta_E \,|\, \beta_W}{\gamma} \in D \;\middle|\; \begin{array}{l} \alpha_W \in W, \quad \alpha_E \in E_i, \quad \alpha_C \in C_i, \\ \neg\beta_C \notin C, \quad \neg\beta_E \notin E, \quad \neg\beta_W \notin W \end{array} \right\}$$

$$E_{i+1} \;=\; Th(W \cup Conseq(\Delta_i))$$
$$C_{i+1} \;=\; Th_{W \cup Conseq(\Delta_i) \cup Justif_C(\Delta_i)} \left(Justif_E(\Delta_i) \right)$$

Then, (E, C) is a contextual extension of (D, W) if $(E, C) = (\bigcup_{i=0}^{\infty} E_i, \bigcup_{i=0}^{\infty} C_i)$.

The extension E is built by successively introducing the consequents of all applying contextual default rules. Also, the deductive closure is computed at each stage. For each partial context C_{i+1}, the partial extension E_{i+1} is unioned with the C-justifications of all applying contextual default rules. This set is unioned in turn with each E-justification of all applying contextual default rules. Again, the deductive closure is computed when appropriate. In this way, each partial context C_{i+1} is built upon its "kernel", $Th(E_{i+1} \cup Justif_C(\Delta_i))$. That is, given a contextual extension (E, C), the contexts C contains the deductive closure of E and all formulas involved in joint consistency requirements. In symbols,[4] $Th\left(E \cup Justif_C\left(GD_{(D,W)}^{(E,C)} \right) \right) \subseteq C$. Since this set is shared by all subcontexts of a context, we call it the *kernel* of a context. With it, a context can alternatively be described as the pointwise closure of the E-justifications under the kernel.

As we detail in Section 5.3, contextual default logic allows for handling both the "broken-arms" as well as the "holidays" example. More interestingly, however, contextual default logic allows for combining the two previous examples: We have argued above that the "broken arms" example is best accomplished in the presence of strong regularity (thus interpreting justifications as joint consistency requirements), while the "holidays" example is treated more intuitively in a weakly regular default logic (that uses justifications as individual consistency requirements). Merging the corresponding contextual default rules results in the following contextual default theory.

---

[3] This is no real restriction, but it simplifies matters.
[4] See Definition 3.3.1 for a definition of $GD_D^{(E,C)}$.

$$\left(\left\{\begin{array}{cc} \dfrac{\|:\neg\mathsf{Bl}\,\|}{\mathsf{Ul}}, & \dfrac{\|:\neg\mathsf{Br}\,\|}{\mathsf{Ur}} \\[2ex] \dfrac{\|:|\mathsf{W}|}{\mathsf{T}}, & \dfrac{\|:|\mathsf{C}|}{\mathsf{S}} \end{array}\right\}, \left\{\begin{array}{c} \mathsf{Bl}\vee\mathsf{Br} \\ \neg\mathsf{W}\vee\neg\mathsf{C} \end{array}\right\}\right) \tag{5.3}$$

With this contextual default theory, we arrive at the so-called "holidays with broken arms" example. Notably, this example cannot be treated adequately by any existing default logic. This is so because no existing default logic is able to account for the variety of contexts (or implicit consistency assumptions, respectively) that is needed for an appropriate treatment of this example.

The first extension

$$Th(\{\neg\mathsf{W}\vee\neg\mathsf{C},\mathsf{Bl}\vee\mathsf{Br},\mathsf{T},\mathsf{S},\mathsf{Ul}\}) \tag{5.4}$$

is formed while reasoning in context

$$Th(\{\mathsf{W},\neg\mathsf{C},\mathsf{T},\mathsf{S},\neg\mathsf{Bl},\mathsf{Br},\mathsf{Ul}\}) \cup Th(\{\neg\mathsf{W},\mathsf{C},\mathsf{T},\mathsf{S},\neg\mathsf{Bl},\mathsf{Br},\mathsf{Ul}\})\,; \tag{5.5}$$

and the second extension

$$Th(\{\neg\mathsf{W}\vee\neg\mathsf{C},\mathsf{Bl}\vee\mathsf{Br},\mathsf{T},\mathsf{S},\mathsf{Ur}\})$$

is embedded in context

$$Th(\{\mathsf{W},\neg\mathsf{C},\mathsf{T},\mathsf{S},\mathsf{Bl},\neg\mathsf{Br},\mathsf{Ur}\}) \cup Th(\{\neg\mathsf{W},\mathsf{C},\mathsf{T},\mathsf{S},\mathsf{Bl},\neg\mathsf{Br},\mathsf{Ur}\})\,.$$

Both extensions direct us to take both a T-shirt and a sweater on our trip to Rennes. However, in the first extension, we believe that the left arm is usable, while we believe the same for the right arm in the second extension.

Now, let us detail the case of the first contextual extension. This extension is obtained by applying contextual default rules

$$\dfrac{\|:\ \neg\mathsf{Bl}\,\|}{\mathsf{Ul}},\qquad \dfrac{\|:|\mathsf{W}|}{\mathsf{T}}\quad\text{and}\quad \dfrac{\|:|\mathsf{C}|}{\mathsf{S}}. \tag{5.6}$$

The C-justification of the first contextual default rule, $\neg\mathsf{Bl}$, is a joint consistency requirement. Therefore, it belongs to each subcontext in (5.5). Each subcontext in turn is originated by the E-justifications of the last two contextual default rules, namely W and C. They have to be individually consistent which is ensured by the respective subcontext that they have in common with the extension at hand. In the same way, we obtain the second contextual extension.

5.3 Embedding existing default logics

This section shows that classical, justified, rational, and constrained default logic are embedded in contextual default logic. Via Theorem 4.2.1 and 4.2.7, this extends moreover to their assertional counterparts, like cumulative and rational cumulative default logic.

In order to relate classical with contextual default logic, let us agree on identifying default theories in classical default logic with contextual default theories as follows [BS93].

Definition 5.3.1 (Classical default logic). *Let* (D, W) *be a default theory. We define*

$$\Phi_{DL}(D, W) = \left(\left\{ \frac{|\alpha|:|\beta|}{\gamma} \;\middle|\; \frac{\alpha:\beta}{\gamma} \in D \right\}, Th(W) \right).$$

Then, classical default logic corresponds to this fragment of contextual default logic [BS93].

Theorem 5.3.1. *Let* (D, W) *be a default theory and let* E *be a set of formulas and* $C_E = \left\{ \beta \;\middle|\; \frac{\alpha:\beta}{\gamma} \in D, \; \alpha \in E, \neg\beta \notin E \right\}$. *Then,* E *is a classical extension of* (D, W) *and* $C = Th_E(C_E)$ *iff* (E, C) *is a contextual extension of* $\Phi_{DL}(D, W)$.

Given a classical extension E, the context C is the pointwise closure of the justifications, C_E, of the generating default rules under E.

Consider the contextual counterpart of Default theory (5.1):

$$\left(\left\{ \frac{||:|W|}{T}, \frac{||:|C|}{S} \right\}, \{\neg W \vee \neg C\} \right)$$

We obtain one contextual extension

– $(Th(\{\neg W \vee \neg C, T, S\}), Th(\{W, \neg C, T, S\}) \cup Th(\{\neg W, C, T, S\}))$

whose extension corresponds to the classical extension of Default theory (5.1). The first subcontext, $Th(\{W, \neg C, T, S\})$, contains the E-justification of the first contextual default rule, whereas the second one, $Th(\{\neg W, C, T, S\})$, contains the E-justification of the second contextual default rule. In addition, a common kernel of the two subcontexts of the context is given by the actual extension.

A default theory in constrained default logic is identified with a contextual default theory in the following way [BS93].

Definition 5.3.2 (Constrained default logic). *Let* (D, W) *be a default theory. We define*

$$\Phi_{CDL}(D, W) = \left(\left\{ \frac{|\alpha|:\beta\wedge\gamma||}{\gamma} \;\middle|\; \frac{\alpha:\beta}{\gamma} \in D \right\}, Th(W) \right).$$

This yields the following correspondence [BS93].

Theorem 5.3.2. *Let* (D, W) *be a default theory and let* E *and* C *be sets of formulas. Then,* (E, C) *is a constrained extension of* (D, W) *iff* (E, C) *is a contextual extension of* $\Phi_{CDL}(D, W)$.

(Theorem 4.2.1 extends this correspondance to cumulative default logic.) Notice that C is always deductively closed whenever (E, C) is an extension in either sense.

For illustration, consider the contextual counterpart of Default theory (3.1) from the perspective of constrained default logic:

$$\left(\left\{ \frac{||:\neg Bl||}{Ul}, \frac{||:\neg Br||}{Ur} \right\}, \{Bl \vee Br\} \right)$$

As a result, we obtain two contextual extensions:

- $(Th(\{BI \vee Br, UI\}), Th(\{\neg BI, Br, UI\}))$
- $(Th(\{BI \vee Br, Ur\}), Th(\{BI, \neg Br, Ur\}))$

These are identical to the respective constrained extensions, given in (3.2) on Page 25.

Actually, the same extensions are obtained when using the transformation embedding rational default logic into the framework of contextual default logic [LS96]:

Definition 5.3.3 (Rational default logic). *Let* (D, W) *be a default theory. We define*

$$\Phi_{\mathsf{RDL}}(D, W) = \left(\left\{ \frac{|\alpha|: \beta\,||}{\gamma} \;\middle|\; \frac{\alpha:\beta}{\gamma} \in D \right\}, Th(W) \right).$$

The correspondence of this contextual fragment to rational default logic is shown in [LS96]; it is analogous to that given in Theorem 5.3.2. As above, this correspondence extends to the assertional counterpart of rational default logic, here, by appeal to Theorem 4.2.7.

Further evidence for the generality of this approach is that it can capture justified default logic. Let us identify default theories in justified default logic with contextual default theories in the following way [BS95a].

Definition 5.3.4 (Justified default logic). *Let* (D, W) *be a default theory. We define*

$$\Phi_{\mathsf{JDL}}(D, W) = \left(\left\{ \frac{|\alpha|: \gamma\,|\beta\wedge\gamma|}{\gamma} \;\middle|\; \frac{\alpha:\beta}{\gamma} \in D \right\}, Th(W) \right).$$

This leads to the following correspondence [BS95a].

Theorem 5.3.3. *Let* (D, W) *be a default theory and let* $E, J,$ *and* C *be sets of formulas. Then,* (E, J) *is a justified extension of* (D, W) *and* $C = Th_E(J)$ *iff* (E, C) *is a contextual extension of* $\Phi_{\mathsf{JDL}}(D, W)$.

Note that J consists of the justifications of the generating[5] default rules for E, whereas C is given by the pointwise closure of the same set of justifications under E.

It is interesting to observe how the relatively complicated consistency check in justified default logic is accomplishable in contextual default logic. For a justified extension (E, J) and a default rule $\frac{\alpha:\beta}{\gamma}$ the condition is $\forall \eta \in J \cup \{\beta\}. E \cup \{\gamma\} \cup \{\eta\} \not\vdash \bot$. In fact, it is two-fold: It consists of a joint and an individual consistency check, ie. $\forall \eta \in J. E \cup \{\gamma\} \cup \{\eta\} \not\vdash \bot$ and $E \cup \{\gamma\} \cup \{\beta\} \not\vdash \bot$. Transposed to the case of a contextual extension (E, C) the two subconditions are $\neg\gamma \notin C$ and $\neg(\beta \wedge \gamma) \notin E$. The first check cares about the joint consistency of the consequent γ, whereas the second one checks whether the conjunction of the justification and consequent of the default rule is individually consistent.

Now, let us see what happens to Default theory (4.1) if we apply translation Φ_{JDL}:

---

[5] In the sense of justified default logic.

$$\left(\left\{ \frac{\| : \ C \mid B \wedge C \mid}{C}, \frac{\| : \ D \mid \neg B \wedge D \mid}{D}, \frac{\| : \ E \mid \neg C \wedge \neg D \wedge E \mid}{E} \right\}, Th(\emptyset) \right)$$

As with justified default logic, we obtain two contextual extensions:

- $(Th(\{C, D\}), Th(\{C, D, B\}) \cup Th(\{C, D, \neg B\}))$,
- $(Th(\{E\}), Th(\{E, \neg C, \neg D\}))$,

whose extensions correspond to the extensions obtained in justified default logic. It is interesting to observe that the respective subcontexts differ exactly in the justifications attached to the extensions in justified default logic.

Apart from the treatment of existing variants of default logics, contextual default logic allows for integrating other well-known concepts in commonsense reasoning, namely first-order derivability and the closed world assumption by means of W-prerequisites and W-justifications, respectively. A general discussion on the expressiveness of contextual default logic is given in [BS95a]. Zaverucha takes up the idea of C-prerequisites in [Zav94] in order to address certain anomalous phenomena discussed in the default logic literature.

5.4 Formal properties

Let us now turn to the formal properties of contextual default logic. We have noticed in Chapter 2 that many interesting properties are not present in Reiter's original default logic in its full generality. Rather we have encountered several restricted subclasses enjoying one or another property. Hence we cannot expect that contextual default logic improves this situation since it is more expressive than any variant of default logic. Many formal properties of restricted subclasses in contextual default logic can be obtained by looking at the subclasses corresponding to existing variants of default logic. See [BS95a] for details on this.

[BS95a] isolate a large subclass of contextual default theories, which goes beyond those subclasses characterizing existing default logics and which enjoys some interesting properties:

Theorem 5.4.1. *Let* (D, W) *be a contextual default theory such that*

$$D \subseteq \left\{ \frac{\alpha_W \mid \alpha_E \mid \alpha_C \ : \ \alpha \wedge \beta \wedge \gamma \mid \gamma \mid}{\beta \wedge \gamma} \ \middle| \ \alpha_W, \alpha_E, \alpha_C, \alpha, \beta, \gamma \ formulas \right\}.$$

Existence. (D, W) *has a consistent contextual extension.*
Semi-monotonicity. contextual default logic is semi-monotonic,
*   when restricted to contextual default rules as in* D.

Moreover, we can merge contextual default rules belonging to different classes representing default theories in existing default logics, which guarantee existence and semi-monotonicity, without loosing the latter properties. For instance, any contextual default theory, whose contextual default rules belong to the fragments of contextual default logic corresponding to "normal classical" or full constrained default logic, has a consistent contextual extension.

Another interesting result deals with the property of orthogonality.

Theorem 5.4.2. *Let* (E, C) *and* (E', C') *be distinct contextual extensions of the contextual default theory* (D, W). *Let* C_K *and* C'_K *be the kernels of* C *and* C'. *Then, we have that either* $C_K \cup C'_{\beta'}$ *is inconsistent for* $C'_{\beta'} = Th(E' \cup \{\beta'\})$ *and some* $\beta' \in Prereq_E \left(GD_{(D,W)}^{(E',C')} \right)$ *or* $C'_K \cup C_\beta$ *is inconsistent for* $C_\beta = Th(E \cup \{\beta\})$ *and some* $\beta \in Prereq_E \left(GD_{(D,W)}^{(E,C)} \right)$.

The theorem shows that multiple extensions stem from incompatibilities between kernels, like C_K or C'_K, and subcontexts, $C'_{\beta'}$ or C_β, of different contextual extensions.

As a corollary, we obtain that contexts of distinct contextual extensions are always mutually contradictory. That is, we obtain the property of weak orthogonality as formulated in Theorem 3.3.4.

A formal semantics for contextual default logic is described in Section 6.5.

5.5 Conclusion

Contextual default logic is not yet another default logic. Rather it provides a unified framework for default logics by extending the notion of a default rule and supplying each extension with a context. Such contexts are formed by pointwisely closing certain consistency assumptions under a given extension.

In this chapter, we have isolated six different application conditions for default rules. Even more such application conditions are discussed in [BS95a].

From a synthetic point of view, contextual default logic integrates existing default logics along with other concepts like the closed world assumption. But apart from the separate integration of these approaches, we moreover gain expressiveness by combining them. From an analytical point of view, the key advantage of contextual default logic is that it provides a syntactical instrument for comparing existing default logics in a unified setting. In particular, contextual default logic has explicated the context-dependency of default logics and thus revealed that existing default logics differ mainly in the way they deal with an explicit or implicit underlying context. As a result, we have seen, for instance, that justified default logic compromises individual and joint consistency, whereas other variants strictly employ either of them. Thus, contextual default logic is obviously of theoretical importance. Moreover, it may be of great practical relevance in the future since it may serve as a common implementation platform for default logics. This may even result in an abstract machine for default logics and similar approaches.

6. Possible worlds semantics for default logics

Any syntactic manipulation of symbols must have some formal semantical under-pinnings provided that the manipulated symbols should convey any meaning. This general principle applies in particular to syntactic methods formalizing some kind of reasoning. In contrast to this, it took seven years until a first formal semantics was given for classical default logic in its full generality. The situation was even worse in several variants of default logic, which were either proposed without semantics or by using syntactical entities. As a consequence, there was no semantical discipline present in the field of default logics. This deplorable state of affairs was remedied in [BS92, BS94] where a uniform semantical approach framework for existing default logics was proposed. This semantical framework allows for comparing existing default logics in a simple but very substantial manner. Moreover, the approach remedies several difficulties encountered in former proposals aiming at individual default logics. This is accomplished by appeal to so-called Kripke structures, which were originally conceived for providing semantics for modal logics.

6.1 Motivation

We have seen in Section 2.3 that despite its intuitiveness, it took several years until first semantical underpinnings for default logic were developed. A first step towards a formal semantics was made by Łukaszewicz in [Łuk85] by providing a semantical characterization for normal default theories. In all, it took seven years until a first model-theoretic semantics for the original approach to default logic was proposed in [Eth87]. Moreover, there has been no coherent semantical approach capturing the variants of default logic in a homogeneous way, even though there where individual attempts dealing separately with certain variants. The focused models structures, described in Section 3.4, provides model-theoretic semantics for constrained and cumulative default logic (via Theorem 4.2.1). Also, Łukaszewicz proposed in [Łuk88] a semantics for justified default logic (yet by appeal to sets of formulas). Hence there was no coherent semantical approach to default logics capturing the different approaches to default logic.

Looking at the descendants of classical default logic, we observe that a common feature is their use of constraints, either on formulas, as in cumulative default logic, or on sets of formulas, as in justified and constrained default logic (cf. Section 3.4).

In other words, all of these variants employ more additional "structures" for achieving their desired results. In a similar way, Etherington's semantics for classical default logic has been extended in order to account for the additional syntactical structures. For instance, two-fold semantics, like the focused models structures, were proposed, whose second component was intended to capture the enriched structure in constrained default logic.

Although the elements of these two-fold semantics are standard first-order interpretations, splitting the semantical characterizations of the extension and its underlying constraints might appear to be artificial. On the other hand, Kripke structures (cf. [Bow79]) provide a means to establish relations between first-order interpretations: A Kripke structure has a distinguished world, the s"actual" world, and a set of worlds accessible from it (each world is associated with a first-order interpretation). As a consequence, a first aim of this work is to avoid two-fold semantics by characterizing extensions in default logics by means of Kripke structures, thereby somehow absorbing the additional syntactical structures used in each variant of classical default logic. In fact, this approach turns out to be very general, so that we obtain a uniform semantical framework for comparing existing default logics in a unified setting.

The idea of the approach is roughly as follows. In default logics, our beliefs consist of the conclusions given by the applying default rules, and the constraints on our beliefs stem from the justifications provided by the same default rules. Accordingly, the intuition behind this semantics is very natural: The actual worlds of a considered class of Kripke structures exhibits what we believe and the accessible worlds exhibit what constraints we have imposed upon our beliefs. Hence, the actual world is our envisioning of how things are and, therefore, characterizes an extension, whereas the surrounding worlds additionally deal with the constraints and, therefore, provide a context in which that envisioning takes place.

Let us put this in more concrete terms by means of constrained default logic. In constrained default logic, a set of constraints C is attached to an extension E. Given a constrained extension (E, C) and a Kripke structure $\mathfrak{k}$, we require that the actual world be a model of the extension, E, and demand that each world accessible from the actual world be a model of the constraints, C. That is, $\mathfrak{k} \models E \wedge \Box C$.[1]

In what follows, we detail semantical characterizations for constrained classical, and justified default logic. A corresponding semantics for rational default logic is obtained through that of contextual default logic, which is described in Section 6.5. Semantical characterizations for assertional default logics are obtained by appeal to the equivalence results given in Section 4.2. More general semantical insights, like the semantics of lemma default rules, and a comparative study of the various approaches from the semantical viewpoint are given in [BS94].

We follow the definitions (cf. Appendix A.2) in [Bow79] of a Kripke structure (called K–model in the sequel). As in Appendix A.2, we use $\mathfrak{k}$ to denote K-models, $\mathfrak{K}$ to denote classes of K–models, and $\models$ to denote the modal entailment relation. We

---

[1] Given a set of formulas S let $\Box S$ stand for $\wedge_{\alpha \in S} \Box \alpha$.

extend the modal entailment relation $\models$ to classes of K–models $\mathfrak{K}$ and write $\mathfrak{K} \models \alpha$ to mean that each element in $\mathfrak{K}$ (that is, a K–model) entails α.

6.2 Possible worlds semantics for constrained default logic

In Section 3.4, we characterized constrained extensions (E, C) by means of focused models structures $(\mathfrak{m}, \breve{\mathfrak{m}})$, which are pairs of classes of first-order interpretations. The first class, $\mathfrak{m}$, characterizes E and the second class, $\breve{\mathfrak{m}}$, characterizes C. However, such focused models structures suggest that the ordering induced by a default rule has a modal nature with the corresponding semantical approach being based on Kripke structures. Intuitively, a pair $(\mathfrak{m}, \breve{\mathfrak{m}})$ is to be rendered as a class $\mathfrak{K}$ of Kripke structures such that $\mathfrak{m}$ is captured by the actual worlds in $\mathfrak{K}$ and $\breve{\mathfrak{m}}$ by the accessible worlds in $\mathfrak{K}$. Ie. consider a non–modal formula α: It is valid in $\mathfrak{m}$ iff α is valid in $\mathfrak{K}$ and it is valid in $\breve{\mathfrak{m}}$ iff $\Box\alpha$ is valid in $\mathfrak{K}$.

Correspondingly, the counterpart to a maximal focused models structure happens to be a class $\mathfrak{K}$ of Kripke structures such that

$$(\{\alpha \text{ non–modal} \mid \mathfrak{K} \models \alpha\}, \{\alpha \text{ non–modal} \mid \mathfrak{K} \models \Box\alpha\})$$

forms a constrained extension of the default theory under consideration. As always, the first set establishes the extension whereas the second set characterizes its constraints.

In order to characterize constrained extensions semantically, we now define a family of strict partial orders on classes of K–models. Analogously to the semantics of Section 2.3 and 3.4, given a default rule δ, its application conditions and the result of applying it are captured by an order $\succ_\delta$ as follows.

Definition 6.2.1. *Let* $\delta = \frac{\alpha : \beta}{\gamma}$. *Let* $\mathfrak{K}$ *and* $\mathfrak{K}'$ *be distinct classes of K–models. We define* $\mathfrak{K} \succ_\delta \mathfrak{K}'$ *iff*

$$\mathfrak{K} = \{\mathfrak{k} \in \mathfrak{K}' \mid \mathfrak{k} \models \gamma \wedge \Box(\gamma \wedge \beta)\}$$

and

1. $\mathfrak{K}' \models \alpha$
2. $\mathfrak{K}' \not\models \Box\neg(\gamma \wedge \beta)$

Given a set of default rules D, the strict partial order $\succ_D$ amounts to the union of the strict partial orders $\succ_\delta$ as follows. $\mathfrak{K} \succ_D \mathfrak{K}'$ iff there exists an enumeration $\langle \delta_i \rangle_{i \in I}$ of some $D' \subseteq D$ such that $\mathfrak{K}_{i+1} \succ_{\delta_i} \mathfrak{K}_i$ for some sequence $\langle \mathfrak{K}_i \rangle_{i \in I}$ of subclasses of $\mathfrak{K}'$ satisfying $\mathfrak{K}' = \mathfrak{K}_0$ and $\mathfrak{K} = \bigcap_{i \in I} \mathfrak{K}_i$.

Moreover, we define the class of K–models associated with W as $\mathfrak{K}_W = \{\mathfrak{k} \mid \mathfrak{k} \models \gamma \wedge \Box\gamma, \gamma \in W\}$ and refer to $\succ_D$–maximal classes of K–models above $\mathfrak{K}_W$ as the *preferred* classes of K–models wrt (D, W).

As for modal logic, observe that the K–models define the modal system K. It makes sense because the only property needed is distributivity for the modal operator $\Box$ to ensure that the constraints are deductively closed. With K, we have chosen the most general modal logic, since it imposes no restrictions on the accessibility relation.

As a reminder, we give below the axiom schema (K) and inference rule (NEC) that must be added to a classical first order system in order to obtain K:

$$(K) \qquad \Box(\alpha \to \beta) \to (\Box\alpha \to \Box\beta)$$

$$(NEC) \qquad \frac{\alpha}{\Box\alpha}$$

We give a detailed example illustrating the main idea. Consider Default theory $(\{\frac{A:B}{C}\}, \{A\})$ that yields the constrained extension $(Th(\{A, C\}), Th(\{A, B, C\}))$. In order to characterize this semantically, we start with

$$\mathbb{K}_W \models A \wedge \Box A.$$

Since $\mathbb{K}_W \models A$ it remains to ensure that $\mathbb{K}_W \not\models \Box\neg(C \wedge B)$, which is obvious. Hence, we obtain a class of K–models $\mathbb{K}$ such that

$$\mathbb{K} \models A \wedge \Box A \wedge C \wedge \Box(C \wedge B).$$

So, the actual worlds of our K–models satisfy the formulas of extension $Th(\{A, C\})$ whereas the surrounding worlds additionally fulfill the constraints, given by the set $Th(\{A, B, C\})$.

Notice that Condition 2 in Definition 6.2.1 is equivalent to

$$\exists \mathfrak{k} \in \mathbb{K}'. \mathfrak{k} \models \Diamond(\gamma \wedge \beta). \tag{6.1}$$

That is, the consistency condition in constrained default logic corresponds semantically to the requirement that there is a K–model which has some accessible world that satisfies $\gamma \wedge \beta$.

Another interesting point concerning Definition 6.2.1 is that finding a non–empty $\mathbb{K} \subseteq \mathbb{K}'$ such that $\mathbb{K} \models \Box(\gamma \wedge \beta)$ whenever $\mathbb{K}' \not\models \Box\neg(\gamma \wedge \beta)$ might appear to be impossible, hence the next result [BS94].

Theorem 6.2.1. *The empty class of K–models is never preferred wrt (D, W) whenever W is consistent.*

As a corollary we obtain that the existence of constrained extensions is guaranteed.

In order to have a comprehensive example throughout this chapter, let us revisit Default theory (4.1), already discussed in Chapter 4. We have seen that Default theory (4.1)

$$\left(\left\{\frac{: B}{C}, \frac{: \neg B}{D}, \frac{: \neg D \wedge \neg C}{E}\right\}, \emptyset\right)$$

gives indeed rise to three constrained extensions, namely $(Th(\{C\}), Th(\{B, C\}))$, $(Th(\{D\}), Th(\{\neg B, D\}))$, and $(Th(\{E\}), Th(\{\neg D, \neg C, E\}))$. On the semantical side, Default theory (4.1) induces three preferred classes of K-models:

- $\{\mathfrak{k} \mid \mathfrak{k} \models C \wedge \square(B \wedge C)\}$,
- $\{\mathfrak{k} \mid \mathfrak{k} \models D \wedge \square(\neg B \wedge D)\}$,
- $\{\mathfrak{k} \mid \mathfrak{k} \models E \wedge \square(\neg D \wedge \neg C \wedge E)\}$.

Let us examine the way these K-models are obtained in some detail. $\mathfrak{K}_W$ is the class of all K-models and clearly, we have $\mathfrak{K}_W \not\models \square\neg(C \wedge B)$, $\mathfrak{K}_W \not\models \square\neg(D \wedge \neg B)$, and $\mathfrak{K}_W \not\models \square\neg(E \wedge \neg D \wedge \neg C)$. Therefore, all three default rules are potentially "applicable".

Let us detail the case of the first preferred class of K-models, say $\mathfrak{K}$. We obtain a $\succ_{\{\frac{:B}{C}\}}$-greater class

$$\mathfrak{K} \models C \wedge \square(C \wedge B).$$

In order to show that there is a $\succ_{\{\frac{:B}{C}, \frac{:\neg B}{D}\}}$-greater class, we would have to show that $\mathfrak{K} \not\models \square\neg(D \wedge \neg B)$. But since $\square(C \wedge B) \models \square B$, we have $\mathfrak{K} \models \square(B \vee \neg D)$, which prevents us from "applying" the second default rule. Analogously, we do not obtain a $\succ_{\{\frac{:B}{C}, \frac{:\neg D \wedge \neg C}{E}\}}$-greater class.

The notion of a preferred class of K–models illustrated above is put into a precise correspondence with constrained extensions in the following theorem [BS94].

Theorem 6.2.2 (Correctness & Completeness). *Let* (D, W) *be a default theory. Let* $\mathfrak{K}$ *be a class of K–models and E, C deductively closed sets of formulas such that*

$$\mathfrak{K} = \{\mathfrak{k} \mid \mathfrak{k} \models E \wedge \square C\}.$$

Then, (E, C) is a constrained extension of (D, W) iff $\mathfrak{K}$ is a $\succ_D$–maximal class above $\mathfrak{K}_W$.

Then our possible worlds approach amounts to the focused model semantics presented in Section 3.4: the first order interpretations associated with the accessible worlds take over the role of the focused models.

Corollary 6.2.1. *Let* (D, W) *be a default theory, $(\mathfrak{M}, \breve{\mathfrak{M}})$ a $\succeq_D$–maximal focused models structure above $(\{\mathfrak{m} \mid \mathfrak{m} \models W\}, \{\mathfrak{m} \mid \mathfrak{m} \models W\})$ and $\mathfrak{K}$ a preferred class of K–models wrt (D, W). Then, for α, β non–modal $\mathfrak{M} \models \alpha$ iff $\mathfrak{K} \models \alpha$ and $\breve{\mathfrak{M}} \models \beta$ iff $\mathfrak{K} \models \square\beta$.*

6.3 Possible worlds semantics for classical default logic

The possible worlds approach to default logic presented above turns out to be very general. The first evidence of this arises from the fact that the above semantical characterization carries over easily to classical default logic. Indeed, the analogue to Definition 6.2.1 can be defined as follows.[2]

---

[2] Given a set of formulas S let $\diamond S$ stand for $\wedge_{\alpha \in S} \diamond \alpha$.

Definition 6.3.1. *Let* $\delta = \frac{\alpha : \beta}{\gamma}$. *Let* $\mathfrak{K}$ *and* $\mathfrak{K}'$ *be distinct classes of K–models. We define* $\mathfrak{K} >_\delta \mathfrak{K}'$ *iff*

$$\mathfrak{K} = \{\mathfrak{k} \in \mathfrak{K}' \mid \mathfrak{k} \models \gamma \wedge \Box\gamma \wedge \Diamond\beta\}$$

and

1. $\mathfrak{K}' \models \alpha$
2. $\mathfrak{K}' \not\models \Box\neg\beta$

The order $>_D$ is defined analogously to that in Section 6.2.

Even though classical default logic does not employ explicit constraints, there is a natural counterpart given by the justifications of the generating default rules over a set of formulas E:

$$C_E = \left\{ \beta \ \middle| \ \frac{\alpha : \beta}{\gamma} \in D, \ \alpha \in E, \neg\beta \notin E \right\}^3$$

We obtain a semantical characterization that yields a one–to–one correspondence between consistent extensions and non–empty $>_D$–preferred classes of K–models (an inconsistent extension trivially corresponds to $\mathfrak{K}_W$ being preferred while being empty).

Theorem 6.3.1 (Correctness & Completeness). *Let* (D, W) *be a default theory. Let* $\mathfrak{K}$ *be a class of K–models and E be a deductively closed set of formulas such that*

$$\mathfrak{K} = \{\mathfrak{k} \mid \mathfrak{k} \models E \wedge \Box E \wedge \Diamond C_E\}.$$

Then, E is a consistent classical extension of (D, W) *iff* $\mathfrak{K}$ *is a* $>_D$*–maximal non-empty class above* $\mathfrak{K}_W$.

Comparing Definition 6.3.1 with Definition 6.2.1, we observe two basic differences, reflecting the fact that constrained default logic employs a stronger consistency check than classical default logic. For one thing, the second condition on $\mathfrak{K}'$ is weakened such that only β instead of $\gamma \wedge \beta$ is required to be satisfied by some accessible world of some K–model in $\mathfrak{K}'$. This becomes perfectly clear by comparing the following formulation of Condition 2 in Definition 6.3.1

$$\exists \mathfrak{k} \in \mathfrak{K}'. \ \mathfrak{k} \models \Diamond\beta \tag{6.2}$$

with the one given in (6.1). For another thing, Definition 6.3.1 requires $\Diamond\beta$ to be valid in $\mathfrak{K}$ whereas Definition 6.2.1 requires $\Box\beta$ to be valid in $\mathfrak{K}$. Stated otherwise, the possible worlds semantics for classical extensions requires only *some* accessible world satisfying the justification β whereas the semantics for constrained default logic requires *all* accessible worlds to satisfy β.

Let us now return to Default theory (4.1). This theory has one preferred class of K-models:

---

3 Observe that the membership qualifying property is exactly the third condition in Definition 2.0.1.

$- \{ \mathfrak{k} \mid \mathfrak{k} \models C \wedge \Box C \wedge \Diamond B \wedge D \wedge \Box D \wedge \Diamond \neg B \}.$

This class of K-models, say $\mathfrak{K}'$, corresponds to the only classical extension, viz. $Th(\{C, D\})$, of Default theory (4.1). Let us examine this example in detail. $\mathfrak{K}_W$ is the class of all K-models and clearly, we have $\mathfrak{K}_W \not\models \Box\neg B$, $\mathfrak{K}_W \not\models \Box\neg(\neg B)$, and $\mathfrak{K}_W \not\models \Box\neg(\neg D \wedge \neg C)$. Thus, as above, all three default rules are potentially "applicable".

From $\mathfrak{K}_W$ we can construct a class of K-models $\mathfrak{K}$ such that $\mathfrak{K} >_{\left\{\frac{:B}{C}\right\}} \mathfrak{K}_W$ and

$$\mathfrak{K} \models C \wedge \Box C \wedge \Diamond B.$$

Accordingly, we can also construct a class of K-models $\mathfrak{K}'$ such that $\mathfrak{K}' >_{\left\{\frac{:B}{C}, \frac{:\neg B}{D}\right\}}$ $\mathfrak{K}_W$ and

$$\mathfrak{K}' \models C \wedge \Box C \wedge \Diamond B \wedge D \wedge \Box D \wedge \Diamond\neg B.$$

But it is impossible to obtain a class $\mathfrak{K}''$ such that $\mathfrak{K}'' >_{\left\{\frac{:B}{C}, \frac{:\neg B}{D}, \frac{:\neg D \wedge \neg C}{E}\right\}} \mathfrak{K}_W$ since $\mathfrak{K}' \models \Box\neg(\neg D \wedge \neg C)$. Therefore, $\mathfrak{K}'$ is a non-empty preferred class of K-models.

From $\mathfrak{K}_W$, selecting first the third default rule leads to a $>_{\left\{\frac{:\neg D \wedge \neg C}{E}\right\}}$-greater class $\dot{\mathfrak{K}}$ such that

$$\dot{\mathfrak{K}} \models E \wedge \Box E \wedge \Diamond(\neg D \wedge \neg C).$$

From $\dot{\mathfrak{K}}$ we can construct a class of K-models $\ddot{\mathfrak{K}}$ such that $\ddot{\mathfrak{K}} >_{\left\{\frac{:\neg D \wedge \neg C}{E}, \frac{:B}{C}\right\}} \mathfrak{K}_W$ and

$$\ddot{\mathfrak{K}} \models E \wedge \Box E \wedge \Diamond(\neg D \wedge \neg C) \wedge C \wedge \Box C \wedge \Diamond B.$$

However, $\ddot{\mathfrak{K}}$ is the empty set of K-models because $\Diamond(\neg D \wedge \neg C) \models \Diamond\neg C$ and $\Box C \wedge \Diamond\neg C \models \bot$.

In contrast to Theorem 6.2.1, the possible worlds semantics for classical default logic admits the empty set of K–models above some non–empty $\mathfrak{K}_W$. This is the case whenever a default rule is applied whose consequent contradicts the justification of some default rule which is itself applied. In particular, this reflects the failure of semi–monotonicity in classical default logic whereas constrained default logic enjoys semi–monotonicity.

As detailed in [BS92, BS94], this semantical approach overcomes post-filtering conditions, such as the stability criterion encountered in Section 2.3. Other semantics for classical default logic were proposed for instance in [dGC90, Tru91b, MT93a], where the two latter apply transformations into other nonmonotonic logics in order to obtain a semantical characterization.

6.4 Possible worlds semantics for justified default logic

Further evidence for the generality of our approach is that it can easily capture justified default logic. Indeed, the analogue to Definition 6.2.1 and 6.3.1 can be defined as follows.

Definition 6.4.1. *Let* $\delta = \frac{\alpha\,:\,\beta}{\gamma}$. *Let* $\mathfrak{K}$ *and* $\mathfrak{K}'$ *be distinct classes of K-models. We define* $\mathfrak{K} \rhd_\delta \mathfrak{K}'$ *iff*

$$\mathfrak{K} = \{\mathfrak{k} \in \mathfrak{K}' \mid \mathfrak{k} \models \gamma \wedge \Box\gamma \wedge \Diamond\beta\}$$

and

1. $\mathfrak{K}' \models \alpha$
2. $\mathfrak{K}' \not\models \Box\neg\beta \vee \Diamond\neg\gamma$

The order $\rhd_D$ is defined analogously to that in Section 6.2.

Compared to the order $>_\delta$ given for classical default logic, the only difference is that Condition $\mathfrak{K}' \not\models \Box\neg\beta$ has become $\mathfrak{K}' \not\models \Box\neg\beta \vee \Diamond\neg\gamma$, that is, $\mathfrak{K}' \not\models \neg(\Box\gamma \wedge \Diamond\beta)$. Again, this becomes apparent by regarding Condition 2 in Definition 6.4.1, namely

$$\exists \mathfrak{k} \in \mathfrak{K}'.\, \mathfrak{k} \models \Diamond\beta \wedge \Box\gamma. \tag{6.3}$$

In classical default logic, there has to be a K-model which has some accessible world satisfying β (see (6.2) above). In justified default logic, however, all accessible worlds of such a K-model additionally have to satisfy γ.

Indeed, the definition reveals the fact that the same constraints implicitly used in classical default logic (in the form of C_E) are explicitly attached to justified extensions (in the form of J, see Definition 4.1.1) and, moreover, are considered when checking consistency. That is, semantically classical and justified default logic account for the justifications of the applied default rules in form of the modal propositions $\Diamond\beta$, which are entailed by $>_\delta$- and $\rhd_\delta$-greater classes of K-models. However, in classical default logic these modal constraints are discarded when checking consistency.

Łukaszewicz has shown in [Łuk88] that justified default logic guarantees the existence of extensions. Semantically, it is obvious that requiring $\mathfrak{K}' \not\models \neg(\Box\gamma \wedge \Diamond\beta)$ and adding those K-models entailing $\Box\gamma \wedge \Diamond\beta$ makes it impossible to obtain the empty set of K-models (hence the analogue to Theorem 6.2.1 trivially holds). Łukaszewicz has also shown that his variant enjoys semi-monotonicity. In fact, "applying" a default rule $\frac{\alpha\,:\,\beta}{\gamma}$ enforces all $\rhd_D$-greater classes of K-models $\mathfrak{K}$ to entail $\Box\gamma \wedge \Diamond\beta$. Therefore, a later "application" of a default rule $\frac{\alpha'\,:\,\beta'}{\gamma'}$ whose consequent γ' contradicts β (eg. $\gamma' = \neg\beta$) is prohibited since its "application" requires $\mathfrak{K} \not\models \Box\neg\beta' \vee \Diamond\neg\gamma'$.

Analogously to classical default logic, Definition 6.4.1 only requires $\Diamond\beta$ to be valid in $\mathfrak{K}$, which is not enough for justified default logic to strongly commit to assumptions. We have seen on Page 35 that Default theory (4.1) has two justified extensions, $Th(\{C, D\})$ wrt $\{B, \neg B\}$ and $Th(\{E\})$ wrt $\{\neg D \wedge \neg C\}$. This is reflected by two preferred classes of K-models:

- $\{\mathfrak{k} \mid \mathfrak{k} \models C \wedge \Box C \wedge \Diamond B \wedge D \wedge \Box D \wedge \Diamond\neg B, \}$
- $\{\mathfrak{k} \mid \mathfrak{k} \models E \wedge \Box E \wedge \Diamond(\neg D \wedge \neg C)\}$

The first preferred class of K-models is obtained analogously to that in classical default logic. That is, we obtain a preferred class

$$\mathfrak{K}' \models C \wedge \Box C \wedge \Diamond B \wedge D \wedge \Box D \wedge \Diamond \neg B.$$

Also, selecting first the third default rule leads to a class $\dot{\mathfrak{K}} \rhd_{\left\{ \frac{: \neg D \wedge \neg C}{E} \right\}} \mathfrak{K}_W$ with

$$\dot{\mathfrak{K}} \models E \wedge \Box E \wedge \Diamond(\neg D \wedge \neg C).$$

Since we have $\dot{\mathfrak{K}} \models \Diamond\neg C$ and $\dot{\mathfrak{K}} \models \Diamond\neg D$ none of the other default rules is "applicable". Therefore, $\dot{\mathfrak{K}}$ is a (non-empty) preferred class.

Similar to the case of classical default logic, there is a natural account of constraints attached to a set of formulas E justified by J: The justifications of the generating default rules over E and J, which are simply

$$C_{(E,J)} = \left\{ \beta \mid \frac{\alpha : \beta}{\gamma} \in D, \ \alpha \in E, \forall \eta \in J \cup \{\beta\}. \ E \cup \{\gamma\} \cup \{\eta\} \not\vdash \bot \right\}.^4$$

Then, a correctness and completeness result holds as in the former sections [BS92].

Theorem 6.4.1 (Correctness & Completeness). *Let* (D, W) *be a default theory. Let* $\mathfrak{K}$ *be a class of K-models, E a deductively closed set of formulas, and J a set of formulas such that* $J = C_{(E,J)}$ *and* $\mathfrak{K} = \{\mathfrak{k} \mid \mathfrak{k} \models E \wedge \Box E \wedge \Diamond C_{(E,J)}\}$. *Then, E is a justified extension of* (D, W) *wrt J iff* $\mathfrak{K}$ *is a* $\rhd_D$*-maximal class above* $\mathfrak{K}_W$.

The equality $J = C_{(E,J)}$ simply states that the implicit constraints $C_{(E,J)}$ and the explicit constraints J coincide.

This possible worlds semantics is the first semantical characterization of justified default logic which is purely model-theoretic. In [Łuk88], Łukaszewicz had to characterize justified extension by means of pairs $(\mathfrak{m}, J)$, where $\mathfrak{m}$ is a class of first-order interpretations and J is a set of formulas. The reason Łukaszewicz did so is that justified default logic allows for inconsistent sets of individually consistent constraints (so that the focused models semantics cannot be adapted there).

Finally, a remark concerning Definition 6.2.1 and 6.4.1 is appropriate. Let us compare the respective consistency condition, (6.1) and (6.3). We observe that the condition in constrained default logic requires that there is a K-model which has some accessible world satisfying $\gamma \wedge \beta$. In contrast, we are faced with a stronger requirement in justified default logic: There has to be a K-model all of which accessible worlds satisfy γ and some of which accessible world satisfies β. At first glance, this seems to be counterintuitive since constrained default logic has a stronger consistency condition than justified default logic (compare Definition 3.2.1 and 4.1.1). However, consistency or satisfiability are always relative to a given set of formulas or class of models, respectively. In fact, we consider a much more restricted class of K-models $\mathfrak{K}'$ in (6.1) in constrained default logic than in (6.3) in justified default logic. Given a set of default rules D' such that $\mathfrak{K}' \succ_{D'} \mathfrak{K}_W$ and $\mathfrak{K}' \rhd_{D'} \mathfrak{K}_W$, we

---

[4] Observe that the membership qualifying property is exactly the third condition in Definition 4.1.1.

have $\mathfrak{K}' \models W \wedge Conseq(D') \wedge \Box(W \wedge Conseq(D') \wedge Justif(D'))$ in constrained default logic, whereas we encounter a less restricted class of K-models in justified default logic, namely $\mathfrak{K}' \models W \wedge Conseq(D') \wedge \Box(W \wedge Conseq(D')) \wedge \Diamond Justif(D')$. As a consequence, we have to employ a stronger satisfiability condition in justified default logic, as reflected by (6.3).

6.5 Possible worlds semantics for contextual default logic

As above, we semantically characterize contextual extensions by maximal elements of a strict partial order on classes of K-models. Given a contextual default rule δ, its application conditions and the result of applying it are captured by an order $\gg_\delta$ as follows.

Definition 6.5.1. *Let* $\delta = \frac{\alpha_W \mid \alpha_E \mid \alpha_C \,:\, \beta_C \mid \beta_E \mid \beta_W}{\gamma}$. *Let* $\mathfrak{K}$ *and* $\mathfrak{K}'$ *be distinct classes of* K-*models. We define* $\mathfrak{K} \gg_\delta \mathfrak{K}'$ *iff*

$$\mathfrak{K} = \{\mathfrak{k} \in \mathfrak{K}' \mid \mathfrak{k} \models \gamma \wedge \Box\gamma \wedge \Box\beta_C \wedge \Diamond\beta_E\}$$

and

1. $\mathfrak{K}_W \models \alpha_W$
2. $\mathfrak{K}' \models \alpha_E$
3. $\mathfrak{K}' \models \Diamond\alpha_C$
4. $\mathfrak{K}' \not\models \Diamond\neg\beta_C$
5. $\mathfrak{K}' \not\models \neg\beta_E$
6. $\mathfrak{K}_W \not\models \neg\beta_W$

Given a set of contextual default rules D, the strict partial order $\gg_D$ is defined as the transitive closure of the union of all orders $\gg_\delta$ such that $\delta \in D$.

Conditions *1-6* in the preceding definition constitute the semantical counterparts of the six application conditions given in the specification of Δ_i in Definition 5.2.3. Thus, they semantically capture the application conditions of a contextual default rule. The correspondence between the first two and last two conditions in Definition 6.5.1 is obvious, so that we focus on the remaining context-sensitive conditions. Condition *3* accounts for the applicability condition expressing "membership in a context of reasoning". Now, in terms of possible worlds, this boils down to the requirement that all considered K-models possess an accessible world satisfying α_C. According to the aforementioned intuition, this amounts to stipulating that α_C belongs to some subcontext of the context captured by $\mathfrak{K}'$. Condition *4* provides (one half of the) semantical underpinnings for the joint consistency requirement of C-justifications. Notice that this condition is equivalent to

$$\exists \mathfrak{k} \in \mathfrak{K}'. \, \mathfrak{k} \models \Box\beta_C. \tag{6.4}$$

That is, the consistency condition for β_C corresponds semantically to the requirement that there is a K-model in which all accessible worlds satisfy β_C. Hence, following the above intuition, β_C belongs to the kernel of the context induced by all such K-models $\mathfrak{k}$. Observe that Condition (6.4) differs from that given in (6.1) for constrained default logic due to different interactions of modal conditions.

The other half of the semantical characterization of joint (and individual) consistency is expressed in the specification of $\mathfrak{K}$. The K-models in $\mathfrak{K}$ capture the result of applying a contextual default rule by gathering the default's conclusion along with its underlying consistency assumptions. Hence they provide the semantical counterpart to Conditions 7-9 in Definition 5.2.3. This is accomplished by enforcing the satisfiability of the consequent γ in all actual as well as in all worlds accessible from the actual worlds by stipulating $\mathfrak{k} \models \gamma \wedge \Box\gamma$. The joint consistency of β_C is preserved by requiring that all accessible worlds satisfy β_C, ie. $\mathfrak{k} \models \Box\beta_C$. In this way, $\mathfrak{K}$ forms a subset of all models $\mathfrak{k}$ in (6.4). The individual consistency of β_E is preserved by enforcing accessible worlds satisfying β_E along with γ and β_C, ie. $\mathfrak{k} \models \Diamond(\gamma \wedge \beta_C \wedge \beta_E)$. Roughly speaking, such accessible worlds capture the sub-contexts "spanned" by E-justifications like β_E (cf. Theorem 6.5.1 below).

In general, we obtain the following soundness and completeness result that make precise the intuition given at the start of this section.

Theorem 6.5.1. *Let* (D, W) *be a contextual default theory. Let* $\mathfrak{K}$ *be a class of K-models, E a deductively closed set of formulas, C a pointwisely closed set of formulas such that*

$$\mathfrak{K} = \{\mathfrak{k} \mid \mathfrak{k} \models E \wedge \Box C_K \wedge \Diamond C_J\}$$

for

$$C_K = Th\left(E \cup Justif_C\left(GD_{(D,W)}^{(E,C)}\right)\right) \quad and \quad C_J = Justif_E\left(GD_{(D,W)}^{(E,C)}\right).$$

Then, (E, C) is a consistent contextual extension of (D, W) iff $\mathfrak{K}$ is a $\gg_D$-maximal non-empty class above $\mathfrak{K}_W$.

Observe that the requirements on a maximal class of K-models correspond to the aforementioned intuitions. Clearly, E is the extension, C the context, C_K the kernel and C_J consists of E-justifications distinguishing the subcontexts from each other.

Let us illustrate this by means of the first contextual extension obtained in the "holidays with broken arms" example, presented in (5.4) and (5.5). In this case, $\mathfrak{K}_W$ is given by the class of all K-models satisfying $\neg W \vee \neg C$, $Bl \vee Br$ and $\Box(\neg W \vee \neg C)$, $\Box(Bl \vee Br)$. By means of the generating contextual default rules listed in (5.6), say δ_1, δ_2 and δ_3, we obtain a maximal class of K-models $\mathfrak{K}$ such that $\mathfrak{K} \gg_{\{\delta_1,\delta_2,\delta_3\}} \mathfrak{K}_W$ and

$$
\begin{aligned}
\mathfrak{K} \models \quad & ((\neg W \vee \neg C) \wedge (Bl \vee Br) \wedge T \wedge S \wedge Ul) \\
& \Box((\neg W \vee \neg C) \wedge (Bl \vee Br) \wedge T \wedge S \wedge Ul \wedge \neg Bl) \\
& \Diamond W \wedge \Diamond C
\end{aligned}
$$

Now, let us decompose the preceding formula in order to isolate the extension E presented in (5.4), the context C presented in (5.5), the kernel C_K and the E-justifications C_J. Clearly, E is given by the non-modal formulas entailed by $\mathfrak{K}$. The kernel C_K is given by all formulas that necessarily hold:

$$\mathfrak{K} \models \Box((\neg W \vee \neg C) \wedge (BI \vee Br) \wedge T \wedge S \wedge UI \wedge \neg BI)$$

They are given by the formulas collectively entailed by the accessible worlds. Interestingly, the accessible worlds differ exactly in the E-justifications given in C_J; they are possibly entailed by $\mathfrak{K}$. To be more precise, we even have

$$\mathfrak{K} \models \Diamond(T \wedge S \wedge UI \wedge \neg BI \wedge W) \wedge \Diamond(T \wedge S \wedge UI \wedge \neg BI \wedge C).$$

Now, each of the two modal conjuncts captures one of the two subcontexts forming the wider common context given in (5.5). In this way, a context is completely described by the set of accessible worlds given in a $\gg_D$-maximal class of K-models, whereas an extension is captured by the set of actual worlds in the same class of K-models.

6.6 Conclusion

We described a uniform semantical framework for default logics. This was accomplished by means of a preference relation on classes of Kripke structures. No other semantics for any default logic offers this generality. Moreover, the approach remedies several difficulties encountered in former proposals aiming at individual default logics: First, the approach avoids post-filtering mechanisms such as the stability condition required in [Eth87] (and [Łuk88]). In contrast, our semantics characterizes extensions strictly by maximal classes of K-models. Second, the approach avoids two-fold semantical structures such as focused models structures or so-called frames [Łuk88]. For a complement, the presented possible worlds semantics allows us to characterize extensions in a very homogeneous way since the increasing structure in default logics is captured by means of possible worlds. Third, the approach provides a semantical characterization of justified default logic which is purely model-theoretic. In [Łuk88], Łukaszewicz characterized the (possibly inconsistent) set of constraints of justified extensions by sets of formulas. Again, this is accomplished by means of possible worlds in our approach.

In addition, we obtain semantical underpinnings for rational default logic (via Transformation $\Phi_{RDL}(D, W)$ in Definition 5.3.3) as well as for the assertional variants of default logic of Section 4.2, such as cumulative and rational cumulative default logic (through Theorem 4.2.1 and 4.2.7).

Other proposals for semantics of classical default logic, among them [dGC90, Tru91b, MT93a], were conceived. The first one gives a reformulation of the fixed-point definition of extensions in terms of classes of first-order interpretations, while the two latter apply transformations into other nonmonotonic logics in order to obtain a semantical characterization. None of them however offers the same universality as the semantical framework described in this chapter. In particular, they merely address Reiter's original approach to default logic.

7. Adding specificity to default logics

The notion of *specificity* is a fundamental principle in commonsense reasoning according to which more specific defaults should be preferred over less specific ones. This principle is however not respected in default logic. That is, given two conflicting default rules from which one is less specific than another one, there is no intrinsic way to give the more specific rule preference over the less specific one. We address this problem by proposing a general approach to specificity in default reasoning. This is accomplished by means of a two-phase system: First, we determine specificity information by appeal to techniques found in conditional logics. Then, we enrich the original default theory with its intrinsic specificity information and obtain a default theory in which specificity is appropriately handled. This approach was introduced in [DS93] and further developed in [DS94a]. Due to the generality of the approach, it has been successfully applied in [DS94a, DS94b] to other approaches to nonmonotonic reasoning, like autoepistemic logic [Moo85] and even circumscription [McC80].

7.1 Motivation

We have seen in the previous chapters that in default logic many desirable properties are obtainable in certain restricted subclasses. For instance, normal default theories enjoy semi-monotonicity and orthogonality. There is however a very important notion in commonsense reasoning that is not addressable inside the framework of default logic, namely the concept of *specificity*. This notion is a fundamental principle in commonsense reasoning according to which more specific defaults should be preferred over less specific ones. Consider a variant of the example on Page 13 in Chapter 2 where birds fly, birds have wings, penguins are birds, and penguins don't fly given.

$$\left(\left\{ \frac{B : F}{F}, \frac{B : W}{W}, \frac{P : B}{B}, \frac{P : \neg F}{\neg F} \right\}, \{P\} \right) \tag{7.1}$$

From this theory, one would want to conclude $\neg F$ by default. Intuitively, being a penguin is a more specific notion than that of being a bird, and, in the case of a conflict, we would want to use the more specific default. On the contrary, we have already seen in the introductory section that the obvious representation of this theory yields two extensions, one extension in which $\neg F$ is true and another one in which F is true. The usual fix (cf. [RC81]) is to establish a precedence among these two interacting defaults by adding the exception P to the justification of the less specific default rule. This amounts to replacing $\frac{B:F}{F}$ by $\frac{B:F\wedge\neg P}{F}$ in Default theory (7.1) which then yields the desired result, namely a single extension containing P, B, W, and $\neg F$.

Since the determination of specificity information is independent of the approach of default logic, we have to address this issue outside the framework of default logic. Moreover, there are approaches, namely conditional logics like [Del87, Pea90, Bou92][1] that allow for isolating specificity information from a given set of conditionals.

Our approach [DS93, DS94a] is to use the specificity information given by a conditional system to generate a default theory in default logic, where specificity is appropriately handled. Hence we address two related but essentially independent questions:

1. How can a conditional system be used to isolate specific interacting defaults?
2. How can this information be uniformly incorporated in a theory expressed in default logic?

For concreteness, we develop the approach by considering System $\mathbf{Z}$ [Pea90] as an example of a conditional system, and classical default logic; however in [DS94a, DS94b], we furthermore consider the application of the approach to other systems, like constrained default logic and even autoepistemic logic [Moo85] and circumscription [McC80]. The general idea is to combine the techniques of System $\mathbf{Z}$ and default logic in a principled fashion to obtain a general hybrid approach for defeasible reasoning.

7.2 Determination of specificity information

In System $\mathbf{Z}$ [Pea90] a set of rules R representing default conditionals is partitioned into an ordered list of mutually exclusive sets of rules $R_0, \ldots, R_n$. Lower ranked rules are considered more normal (or less specific) than higher ranked rules. In [DS94b], we propose an extension to System $\mathbf{Z}$ distinguishing strict and defeasible conditionals. For simplicity, however, we deal below with basic System $\mathbf{Z}$ as introduced in [Pea90] and therefore deal with defeasible rules only. One begins then with a set $R = \{r \mid \alpha_r \rightarrow \beta_r\}$ where each α_r and β_r are propositional formulas over a finite alphabet. A set $R' \subseteq R$ *tolerates* a rule r if $\{\alpha_r \wedge \beta_r\} \cup R'$ is satisfiable. We assume in what follows that R is $\mathbf{Z}$-*consistent*,[2] ie. for every non-empty $R' \subseteq R$, some $r' \in R'$ is tolerated by $R' - \{r'\}$. Using this notion of tolerance, a so-called $\mathbf{Z}$-*ordering* on the rules in R is defined:

1. First, find all rules tolerated by R, and call this subset R_0.
2. Next, find all rules tolerated by $R - R_0$, and call this subset R_1.

---

[1] See [DS94a] for a detailed discussion on these approaches.
[2] Pearl uses the term *consistent* [Pea90].

3. Continue in this fashion until all rules have been accounted for.

In this way, we obtain a *partition* $(R_0, \ldots, R_n)$ of R, where

$$R_i = \{r \mid r \text{ is tolerated by } R - R_0 - \cdots - R_{i-1}\}$$

for $1 \leq i \leq n$. More generally, we write R_i to denote the ith set of rules in the partition of a set of conditionals R. A set of rules R is called *trivial* iff its partition consists only of a single set of rules.

From this point, [Pea90] defines a ranking on models, determined by which rules are falsified in the model; subsequently a notion of default inference is obtained. These considerations need not concern us here, since it is just the ordering that we make use of.[3]

For the time being,[4] let us agree on identifying a normal default rule of the form $\frac{\alpha : \beta}{\beta}$ with a rule of the form $\alpha \rightarrow \beta$. For our default theory in (7.1), we obtain then the **Z**-ordering

$$R_0 = \{\mathsf{B} \rightarrow \mathsf{F}, \mathsf{B} \rightarrow \mathsf{W}\}, \qquad\qquad R_1 = \{\mathsf{P} \rightarrow \mathsf{B}, \mathsf{P} \rightarrow \neg\mathsf{F}\}. \qquad (7.2)$$

As mentioned previously, we gather information extracted from certain **Z**-orderings in order to (ultimately) generate a default theory: A **Z**-ordering provides specificity information, and so for example, tells us that $\mathsf{P} \rightarrow \neg\mathsf{F}$ is a more specific rule than $\mathsf{B} \rightarrow \mathsf{F}$. However, we do not use the full **Z**-ordering (since it may introduce unwanted specificities, as shown in [DS94a]), but rather we determine minimal sets of rules that conflict, and use these sets to sort out specificity information.

Consider our example in (7.1), expressed as a **Z**-ordering in (7.2). First we locate the minimal sets of conditionals, such that there is a non-trivial **Z**-ordering for this set of conditionals. In our example this set $C = C_1 \cup C_2$ consists solely of:

$$C_0 = \{\mathsf{B} \rightarrow \mathsf{F}\} \qquad\qquad C_1 = \{\mathsf{P} \rightarrow \mathsf{B}, \mathsf{P} \rightarrow \neg\mathsf{F}\} \qquad (7.3)$$

Any such set is called a *minimal conflicting set* of defaults. Such a set has a non-trivial **Z**-ordering, but for any subset there is no non-trivial **Z**-ordering. What this in turn means is that if all the rules in such a set are jointly applicable, then, one way or another there will be a conflict.[5]

For our formal analysis, we consider a **Z**-consistent set of default conditionals $R = \{r \mid \alpha_r \rightarrow \beta_r\}$ where each α_r and β_r are propositional formulas over a finite alphabet. We write *Prereq*(R) for $\{\alpha_r \mid \alpha_r \rightarrow \beta_r \in R\}$, and *Conseq*$(R)$ for $\{\beta_r \mid \alpha_r \rightarrow \beta_r \in R\}$.

For a set of rules R, the set of its minimal conflicting sets represents conflicts among rules in R due to disparate specificity [DS93].

---

[3] Indeed, as shown in [DS94a], System **Z** as a whole is too strong for our requirements.

[4] See Page 82 for an alternative encoding.

[5] If the rules were represented as normal default rules in default logic for example, one would obtain multiple extensions.

Definition 7.2.1. *Let R be a Z-consistent set of rules. $C \subseteq R$ is a minimal conflicting set in R iff C has a non-trivial Z-ordering and any $C' \subset C$ has a trivial Z-ordering.*

Observe that adding new rules to R cannot alter or destroy any existing minimal conflicting sets. That is, for default theories R and R', where $C \subseteq R \subseteq R'$, we have that if C is a minimal conflicting set in R then C is a minimal conflicting set in R'.

The next theorem shows that any minimal conflicting set has a binary partition [DS93]:

Theorem 7.2.1. *Let C be a minimal conflicting set in R. Then, the Z-ordering of C is (C_0, C_1) for some non-empty sets C_0 and C_1 with $C = C_0 \cup C_1$.*

Moreover, a minimal conflicting set entails the negations of the antecedents of the higher-level rules [DS93]:

Theorem 7.2.2. *Let C be a minimal conflicting set in R. Then, if $\alpha \to \beta \in C_1$ then $C \models \neg\alpha$.*

Hence, given the rule set in (7.2),

$$R = \{\mathsf{B} \to \mathsf{F},\ \mathsf{B} \to \mathsf{W},\ \mathsf{P} \to \mathsf{B},\ \mathsf{P} \to \neg\mathsf{F}\},$$

there is one minimal conflicting set

$$C = \{\mathsf{B} \to \mathsf{F},\ \mathsf{P} \to \mathsf{B},\ \mathsf{P} \to \neg\mathsf{F}\}.$$

As shown in (7.3), the first conditional constitutes C_0 and the last two C_1 in the Z-order of C. The set $\{\mathsf{B} \to \mathsf{F},\ \mathsf{P} \to \neg\mathsf{F}\}$ for example, is not a minimal conflicting set since alone it has a trivial Z-order. It is easy to see that $C \models \neg\mathsf{P}$.

Intuitively, a minimal conflicting set consists of three mutually exclusive sets of rules: the least specific or *minimal conflicting rules* in C, $min(C)$; the most specific or *maximal conflicting rules* in C, $max(C)$; and the remaining rules providing a minimal inferential relation between these two sets of rules, $inf(C)$. The following definition provides a very general formal frame for these sets [DS93]:

Definition 7.2.2. *Let R be a set of rules and let $C \subseteq R$ be a minimal conflicting set in R. We define $max(C)$ and $min(C)$ to be non-empty subsets of R such that*

$$\begin{aligned}
min(C) &\subseteq C_0 \\
max(C) &\subseteq C_1 \\
inf(C) &= C - (min(C) \cup max(C))
\end{aligned}$$

We observe that *min*, *max*, and *inf* are exclusive subsets of C such that $C = min(C) \cup inf(C) \cup max(C)$. We show below that the rules in $max(C)$ and $min(C)$ are indeed conflicting due to their different specificity. Note however that the following three theorems are independent of the choice of $min(C)$, $inf(C)$, and $max(C)$. Yet after these theorems we argue in Definition 7.2.3 for a specific choice for these sets that complies with the intuitions described in the previous section.

First, the antecedents of the most specific rules in $min(C)$ imply the antecedents of the least specific rules in $max(C)$ modulo the "inferential rules":

Theorem 7.2.3. *Let C be a minimal conflicting set in a set of rules R. Then,* $inf(C) \cup max(C) \models Prereq(max(C)) \supset Prereq(min(C))$.

In fact, $inf(C) \cup max(C)$ is the weakest precondition under which the last entailment holds. This is important since we deal with a general setting for minimal conflicting sets. Observe that omitting $max(C)$ would eliminate rules, like $\mathsf{P} \rightarrow \mathsf{B}$ that may belong to $max(C)$, yet provide "inferential relations". The next theorem shows that the converse of the previous one does not hold in general.

Theorem 7.2.4. *Let C be a minimal conflicting set in a set of rules R. Then, for any set of rules R' such that $C \subseteq R'$ and any set of rules $R'' \subseteq min(C)$ such that $R' \cup Prereq(R'')$ is satisfiable, we have: $R' \not\models Prereq(R'') \supset Prereq(max(C))$.*

The reason for considering consistent subsets of $min(C)$ is that its entire set of prerequisites might be equivalent to those in $max(C)$. Then, however, $C \cup Prereq(min(C))$ and so $R' \cup Prereq(min(C))$ is inconsistent. In fact, R' is the strongest precondition under which the above theorem holds. Finally, we demonstrate that these rules are indeed conflicting.

Theorem 7.2.5. *Let C be a minimal conflicting set in a set of rules R. Then, for any $\alpha \rightarrow \beta \in max(C)$, we have: $inf(C) \cup \{\alpha\} \models \neg(Conseq(min(C)) \wedge Conseq(max(C)))$.*

As above, $inf(C) \cup \{\alpha\}$ is the weakest precondition under which the last entailment holds. In all, the last three theorems demonstrate that the general framework given for minimal conflicting sets (already) provides an extremely expressive way of isolating rule conflicts due to their specificity.

We note however that in the worst case the number of minimal conflicting sets grows exponentially with the size of a set of rules. This though is an artifact of the problem in general, rather than the specific approach at hand—there may simply be an exponential number of ways in which a set of defaults conflict.

As indicated above, we require further restrictions on the choice of $min(C)$ and $max(C)$ for our translation into default logic. For a minimal conflicting set $C = (C_0, C_1)$, we have the information that the rules in C_0 are less specific than those in C_1. However we wish to isolate those rules in C_0 whose application would conflict with applications of rules in C_1. Such a set is referred to as a *conflicting core* of a minimal conflicting set. This leads [DS93] to the following definition:

Definition 7.2.3. *Let $C = (C_0, C_1)$ be a minimal conflicting set. A conflicting core of C is a pair of least sets $(min(C), max(C))$ where*

1. *$min(C) \subseteq C_0$,*
2. *$max(C) \subseteq C_1$,*
3. *$\{\alpha_r \wedge \beta_r \mid r \in max(C) \cup min(C)\} \models \perp$,*

provided that $min(C)$ and $max(C)$ non-empty.

This definition specializes the general setting of Definition 7.2.2. So, $\alpha_r \rightarrow \beta_r$ is in $min(C)$ if its application conflicts with the application of a rule (or rules) in C_1.

So in our example the rules $B \to F$ and $P \to \neg F$ yield the conflicting core $(\{B \to F\}, \{P \to \neg F\})$.

Note that a conflicting core need not necessarily exist for a specific minimal conflicting set. For example, consider the minimal conflicting set (expressed as a Z-order):

$$C_0 = \{Q \to P, R \to \neg P\}$$
$$C_1 = \{Q \wedge R \to C\}$$

Thus Quakers are pacifists while republicans are not; Quakers that are republicans are conservative. Here the conflict is between two defaults at the same level (viz. $Q \to P$ and $R \to \neg P$) that manifests itself when a more specific default is given.

[DS93] gives the following result however.

Theorem 7.2.6. *For minimal conflicting set C in a set of rules R, if $\{\alpha_r \wedge \beta_r \mid r \in min(C)\} \not\models \bot$ and $\{\alpha_r \wedge \beta_r \mid r \in max(C)\} \not\models \bot$ then C has a conflicting core.*

Note that while in "normal" cases a minimal conflicting set (apparently) has a unique conflicting core, this is not always the case. In the sequel, for simplicity we restrict our attention to minimal conflicting sets having a unique conflicting core. Non-unique conflicting cores are easily handled in Definition 7.3.1 by considering each minimal conflicting set/conflicting core pair separately.

More examples and a more detailed discussion can be found in [DS94a].

7.3 Compiling specificity into default theories

This section describes a strategy, based on the notions of specificity and conflict developed in the previous section, for producing a standard semi-normal default theory, and which provable maintains this notion of specificity. The transformation is succinctly defined:

Definition 7.3.1. *Let R be a set of rules and let $\langle C^i \rangle_{i \in I}$ be the family of all minimal conflicting sets in R. For each $r \in R$, we define*

$$\delta_r = \frac{\alpha_r : \beta_r \wedge \bigwedge_{r' \in R_r}(\alpha_{r'} \supset \beta_{r'})}{\beta_r} \qquad (7.4)$$

where $R_r = \{r' \in max(C^i) \mid r \in min(C^i) \text{ for } i \in I\}$. We define $D_R = \{\delta_r \mid r \in R\}$.

In what follows, we adopt the latter notation and write $D_{R'} = \{\delta_r \mid r \in R'\}$ for any subset R' of R.

The most interesting point in the preceding definition is the formation of the justifications of the (sometimes) semi-normal defaults. Given a rule r, the justification of δ_r is built by looking at all minimal conflicting set, C^i, in which r occurs as a least specific rule (ie. $r \in min(C^i)$). Then, the consequent of r is conjoined with the strict counterparts of the most specific rules in the same sets (viz.

$(\alpha_{r'} \supset \beta_{r'})$ for $r' \in max(C^i)$). Hence, for the minimal conflicting rules we obtain semi-normal defaults; all other defaults are normal (since then $R_r = \emptyset$). So for any minimal conflicting set C in R, we transform the rules in $min(C)$ into semi-normal defaults, whereas we transform the rules in $inf(C) \cup max(C)$ into normal defaults, provided that they do not occur elsewhere as a minimal conflicting rule.

As suggested in the previous section, we are only interested in minimal and maximal conflicting rules forming a conflicting core. That is, given a minimal conflicting set C, we stipulate that $(min(C), max(C))$ forms a conflicting core of C. According to Definition 7.3.1, we get in our example $R_{\mathsf{B} \rightarrow \mathsf{F}} = \{\mathsf{P} \rightarrow \neg \mathsf{F}\}$. This results in a single semi-normal default rule

$$\frac{\mathsf{B} \,:\, \mathsf{F} \wedge (\mathsf{P} \supset \neg \mathsf{F})}{\mathsf{F}}, \qquad \text{or} \qquad \frac{\mathsf{B} \,:\, \mathsf{F} \wedge \neg \mathsf{P}}{\mathsf{F}}.$$

Observe that we obtain $\frac{\mathsf{P} \,:\, \mathsf{B}}{\mathsf{B}}$ and $\frac{\mathsf{P} \,:\, \neg \mathsf{F}}{\neg \mathsf{F}}$ for $\mathsf{P} \rightarrow \mathsf{B}$, and $\mathsf{P} \rightarrow \neg \mathsf{F}$ since these rules do not occur elsewhere as minimal rules in a conflicting core. More examples and a more detailed discussion can be found in [DS94a].

We obtain the following results. GD_D^E stands for the generating defaults of E with respect to D, ie. $GD_D^E = \{\frac{\alpha \,:\, \beta}{\omega} \in D, \mid \alpha \in E, \neg\beta \notin E\}$. Note that Theorem 7.3.1 is with respect to the general theory of minimal conflicting sets while Theorem 7.3.2 is with respect to the specific development involving conflicting cores [DS93].

Theorem 7.3.1. *Let R be a set of rules and let W be a set of formulas. Let C be a minimal conflicting set in R. Let E be a consistent extension of (D_R, W). Then,*

1. if $D_{max(C)} \cup D_{inf(C)} \subseteq GD_D^E$ then $D_{min(C)} \not\subseteq GD_D^E$,
2. if $D_{min(C)} \cup D_{inf(C)} \subseteq GD_D^E$ then $D_{max(C)} \not\subseteq GD_D^E$.

Let us relate this theorem to the underlying idea of specificity: Observe that in the first case, where $D_{max(C)} \cup D_{inf(C)} \subseteq GD_D^E$, we also have

$$Prereq(min(C)) \subseteq E$$

by Theorem 7.2.3. That is, even though the prerequisites of the minimal conflicting defaults are derivable, they do not contribute to the extension at hand. This is so because some of the justifications of the minimal conflicting defaults are not satisfied. In this way, the more specific defaults in $D_{max(C)}$ take precedence over the less specific defaults in $D_{min(C)}$. Conversely, in the second case, where $D_{min(C)} \cup D_{inf(C)} \subseteq GD_D^E$, the less specific defaults apply only if the more specific defaults do not contribute to the given extension [DS93] .

Theorem 7.3.2. *Let R be a set of rules and let W be a set of formulas. Let $(min(C), max(C))$ be a conflicting core of some minimal conflicting set C in R. Let E be a consistent extension of (D_R, W). Then,*

1. if $D_{max(C)} \subseteq GD_D^E$ then $D_{min(C)} \not\subseteq GD_D^E$,
2. if $D_{min(C)} \subseteq GD_D^E$ then $D_{max(C)} \not\subseteq GD_D^E$.

Thus in this case we obtain that the defaults in a conflicting core are not applicable, independent of the "linking defaults" in $D_{inf(C)}$.

Given a set of formulas W representing our world knowledge and a set of default conditionals R, we can apply Definition 7.3.1 in order to obtain a so-called **Z**-*default theory* (D_R, W). The following theorem gives an alternative characterization for extensions of **Z**-default theories. In particular, it clarifies further the effect of the set of rules R_r associated with each rule r. Recall that in general, however, such extensions are computed in the classical framework of default logic [DS93].

Theorem 7.3.3. *Let R be a set of rules, let $D_N = \left\{ \frac{\alpha_r : \beta_r}{\beta_r} \;\middle|\; \alpha_r \to \beta_r \in R \right\}$, and let W and E be sets of formulas. Define $E_0 = W$ and for $i \geq 0$ (and R_r as in Definition 7.3.1)*

$$
E_{i+1} \;=\; Th(E_i) \cup \left\{ \beta_r \;\middle|\; \frac{\alpha_r : \beta_r}{\beta_r} \in D_N, \; \alpha_r \in E_i, \right.
$$
$$
\left. E \cup \{\beta_r\} \cup \bigcup_{r' \in R_r} (\alpha_{r'} \supset \beta_{r'}) \not\vdash \bot \right\}
$$

Then, E is an extension of (D_R, W) iff $E = \bigcup_{i=0}^{\infty} E_i$.

Finally we note that the preceding exposition was dominated by the view that rules, like $\alpha \to \beta$, are associated with defaults having prerequisite α and consequent β. This view underlies for instance the approaches in [BH93] and [Bre94a]. That is, they rely on the existence of prerequisites. As we showed in [DS94a] in detail, we can treat these rules as strict implications, and so compile them into a prerequisite-free variant of default logic (and so, for example, obtain reasoning by cases). To this end, we replace the definition of δ_r in Definition 7.3.1 by

$$
\zeta_r = \frac{: (\alpha_r \supset \beta_r) \wedge \bigwedge_{r' \in R_r} (\alpha_{r'} \supset \beta_{r'})}{(\alpha_r \supset \beta_r)}.
$$

Similarly we have shown in [DS94a, DS94b] how to compile prioritized rules into Theorist [Poo88], constrained default logic or other approaches, such as autoepistemic logic [Moo85] and circumscription [McC80]. Also, we have to refer the reader to [DS94a, DS94b] for a detailed comparison of our work to other approaches dealing with prioritization, like [Bou92, Lif85b, Gro91, BH93, Bre94a].

7.4 Conclusion

We described a two-phase approach addressing the notion of specificity in default reasoning. The goal is to produce a default theory, where conflicts arising from differing specificities are resolved. The approach is to use the techniques of a conditional system, as exemplified by System **Z**, to isolate minimal sets of conflicting defaults. From the specificity information intrinsic in these sets, a default theory is derived. In contrast to previous work, like [BH93, Bre94a], the approach avoids stepping outside the machinery of default logic. Thus we do not obtain an explicit global partial order on default rules, but rather a classical default theory where local conflicts are resolved by semi-normal defaults.

This approach is modular, in that we separate the *determination* of conflicts from the *resolution* of conflicts among rules. Thus either module could be replaced by some other approach. Alternately, conflicts could be determined using minimal conflicting sets via System Z, and then an ordered default theory as described in [BH93] could be generated. The approach may be seen as generalizing that of [RC81]. Also, for example, [ER83] and [Bre94a] may be seen as falling into the same general framework.

A full account of the approach can be found in [DS93, DS94a].

8. Adding lemma handling to default logics

The caching of frequently used—often intermediate—information is an indispensable means in many domains of computer science. For instance, in automated theorem proving, one often caches so-called *lemmas*, ie. auxiliary propositions used in the demonstration of another proposition, in order to reduce computational efforts. Such a technique is however not applicable to default logics, since the addition of derived propositions may change the entire set of conclusions. We address this problem by proposing a general approach to deal with lemmas in default logics. The idea is to change the status of a default conclusion whenever it is added to a world-description by turning it into a new default rule. This default rule contains information about the default proof of the original conclusion and so tells us when this proof is not valid any more.

8.1 Motivation

Section 2.1 and 4.2 already dealt with the formal aspects of the property of cumulativity. There, we have stressed the theoretical importance of this property. In this chapter, we address a severe practical shortcoming induced by the lack of cumulativity in default logics, namely the failure of default logics to handle lemmas.

Hence cumulativity is moreover of great practical relevance. This is because a cumulative consequence relation allows for the use of lemmas needed for reducing computational efforts. Clearly, cumulativity holds for any monotonic logic. Accordingly, the resulting theorem provers are free to store and then to use any intermediate conclusion. Since computation in default logics does not only involve deduction but also expensive consistency checks, the need to incorporate lemmas is even greater in default logic theorem proving than in standard theorem proving.

As discussed in Section 4.2, cumulativity fails in default logics because the implicit consistency assumptions are lost, whenever a conclusion is added to the set of premises. Therefore, we can trace back the failure of cumulativity to default logic's inability to be aware of the consistency assumptions underlying a default conclusion. Recall default theories (2.5) and (2.6) on Page 15. There, we have observed how the addition of derived default conclusions to the facts can change dependencies between default rules. This may result in new extensions which then change the set of conclusions and, therefore, destroy cumulativity.

As discussed in [Sch93], an extremely simple solution to lemma handling in constrained default logic is offered by pre-constrained default logic, as introduced in Section 3.5. The idea is as follows. For turning a default conclusion into a default lemma, we add the actual lemma to the facts, and its underlying consistency assumptions to the pre-constraints of the pre-constrained default theory at hand.

Let us see what happens while lemmatizing a default conclusion according to the above recipe. Consider Default theory (2.5) on Page 15. This theory yields conclusion A and thus also A ∨ B. Lemmatizing the latter default conclusion as described above yields a pre-constrained default theory, whose facts contain default lemma A ∨ B and whose pre-constraints contain the consistency assumptions made while deriving it. These are given by justification A of default rule $\frac{:A}{A}$. This yields theory

$$\left(\left\{\frac{:A}{A}, \frac{A \vee B : \neg A}{\neg A}\right\}, \{A \vee B\}, \{A\}\right)$$

which has the same extension as Default theory (2.5) and no others. Even though the prerequisite of the default rule $\frac{A \vee B : \neg A}{\neg A}$ is now derivable, its justification is inconsistent with the pre-constraints. So, this default rule is blocked and does not produce a second extension.

In order to lemmatize a default conclusion α in general, we have to take α, a set of default rules D_α used for deriving α, and then we add α to the facts and add the justifications and consequents of the default rules in D_α to the pre-constraints. This approach does neither produce any new nor modify any previous extensions.

This solution offers the following advantages. First, the approach simply deals with first-order formulas and thus avoids an extended language as encountered in cumulative default logic. Second, the use of pre-constraints eliminates extensions which are inconsistent with the default lemma or even its underlying assumptions. However, we encounter the same drawback as found in cumulative default logic [Bre91c]: We obtain an inconsistent system whenever we are faced with new facts contradicting formerly lemmatized conclusions or their underlying assumptions.

8.2 Lemma handling in constrained default logic

A more sophisticated and general approach to handle default lemmas has been developed in [Sch91b, Sch92b] for classical and constrained default logic. Let us first look at the case of constrained default logic due to its closeness to cumulative default logic: Inspired by default logic's natural distinction between facts and defaults, this approach views default lemmas as abbreviations for the corresponding default inferences. According to this philosophy, it becomes natural to add them as default rules, which results in the notion of a *lemma default rule*. That is, informally, in order to lemmatize[1] a default theorem, we take this theorem along with one of its default proofs and construct the corresponding lemma default rule in a certain way.

---

[1] Ie. to introduce a derivable theorem as a lemma by adding it to the initial theory.

But before introducing lemma default rules themselves, we have to account for the notion of a *default proof*[2] in constrained default logic.

Definition 8.2.1. *Let (E, C) be a constrained extension of a default theory (D, W). A default proof of ℓ in (E, C) from (D, W) is a set of default rules $D_\ell \subseteq GD_{(D,W)}^{(E,C)}$ such that D_ℓ is grounded in W and $W \cup Conseq(D_\ell) \vdash \ell$.*

Note that, given an extension E, by compactness and groundedness any formula $\gamma \in E$ has a finite default proof being composed of a finite set of default rules.

Then, a conclusion's lemma default rule is defined in constrained default logic as follows.

Definition 8.2.2. [Sch92b] *Let (D, W) be a default theory and let (E, C) be a constrained extension of (D, W). Let $\ell \in E$ and D_ℓ be a default proof of ℓ in (E, C) from (D, W). We define a lemma default rule δ_ℓ for ℓ as*

$$\delta_\ell = \frac{: \bigwedge_{\delta \in D_\ell} Justif(\delta) \wedge \bigwedge_{\delta \in D_\ell} Conseq(\delta)}{\ell}.$$

The main idea behind lemma default rules is expressed in the following theorem. With it, we have passed the halfway stage to the main result given in Theorem 8.2.2.

Theorem 8.2.1. *Let (D, W) be a default theory and let (E, C) and (E', C') be constrained extensions of (D, W). Let D_ℓ be a default proof of ℓ in (E', C') and let δ_ℓ be the corresponding lemma default rule for ℓ. Then, $\delta_\ell \in GD_{(D \cup \{\delta_\ell\}, W)}^{(E,C)}$ iff $D_\ell \subseteq GD_{(D,W)}^{(E,C)}$.*

Accordingly, we have the following theorem stating that the addition of lemma default rules does not alter the constrained extensions of a given default theory.

Theorem 8.2.2. [Sch92b] *Let (D, W) be a default theory and let (E', C') be a constrained extension of (D, W). Let δ_ℓ be a lemma default rule for $\ell \in E'$. Then, (E, C) is a constrained extension of (D, W) iff (E, C) is a constrained extension of $(D \cup \{\delta_\ell\}, W)$.*

The approach provides a simple solution for generating and using default lemmas. Also, it clarifies the notion of default lemmas by distinguishing between them and their original theorems. Whenever we lemmatize a conclusion, we change its representation into a default rule and add it to the default rules of a considered default theory.

Consider again Default theory (2.5) on Page 15. Clearly, the default proof of default conclusion A ∨ B is simply $\left\{ \frac{:A}{A} \right\}$. Accordingly, the lemma default rule for A ∨ B is $\frac{:A}{A \vee B}$. Adding this lemma default rule for default theorem A ∨ B to the set of default rules yields Default theory

---

[2] A proof-theoretic definition of a default proof in constrained default logic is given in Definition 9.2.1 along with its refinement in Definition 9.5.1; the present notion simply relies on an existing extension along with its generating default rules.

$$\left(\left\{\frac{: A}{A}, \frac{A \vee B : \neg A}{\neg A}, \frac{: A}{A \vee B}\right\}, \emptyset\right) \tag{8.1}$$

which has the same constrained extension as Theory (2.5), $(Th(\{A\}), Th(\{A\}))$. That is, the addition of lemma default rule $\frac{: A}{A \vee B}$ for proposition $A \vee B$ yields the same constrained extension and no others. Although there are still two ways to derive $A \vee B$ (as the prerequisite of default rule $\frac{A \vee B : \neg A}{\neg A}$), both of them rely on the consistency of A and, therefore, prevent the application of default rule $\frac{A \vee B : \neg A}{\neg A}$.

Now, let us consider what happens in the presence of subsequent contradictory information. The following default theory results from adding $\neg(A \vee B)$ to the set of facts of Default theory (8.1).

$$\left(\left\{\frac{: A}{A}, \frac{A \vee B : \neg A}{\neg A}, \frac{: A}{A \vee B}\right\}, \{\neg(A \vee B)\}\right) \tag{8.2}$$

This theory has still a (though trivial) constrained extension, $(Th(\{\emptyset\}), Th(\{\emptyset\}))$. Adding $\neg(A \vee B)$ in the presence of lemma default rule $\frac{: A}{A \vee B}$ just blocks the lemma default rule (along with all other default rules) and does not harm the reasoning process itself. We see that the lemma default rule is retractable and, therefore, preserves the "smooth" default property of the original default conclusion.

An obvious question arising in the context of cumulativity is, how the approach taken by cumulative default logic is related to that of lemma default rules. First, the major difference between the addition of assertions to the assertional facts and the addition of lemma default rules to the set of default rules is that once we have added an assertion to the premises it is not "retractable" any more whenever an inconsistency arises. As an example, take the assertional default theory obtained from (4.5) after lemmatizing assertion $\langle A \vee B, \{A\}\rangle$. Adding $\langle \neg(A \vee B), \emptyset\rangle$ yields now a "hard" contradiction since $Form(\langle A \vee B, \{A\}\rangle) \cup Form(\langle \neg(A \vee B), \emptyset\rangle) \vdash \bot$. As a result, the assertional counterpart of Default theory (8.2), viz.

$$\left(\left\{\frac{: A}{A}, \frac{A \vee B : \neg A}{\neg A}\right\}, \{\langle A \vee B, \{A\}\rangle, \langle \neg(A \vee B), \emptyset\rangle\}\right),$$

has an inconsistent assertional extension.

Thus, in assertional default theories, the smooth automatic retraction of default conclusions in case of inconsistencies is lost. However, adding $\neg(A \vee B)$ in the presence of lemma default rule $\frac{: A}{A \vee B}$ just blocks the default rule and does not harm the reasoning process itself, as we have seen in (8.1) and (8.2). Consequently, the addition of assertions as in cumulative default logic is stronger than that of lemma default rules.

Second, the approach taken by cumulative default logic guarantees only the continued existence of assertional extensions compatible with the lemmatized assertion. All extensions inconsistent with the asserted formula or even its support are eliminated after its addition. Consequently, the generation of credulous default lemmas may eliminate incompatible assertional extensions. For instance, Assertional default theory

$$\left(\left\{\frac{: A}{C}, \frac{C : B}{D}, \frac{: \neg C}{\neg C}\right\}, \emptyset\right)$$

yields initially two assertional extensions: $\widehat{Th}(\{\langle C, \{A, C\}\rangle, \langle D, \{A, B, C, D\}\rangle\})$ and $\widehat{Th}(\{\langle \neg C, \{\neg C\}\rangle\})$. But adding subsequently assertion $\langle D, \{A, B, C, D\}\rangle$ as a credulous default lemma (which is solely contained in the first assertional extension) results in the elimination of the second assertional extension: Assertional default theory

$$\left(\left\{\frac{: A}{C}, \frac{C : B}{D}, \frac{: \neg C}{\neg C}\right\}, \{\langle D, \{A, B, C, D\}\rangle\}\right)$$

has one assertional extension: $\widehat{Th}(\{\langle C, \{A, C\}\rangle, \langle D, \{A, B, C, D\}\rangle\})$. At first, default rule $\frac{: \neg C}{\neg C}$ has generated the second assertional extension. However, this default rule is now blocked, since its justification (or its consequent) is inconsistent with the support of assertion $\langle D, \{A, B, C, D\}\rangle$.

In contrast, lemma default rules preserve *all* extensions and therefore their purpose is more that of a compact representation of default proofs for improving computational efforts. An advantage of the approach taken by lemma default rules is that, since the addition of lemma default rules does not change the extensions of an initial default theory, it allows for the use of skeptical as well as credulous default lemmas. That is, we can also introduce lemmas for default conclusions which do not belong to all extensions.

What has been achieved? One of the original postulates of default formalisms was to "jump to conclusions" in the absence of information. But since the computation of default conclusions involves not only deduction but also expensive consistency checks, the need to incorporate lemmas is even greater in default theorem proving than in standard theorem proving. Hence, default lemmas can be seen as a step in this direction. This becomes obvious by means of Definition 3.2.1: It is possible to jump to a conclusion ρ normally derived in layer E_k by skipping all previous layers E_0 to E_{k-1} and solely applying the (prerequisite-free) lemma default rule.

Let us look at a simplified default proof of a default theorem ρ consisting of a chain of default rules

$$\left\{\frac{\alpha_0 : \beta_0}{\gamma_0}, \ldots, \frac{\alpha_i : \beta_i}{\gamma_i}, \ldots, \frac{\alpha_n : \beta_n}{\rho}\right\}$$

such that $W \vdash \alpha_0$, $W \cup \{\gamma_i\} \vdash \alpha_{i+1}$ for $0 \leq i < n$ and $W \cup \{\gamma_{n-1}\} \vdash \rho$. Normally, proving ρ from scratch requires n proofs and n consistency checks. Each consistency check involves the justification as well as the consequent of each default rule. By comparison, applying the corresponding lemma default rule requires *no* proofs since lemma default rules are prerequisite-free. The effort of checking consistency reduces to *one* consistency check. But although the justification of the lemma default rule contains all justifications and consequents of previously applied default rules we have the advantage that their joint consistency has already been proven.

8.3 Lemma handling in classical default logic

This section summarizes the technicalities needed for adding lemma handling to classical default logic. Since the treatment of lemma default rules in constrained default logic carries over to classical default logic in a straightforward way, the following treatment will be necessarily brief.

First, we account for the notion of a default proof in classical default logic:

Definition 8.3.1. *Let E be a classical extension of a default theory (D, W). A default proof of ℓ in E from (D, W) is a set of default rules $D_\ell \subseteq GD^E_{(D,W)}$ such that D_ℓ is grounded in W and $W \cup Conseq(D_\ell) \vdash \ell$.*

Then, we define the lemma default rule for a (default) conclusion as follows.

Definition 8.3.2. [Sch92b] *Let (D, W) be a default theory and let E be a classical extension of (D, W). Let $\ell \in E$ and $D_\ell = \{\delta_1, \ldots, \delta_n\}$ be a default proof of ℓ in E from (D, W). We define a lemma default rule ζ_ℓ for ℓ as*

$$\zeta_\ell = \frac{:\ Justif(\delta_1), \ldots, Justif(\delta_n)}{\ell}\ .$$

Observe that we obtain a non-singular (prerequisite-free) default rule. This is due to the fact that we have to preserve the consistency of each justification separately.

Observe that a lemma default rule, like ζ_ℓ, corresponds to an assertion of the form $\langle \ell, Justif(\delta_1), \ldots, Justif(\delta_n) \rangle$ in Giordano and Martelli's classical cumulative default logic. However, while the addition of the latter to the premises eliminates all extensions inconsistent with the actual assertion or its support (in the sense of the well-definedness criterion), the addition of the lemma default rule does not alter the classical extensions of a given default theory:

Theorem 8.3.1. [Sch92b] *Let (D, W) be a default theory and let E' be a classical extension of (D, W). Let ζ_ℓ be a lemma default rule for $\ell \in E'$. Then, E is a classical extension of (D, W) iff E is a classical extension of $(D \cup \{\zeta_\ell\}, W)$.*

This approach allows us to enrich classical default logic such that it admits the generation and the use of default lemmas without altering the logical formalism as such. The above examples carry over one-to-one to classical default logic, so that we do not repeat them here.

[Ris95b] gives alternative definitions for lemma default rules, in particular, one for justified default logic.

8.4 Conclusion

We have addressed the failure of handling lemmas in default logics by introducing lemma default rules as a general proof-theoretic approach for using and generating default lemmas. For lemmatizing a default conclusion, we take one of its default proofs, from which we extract the underlying assumptions, and construct the corresponding lemma default rule. This approach is elaborated in [Sch91b, Sch92b]. The semantical underpinnings of this approach are given in [BS94]. Implementation techniques for generating and using such lemma default rules are discussed in Section 9.8.1.

Let us conclude this chapter with a final remark on the formal property of cumulativity. Cumulativity is a property of consequence relations. Consequence relations themselves are concerned with sets of formulas. As a consequence, the approach taken by lemma default rules does not account for cumulativity strictly according to formal regulations. Rather it provides extra-logical means that change the representation of default conclusions, whenever they become default lemmas. However, we have argued above that this approach has nonetheless some advantages over those manipulating formulas as the objects of discourse. For instance, it is truly neutral in the sense that it leaves the original set of extensions unaffected. Also, it tolerates subsequent information contradictory to previously lemmatized conclusions.

Brewka has pursued the idea in lemma default rules in [Bre92] by treating default rules as objects of discourse. The lemmatization process then amounts to turning a "derived" default rule into a lemma default rule. A comparative study of approaches addressing the failure of cumulativity can be found in [Ris95b].

9. Query-answering in default logics

In computer science we are primarily concerned with the conception of formal syntactical methods that are computable by a computer in one way or another. The first step in this creative activity is the specification of the process that is to be modeled. In a second step this specification is turned into an algorithm that is finally implemented.

In this treatise, we are concerned with the formalization of reasoning in the absence of information. We have laid the fundamental basis for this in the previous chapters by specifying the corresponding formal methods. This formal specification was thoroughly investigated on the theoretical level. In this chapter, we are working towards the implementation of our formal methods. In fact, we are interested in query-answering from incomplete knowledge-bases.

The fundamental idea is to exploit existing automated reasoning technology by treating default rules as classical implications along with some qualifying conditions restricting the use of such rules while query-answering. We accomplish this by taking advantage of the conception of structure-oriented theorem proving provided by Bibel's connection method [Bib87]. We will see that the structure-sensitive nature of the connection method allows for an elegant characterization of proofs in default logic.

After introducing our basic approach to query-answering, we present a corresponding algorithm and describe its implementation. Both the algorithm and its implementation are obtained by slightly modifying an existing algorithm and an existing implementation of the connection method. In turn, we give a couple of refinements of the basic approach that lead to conceptionally different algorithms. The approach turns out to be extraordinarily qualified for implementations by means of existing automated theorem proving techniques.

9.1 Motivation

We have listed in the introductory chapter various domains, in which default logic has proven to be extremely valuable for formalizing reasoning in the absence of information. Moreover, it provides semantics for truth maintenance systems [Bre91c] and diverse forms of logic programming [GL90]. Hence, default logic is very expressive and thus of theoretical importance. But expressiveness has its costs. Even though default logic captures many practical approaches, corresponding query-answering procedures are hardly implementable in full generality. The major cause for this is that classical default logic lacks several properties, foremost semi-monotonicity, which are indispensable for reasonable proof procedures.

So far, this difficulty has been addressed in two different ways. First, it has led to algorithmic approaches dealing with restricted subclasses of default logic, which enjoy desirable computational properties [Rei80, BQQ83, Sch90b]. Yet there are principally no approaches to query-answering in full-fledged default logic, apart from those approaches computing entire extensions [JK90, SR91, Nie95, MT]. Second, it has led to variants of default logic overcoming several shortcomings encountered in the original approach, as described in Chapter 4. Although these variants are often more easily "implementable" in full generality, this line has been rarely pursued [Ris93].

We address the aforementioned difficulty from a strictly different point of view, namely the one given by existing automated theorem provers for classical logic. Our approach is driven by the desire to obtain a simple yet powerful method for default theorem proving which is easily adaptable by existing implementations of automated theorem provers.

So, the key question is how classical theorem proving differs from default theorem proving. On the one hand, automated theorem provers handle classical logic extremely well. On the other hand, there are a priori no means for dealing with default rules. Thus, the difference between classical theorem proving and default theorem proving rests on the notion of a default rule, like $\frac{\alpha : \beta}{\gamma}$. In contrast to such rules, automated theorem provers deal with classical implications, like $\alpha \rightarrow \gamma$, or their clausal form. Accordingly, the previously-raised question reduces to the one upon the difference between implications and default rules. Roughly speaking, this difference boils down to that between sentential operators and inference rules on the one hand, and an additional condition given by the consistency check on the other hand. The last two notions strongly affect the application and the use of default rules as opposed to classical implications.

As an example, consider the default rule $\frac{A : \neg S}{E}$ saying that adults (A) are typically employed (E) unless they are students (S) along with its sentential counterpart $A \rightarrow E$. Of course, given an adult A (and nothing else) both rules allow us to conclude E. However, given an unemployed person $\neg E$, the implication allows us to conclude $\neg A$ (by contraposition) while this is impossible with the default rule, since an inference rule cannot be applied in reverse order. Also, we can derive E from A and S with implication $A \rightarrow E$ while this is not possible with the default rule, since its justification $\neg S$ is inconsistent with the premises.

The basic idea of our approach is the following one. In order to allow for default theorem proving based on classical automated theorem provers, we treat default rules as classical implications along with some qualifying conditions restricting the use of such rules. In concrete terms, this leads to two restrictions on classical proofs: First, we restrict admissible proofs to those that are structured in a certain way in order to account for the concept of an inference rule. Second, we impose a condition on proofs ensuring the compatible use of default rules preserving their consistency conditions.

In what follows, we develop a new approach to theorem proving in default logics based on the connection method [Bib87]. We have chosen this method since it relies on analyzing the structure of formulas and thus allows for structure-oriented theorem proving. Unlike resolution-based methods that decompose formulas in order to derive a contradiction, the connection method analyzes the structure of formulas for proving their unsatisfiability. This structure-sensitive nature allows for an elegant characterization of the two aforementioned restrictions on classical proofs. As a consequence, we obtain a homogeneous characterization of default proofs at the level of the calculus.

In general, there are two approaches to query-answering in default logics. In the *credulous* approach, we accept a query if it belongs to one extension of a considered default theory, whereas in the *skeptical* approach, we accept a query if it belongs to all extension of the default theory. In the sequel, we exclusively deal with the more basic approach, namely credulous default reasoning. The given approach is extended to skeptical reasoning in [ST95], as summarized in Section 9.8.3.

Even though our method has a general nature, we introduce it here with the example of constrained default logic because this variant enjoys several desirable computational properties needed for reasonable proof procedures. In general, the approach applies to any default logic enjoying semi-monotonicity, as detailed in the following sections.

The chapter is organized as follows. After some formal preliminaries accounting for default logics in Section 3.2, we smooth the way for our approach by providing computational characterizations of extensions, queries, and default theories in Section 9.2. We introduce our basic method for query-answering in default logics in Section 9.3. In the subsequent section, we present a corresponding algorithm and sketch a preliminary yet interesting implementation obtained by carefully modifying an existing connection method theorem prover. This endeavor is driven by our initial desire to obtain a simple yet powerful method for default theorem proving which is easily adaptable by existing implementations of automated theorem provers. To this end, the latter implementation provides an initial case-study in how far an existing theorem prover for the connection method has to be modified in order to allow for query-answering in default logics.

To a turn, we introduce in Section 9.5 an equivalent but conceptually different approach to query-answering in default logics. This results in an algorithm orthogonal to the one introduced in the first part of the chapter. Section 9.6 gives an intermediate summary of our approach. In Section 9.7, we provide simple prototypical implementations of the different mouldings of the approach. These prototypes provide us with some experimental results, which are detailed in [Sch95b] and summarized in Section 9.7. Section 9.8 describes several enhancements and extensions of the approach. Among others, we show how the approach can be enriched by lemma handling and sketch the incorporation of priorities.

In what follows, we deal for simplicity with a propositional language $\mathcal{L}_\Sigma$ over a finite alphabet Σ. Arguably, the restriction to a decidable logic is a necessary one. Otherwise the resulting system would not even be semi-decidable due to the reference to consistency while deriving formulas in default logic (cf. [Rei80]). This agrees with a customary tradition in logic programming, where logic programs with variables are viewed as a shorthand for the set of their ground instances.

9.2 Computational characterizations

This section provides the fundamental basis for our approach to query-answering in default logics. To this end, let us first turn to the two features distinguishing default rules from classical implications, namely the character of an inference rule and the additional consistency check. While the latter is handled in the usual manner by testing satisfiability, the former needs a more subtle treatment. In fact, the character of an inference rule can be captured by the notion of *groundedness*, which distinguishes default rules from classical implications. For instance, the default rule $\frac{A : \neg S}{E}$ is (trivially) not grounded in the set of facts $\{\neg E\}$ so that reasoning by contraposition becomes impossible. That is, $\neg A$ is not derivable from $\neg E$. Moreover, groundedness prevents circular chains of reasoning. Consider the default rules $\frac{A : C}{C}$ and $\frac{C : A}{A}$ and no facts. In this case, neither A nor C is derivable since there is no non-empty grounded sequence of default rules.

So, from the perspective of the introductory section, groundedness and consistency constitute the two qualifying conditions for the application and the use of default rules. In particular, these two notions allow for characterizing extensions in a considerably simpler way. As described in Theorem 3.3.2, we obtain a non-fixed point characterization of constrained extensions, which is indispensable for computational purposes: For a default theory (D, W) and sets of formulas E and C, we have that (E, C) is a constrained extension of (D, W) iff

$$
\begin{aligned}
E &= Th(W \cup Conseq(D')) \\
C &= Th(W \cup Justif(D') \cup Conseq(D'))
\end{aligned}
$$

for a maximal $D' \subseteq D$ such that D' is grounded in W and $W \cup Justif(D') \cup Conseq(D')$ is consistent.

In this way, an extension is characterized as the deductive closure of the set of facts and the consequents of a maximal set of default rules which is grounded and preserves consistency. Accordingly, the computation of a constrained extension boils down to classical deduction along with enforcement of groundedness and consistency.

This suggests the following approach to query-answering in default logics. In order to verify whether a formula φ is in some extension E of a default theory (D, W), we have to find a subset of D that allows for deriving φ and complies with the above requirements. As already noticed in [Rei80], this can only be accomplished in a reasonable way if we can confine ourselves to default rules relevant for deriving φ. The formal counterpart of this observation is given by the property of *semi-monotonicity*—on which also our approach relies. Given this property, it is sufficient to consider a relevant subset of default rules while answering a query, since applying other default rules would only enlarge or preserve the partial extension at hand.[1]

This property leads us to the following notion of a *default proof*,[2] on which we build our formal characterization of query-answering in constrained default logic.

Definition 9.2.1. *Let* (D, W) *be a default theory and* φ *a formula. A default proof* $D_\varphi \subseteq D$ *for* φ *from* (D, W) *is a finite set of default rules such that* $W \cup Conseq(D_\varphi) \vdash \varphi$ *and* D_φ *is grounded in* W *and* $W \cup Justif(D_\varphi) \cup Conseq(D_\varphi)$ *is consistent.*

Observe that a default proof D_φ is implicitly a sequence $\langle \delta_i \rangle_{i \in I}$ of default rules, due to the groundedness condition given in (2.8). This is emphasized in the refinement given below in Definition 9.5.1.

The following corollary to Theorem 3.3.2 assures that a query φ is in some extension of the default theory at hand iff φ has a default proof:

Corollary 9.2.1. *Let* (D, W) *be a default theory. Then,* $\varphi \in E$ *for some constrained extension* (E, C) *of* (D, W) *iff there is a default proof for* φ *from* (D, W).

That is, for verifying whether φ is in some extension of a default theory (D, W), it is enough to determine a grounded and consistent set of default rules $D_\varphi \subseteq D$ that allows for proving φ from the facts in W and the consequents of all default rules in D_φ.

Theorem 3.3.2 and Corollary 9.2.1 provide the fundamental basis for our approach to query-answering in (constrained) default logic. They are strongly rooted in the basic concepts of groundedness and consistency. Observe that in both specifications the latter concepts constitute rather separate constraints on the default rules under consideration. We will stepwisely refine this approach in the two following sections. In particular, Section 9.4 strongly relies on the possibility of separating these concepts for implementing our approach by using existing automated theorem provers.

Another salient feature of the previous specifications is the formation of sequences of default rules. This will come to the fore more and more in the subsequent sections. In particular in Section 9.5, where we provide an alternative approach by meshing together the concepts of groundedness and consistency for forming sequences of default rules. Moreover, we have seen in [Sch94a] that such a combination is very useful for implementing priorities.

We now turn to the issue of default theorem proving using conventional theorem provers. As argued in the introductory section, classical theorem provers cannot

---

[1] This explains why computational approaches to classical default logic deal with entire extensions. This is because the absence of semi-monotonicity enforces the inspection of *all* given default rules anyway.

[2] Observe that this conception differs from that in Definition 8.2.1, insofar as it does not rely on an existing extension.

deal with default rules but conventional clauses only. As a first step, we thus shift information from the default part into the classical part of a default theory in order to facilitate the treatment of default theories. To this end, we transform default theories by substituting default rules by so-called *atomic default rules* consisting of new atomic propositions and by extending the facts with a set of implications relating these propositions to the constituents of the original default rules: For a default theory (D, W) in language $\mathcal{L}_\Sigma$ over some alphabet Σ, let $\mathcal{L}_{\Sigma'}$ be the language over the alphabet Σ', obtained by adding to Σ the new propositions $\alpha_\delta, \beta_\delta, \gamma_\delta$ for each $\delta \in D$. The function τ maps a default theory (D, W) in $\mathcal{L}_\Sigma$ into default theory (D', W') in $\mathcal{L}_{\Sigma'}$, where

$$D' = \left\{ \frac{\alpha_\delta : \beta_\delta}{\gamma_\delta} \;\middle|\; \delta \in D \right\}$$
$$W' = W \cup \{ Prereq(\delta) \to \alpha_\delta, \beta_\delta \to Justif(\delta), \gamma_\delta \to Conseq(\delta) \mid \delta \in D \}.$$

The resulting default theory (D', W') is called the *atomic format* of the original default theory (D, W). That is, (D', W') contains only atomic default rules. The motivations for this format are similar to the ones for definitional clausal form in automated theorem proving [Ede92].

Consider default rule $\frac{S:A}{A}$ (for short δ_1). Applying τ to this theory yields for δ_1 the default rule $\frac{S_{\delta_1} : A_{\delta_1}}{A_{\delta_1}}$ (where S_{δ_1} and A_{δ_1} are new propositional letters)[3] along with the implications $S \to S_{\delta_1}$ and $A_{\delta_1} \to A$.

The transformation of default theories into their atomic format does not affect the computation of queries to the original default theory, as shown in [Rot93]:

Theorem 9.2.1. [Rot93] *Let (D, W) be a default theory in $\mathcal{L}_\Sigma$. Let E, C be sets of formulas in $\mathcal{L}_\Sigma$ and E', C' be sets of formulas in $\mathcal{L}_{\Sigma'}$ such that $E = E' \cap \mathcal{L}_\Sigma$ and $C = C' \cap \mathcal{L}_\Sigma$. Then, (E, C) is a constrained extension of (D, W) iff (E', C') is a constrained extension of $\tau(D, W)$.*

The major advantage of atomic default rules over arbitrary ones is that the constituents of default rules are not spread over several clauses while transforming them into clausal format. Rather each atomic default rule can be represented as a single binary clause, as we will see in the next section. Strictly speaking, this is not absolutely necessary but it simplifies matters drastically. This concerns the formal presentation of the approach and moreover its implementation by existing automated theorem provers. With the above transformation, we can (and will) therefore confine ourselves to default theories with atomic default rules only (without loosing generality).

9.3 A method for query-answering in default logics

In this section, we develop a method for query-answering in default logics based on the connection method [Bib87]. The connection method allows for testing the unsat-

---
[3] For simplicity, we introduce only two new propositional letters, since δ_1 is a normal default rule.

isfiability of formulas in conjunctive normal form (CNF). Unlike resolution-based methods that decompose formulas in order to derive a contradiction, the connection method analyses the structure of formulas for proving their unsatisfiability. This structure-sensitive nature allows for an elegant characterization of proofs in default logic, as we will see below.

9.3.1 The connection method

In the connection method, formulas in CNF are displayed two-dimensionally in the form of *matrices*. A matrix is a set of sets of literals (literal occurrences, to be precise).[4] Such a matrix is given in (9.1) below. Each column of a matrix represents a *clause* of the CNF of the formula. In order to show that a sentence φ is entailed by a sentence W, we prove that $W \wedge \neg\varphi$ is unsatisfiable. In the connection method this is accomplished by path checking: A *path* through a matrix is a set of literals, one from each clause. A *connection* is an unordered pair of literals which are identical except for the negation sign (and possible indexes). A *mating* is a set of connections. A mating *spans* a matrix if each path through the matrix contains a connection from the mating. Finally, a formula, like $W \wedge \neg\varphi$, is unsatisfiable iff there is a spanning mating for its matrix.

Let us briefly illustrate this by verifying whether C is entailed by

$$S \wedge (S \rightarrow A) \wedge (A \rightarrow C).$$

For this, we prove that conjoining the negated query $\neg$C to the latter formula yields an unsatisfiable formula. Transforming the resulting formula into its CNF yields

$$S \wedge (\neg S \vee A) \wedge (\neg A \vee C) \wedge \neg C$$

whose two-dimensional representation is the following one (by ignoring the arcs).

$$\begin{bmatrix} & \neg S & \neg A & \neg C \\ S & A & C & \end{bmatrix} \tag{9.1}$$

This matrix has a spanning mating whose connections are represented by arcs linking the respective literals. This is so because Matrix (9.1) contains four paths, like $\{S, A, \neg A, \neg C\}$, all of which contain at least one connection, like $\{A, \neg A\}$. In this way, we have shown that C is entailed by $S \wedge (S \rightarrow A) \wedge (A \rightarrow C)$.

In the sequel, we sometimes refer to certain submatrices or supermatrices of a given matrix. We call a matrix M' a submatrix of a matrix M if M' is obtainable from M by deleting literals or even clauses in M. The definition of supermatrices is analogous. We call a matrix *complementary* if it has a spanning mating. We say that a path is *complementary* or *closed* if it contains a connection from a given mating.

---

[4] In the sequel, we simply say literal instead of literal occurrences; the latter allow for distinguishing between identical literals in different clauses.

Otherwise, we say that the path is *non-complementary* or *open*. Finally, we call a matrix *complementary* if it has a spanning mating or, in other words, if each path through the matrix contains a connection from a mating at hand.

9.3.2 Complementarity

In this section, we describe how to turn default theories into matrices and how to verify the complementarity of the resulting matrices.

Our approach relies on the idea that a default rule can be decomposed into a classical implication along with two qualifying conditions, one accounting for the character of an inference rule and another one enforcing the respective consistency condition. The computational counterparts of these qualifying conditions are given by the proof-oriented concepts of *admissibility* and *compatibility*, which we will introduce in the two following sections.

In order to find out whether a formula φ is contained in some extension of a default theory (D, W) we proceed as follows. First, we transform the default rules in D into their sentential counterparts. This yields a set of indexed implications

$$W_D = \left\{ \alpha_\delta \to \gamma_\delta \ \middle| \ \tfrac{\alpha_\delta \,:\, \beta_\delta}{\gamma_\delta} \in D \right\}.$$

In what follows, we adopt this notation and write $W_{D'} = \left\{ \alpha_\delta \to \gamma_\delta \ \middle| \ \tfrac{\alpha_\delta \,:\, \beta_\delta}{\gamma_\delta} \in D' \right\}$ for any subset D' of D. Second, we transform both W and W_D into their clausal forms, C_W and C_D. The clauses in C_D, like $\{\neg\alpha_\delta, \gamma_\delta\}$, are called δ-*clauses;* all other clauses like those in C_W are referred to as ω-*clauses.* Now, we are ready for query-answering. That is, a query φ is derivable from (D, W) iff there is a spanning mating for the matrix $C_W \cup C_D \cup \{\neg\varphi\}$ agreeing with the concepts of admissibility and compatibility.[5]

As an example, consider the statements "students are typically adults", "adults usually drive a car", and "adults are typically employed unless they are students" along with a student S. The corresponding default theory is the following one.

$$\left(\left\{ \frac{S \,:\, A}{A}, \frac{A \,:\, C}{C}, \frac{A \,:\, \neg S}{E} \right\}, \{S\} \right) \tag{9.2}$$

In both Reiter's and constrained default logic, this default theory yields a unique extension $Th(\{S, A, C\})$ in which a student is an adult driving a car.

The encoding of the set of default rules yields the following set, W_D, of implications:

$$\{S_{\delta_1} \to A_{\delta_1}, A_{\delta_2} \to C_{\delta_2}, A_{\delta_3} \to E_{\delta_3}\}$$

The indexes denote the respective default rules in Default theory (9.2) from left to right. In order to verify that a student drives a car, C, we first have to transform the fact S (in Default theory (9.2)) and the implications in W_D into their

---

[5] Without loss of generality, we deal with atomic queries only, since any query can be transformed into "atomic format" in the spirit of transformation τ (cf. Section 3.2).

clausal form. The resulting clauses are given two-dimensionally as the first four columns of the matrix in (9.3). The full matrix is obtained by adding the clause containing the negated query, $\neg C$. In fact, the matrix has a spanning mating, $\{\{S, \neg S_{\delta_1}\}, \{A_{\delta_1}, \neg A_{\delta_2}\}, \{C_{\delta_2}, \neg C\}\}$. As above, we have indicated these connections in (9.3) as arcs linking the respective literals.

$$
\begin{bmatrix}
 & \neg S_{\delta_1} & \neg A_{\delta_2} & \neg A_{\delta_3} & \neg C \\
S & A_{\delta_1} & C_{\delta_2} & E_{\delta_3} &
\end{bmatrix}
\tag{9.3}
$$

For simplicity, we have refrained from transforming Default theory (9.2) into atomic format since it already consists of atomic formulas. In such a case, let us rather adopt the following two conventions. First, let us agree on simply labeling components of a default rule and allowing for connections between complementary literals having different indexes (if any at all). Second, let us assume that we can always distinguish between the prerequisite and the consequent in a δ-clause. Observe that both conventions are obsolete as soon as we enforce default theories in atomic format by transformation τ (cf. Section 3.2). First, we obtain in atomic format two standard connections, rather than a "mixed" connection between an indexed and unindexed literal, For instance, instead of two clauses $\{S\}$ and $\{\neg S_{\delta_1}, A_{\delta_1}\}$ (from S, $\frac{S : A}{A}$) along with the "mixed" connection $\{S, \neg S_{\delta_1}\}$, we would obtain three clauses $\{S\}, \{\neg S, S_{\delta_1}\}$, and $\{\neg S_{\delta_1}, A_{\delta_1}\}$ (from S, $S \rightarrow S_{\delta_1}$, $\frac{S_{\delta_1} : A_{\delta_1}}{A_{\delta_1}}$) along with two standard connections $\{S, \neg S\}$ and $\{S_{\delta_1}, \neg S_{\delta_1}\}$. The same applies to the remaining clauses in Matrix (9.3). Second, observe that in atomic format the distinction between prerequisites and consequents of δ-clause is trivial. This is so because the prerequisite is given by the negative literal in the δ-clause and the consequent by the positive literal. We support this in two-dimensional notation by stacking prerequisites over consequents.

The above matrix illustrates yet another point: Not all of the clauses are necessarily involved in providing a spanning mating for a matrix. A useful concept is then that of a *core* of a matrix M wrt a mating Π, which allows for isolating the clauses relevant to the underlying proof. We define the core of M wrt Π as follows.[6]

Definition 9.3.1. *Let Π be a mating for the matrix M. Then, we define the core of M wrt Π as*

$$
\kappa(M, \Pi) = \{c \in M \mid \exists \pi \in \Pi \,.\, c \cap \pi \neq \emptyset\}.
$$

For instance, the core of the preceding matrix relative to the drawn mating is given by the first three and the last clauses.

So far, it might seem that classical theorem proving with ω- and δ-clauses suffices for querying default theories. To see that this is not enough, consider again default rule $\frac{A : \neg S}{E}$ along with the fact $\neg E$. In default logics, there is no way to derive

---

[6] Recall that we deal with literal occurrences.

¬A. However, the resulting matrix, given in (9.4), has a spanning mating, which amounts to deriving ¬A by contraposition.

$$
\left[\begin{array}{cc} & \overset{\frown}{\neg A_{\delta_3} \quad A} \\ \overset{\frown}{\neg E \quad E_{\delta_3}} & \end{array} \right] \tag{9.4}
$$

This example shows that pure deduction with δ-clauses cannot account for the inference rule character of the original default rules.

9.3.3 Admissibility

In default logics, the nature of an inference rule is reflected by the property of groundedness, which relies on forming sequences of default rules. In fact, the connection method allows for imposing a similar restriction on the clausal counterparts of default rules. This leads us to our first qualifying condition on proofs given by the concept of admissibility.

Definition 9.3.2 (Admissibility). *Let C_W be a set of ω-clauses and C_D be a set of δ-clauses and let Π be a mating for $C_W \cup C_D$. Then, we define that $(C_W \cup C_D, \Pi)$ is admissible iff there is an enumeration $\langle \{\neg\alpha_{\delta_i}, \gamma_{\delta_i}\} \rangle_{i \in I}$ of $\kappa(C_D, \Pi)$ such that for $i \in I$, Π is a spanning mating for*

$$
C_W \cup \left(\bigcup_{j=0}^{i-1} \{\{\neg\alpha_{\delta_j}, \gamma_{\delta_j}\}\} \right) \cup \{\{\neg\alpha_{\delta_i}\}\}. \tag{9.5}
$$

Note that sometimes not all connections in Π are needed for showing the unsatisfiability of the submatrices in (9.5). We say that $(C_W \cup C_D, \Pi)$ is admissible at i in an index set I, if (9.5) holds for $i \in I$. Moreover, we say that $(C_W \cup C_D, \Pi)$ is admissible wrt I, if it is admissible at all $i \in I$.

The previous definition may be nicely illustrated by the proof in our student example given in (9.3). There, we obtain the enumeration

$$
\langle \{\neg S_{\delta_1}, A_{\delta_1}\}, \{\neg A_{\delta_2}, C_{\delta_2}\} \rangle,
$$

which in turn leads to the following matrices; each representing a set of clauses as specified in (9.5):

$$
\left[\begin{array}{c} \overset{\frown}{\neg S_{\delta_1}} \\ S \end{array} \right] \qquad \left[\begin{array}{cc} \overset{\frown}{\neg S_{\delta_1}} \;\; \overset{\frown}{\neg A_{\delta_2}} \\ S \quad\; A_{\delta_1} \end{array} \right] \tag{9.6}
$$

Observe that the preceding matrices are in fact submatrices of Matrix (9.3). Clearly, each of these submatrices has a spanning mating, so that the original matrix along with its mating, given in (9.3), constitute an admissible proof.

Observe that the proof in the example involving contraposition violates admissibility. This is so because there is no spanning mating for the submatrix $\{\{\neg E\}, \{\neg A_{\delta_3}\}\}$ of Matrix (9.4).

In the remainder of this subsection, we provide an incremental approach to admissibility. This is made precise in the following theorem.

Theorem 9.3.1. *Let C_W be a set of ω-clauses and $C_D = \{\{\neg \alpha_{\delta_i}, \gamma_{\delta_i}\} \mid i \in I\}$ be a set of δ-clauses. Let Π be a mating for $C_W \cup C_D$ such that $(C_W \cup C_D, \Pi)$ is admissible wrt I. Let $\{\neg \alpha_\delta, \gamma_\delta\}$ be a δ-clause. Then, $(C_W \cup C_D \cup \{\{\neg \alpha_\delta, \gamma_\delta\}\}, \Pi)$ is admissible iff Π is a spanning mating for $C_W \cup \{\{\gamma_{\delta_i}\} \mid i \in I\} \cup \{\{\neg \alpha_\delta\}\}$.*

Informally, this theorem allows us to discard paths through "prerequisites of admissible δ-clauses" while verifying admissibility. Hence, for verifying admissibility of the proof given in (9.3), we can proceed as follows. For illustration, consider also the two submatrices in (9.6). We start with the set of open paths through all ω-clauses. There is only one such path in our example, $\{S\}$. For verifying the admissibility of[7] $\{\neg S_{\delta_1}, A_{\delta_1}\}$, we have to check whether all such open paths contain a literal complementary to $\neg S_{\delta_1}$. Since this is the case, we can proceed by verifying the admissibility of $\{\neg A_{\delta_2}, C_{\delta_2}\}$. For this, we can discard all paths through $\neg S_{\delta_1}$. Thus, we can restrict ourselves to all open paths obtained by adding A_{δ_1} to all open paths through all ω-clauses. There is only one such path in our example, $\{S, A_{\delta_1}\}$. As above, this path has to contain a literal complementary to $\neg A_{\delta_2}$ for confirming the admissibility of the second δ-clause. Clearly, the path $\{S, A_{\delta_1}\} \cup \{\neg A_{\delta_2}\}$ is closed, so that admissibility is confirmed.

Moreover, Theorem 9.3.1 shows that admissibility is indeed the proof-theoretic counterpart of groundedness. That is, if C_W is the clausal representation of W, then there is a spanning mating for $C_W \cup \bigcup_{i=0}^{n}\{\{\gamma_{\delta_i}\}\} \cup \{\{\neg \alpha_\delta\}\}$ iff $W \cup Conseq(\{\delta_0, \ldots, \delta_n\}) \vdash Prereq(\delta)$, where $\gamma_{\delta_i} = Conseq(\delta_i)$. Observe that the latter corresponds to the condition given for groundedness in (2.8).

9.3.4 Compatibility

The second qualifying condition for proofs is given by the concept of compatibility; it relies on the notion of consistency specific to constrained default logic.

Definition 9.3.3 (Compatibility). *Let C_W be a set of ω-clauses and C_D be a set of δ-clauses and let Π be a mating for $C_W \cup C_D$. Then, we define that $(C_W \cup C_D, \Pi)$ is compatible iff there is no spanning mating for*

$$C_W \cup \{\{\beta_\delta\}, \{\gamma_\delta\} \mid \{\neg \alpha_\delta, \gamma_\delta\} \in \kappa(C_D, \Pi), \ \beta_\delta = Justif(\delta)\}.$$

Notably, this is the first place where we refer to a notion specific to constrained default logic; the entire preceding exposition involving the concept of admissibility applies to any (semi-monotonic) default logic.

---

[7] For illustration, we often explicate the respective δ-clauses rather than expressing things in terms of indexes.

Consider again our student example. For compatibility, we have to verify that the matrix $\{\{S\}\} \cup \{\{A_{\delta_1}\}, \{C_{\delta_2}\}\}$ or two-dimensionally

$$\left[\begin{array}{ccc} S & A_{\delta_1} & C_{\delta_2} \end{array} \right] \qquad (9.7)$$

has no spanning mating. This matrix is formed by the facts $\{S\}$ and the justifications A_{δ_1} and C_{δ_2} of the first two default rules in (9.2). Obviously, Matrix (9.7) has no spanning mating, since it has a non-complementary path, $\{S, A_{\delta_2}, E_{\delta_3}\}$. We thus obtain an admissible and compatible proof for the original query, S, asking whether a student drives a car. Note that an open path gives a model of the considered formula.

In order to give an example for an incompatible proof, consider matrix

$$\{\{S\}\} \cup \{\{A\}, \{\neg S\}, \{E\}\}$$

whose compatibility is verified while answering the query E from the fact S and default rules $\frac{S:A}{A}$ and $\frac{A:\neg S}{E}$. This matrix has a spanning mating $\{\{S, \neg S\}\}$ indicating an incompatible use of default rules.

In principle, compatibility is separate from admissibility. However, the next theorem shows that compatibility can be verified on (almost) the same matrices as used for verifying complementarity and admissibility.

Theorem 9.3.2. *Let C_W be a set of ω-clauses and C_D be a set of δ-clauses. Let Π be a mating for $C_W \cup C_D$ such that $(C_W \cup C_D, \Pi)$ is admissible. Then, Π is a spanning mating for $C_W \cup C_D \cup \{\{\beta_\delta\} \mid \{\neg\alpha_\delta, \gamma_\delta\} \in C_D, \beta_\delta = Justif(\delta)\}$ iff Π is a spanning mating for $C_W \cup \{\{\beta_\delta\}, \{\gamma_\delta\} \mid \{\neg\alpha_\delta, \gamma_\delta\} \in C_D, \beta_\delta = Justif(\delta)\}$.*

This theorem offers the computational advantage of structure *and* information sharing while query-answering.

Above, we have verified the compatibility of the proof obtained in our student example by regarding the matrix given in (9.7). Theorem 9.3.2 tells us that this is equivalent to checking whether the following admissible supermatrix of (9.7) has no spanning mating.

$$\left[\begin{array}{ccc} & \neg S_{\delta_1} & \neg A_{\delta_2} \\ S & A_{\delta_1} & C_{\delta_2} \end{array} \right] \qquad (9.8)$$

Even though the latter matrix is larger than the one in (9.7), it shares the structure of the matrices used for verifying complementarity and admissibility. In fact, it is at the same time a supermatrix of the largest matrix used for checking admissibility in (9.6) and a submatrix of the actual matrix used for proving the query C in (9.3). That is, Matrix (9.8) is obtained by adding C_{δ_2} to the rightmost clause of the right matrix in (9.6). Analogously, we obtain the proof for C in (9.3) by adding the query clause $\{\neg C\}$ to Matrix (9.8). We will take up these ideas in Section 9.5.

9.3.5 Characterizing default proofs

In Section 9.2, we have decomposed default theorem proving in default logic into classical deduction along with the concepts of groundedness and consistency. In the previous subsections, we have carefully mapped these notions onto the connection method. We have accomplished this by identifying the concepts of complementarity, admissibility, and compatibility, as the proof-theoretic counterparts of classical deduction, groundedness and consistency.

As a result, we obtain the following theorem showing that our method is correct and complete for constrained default logic:

Theorem 9.3.3. *Let* (D, W) *be a default theory in atomic format and* φ *an atomic formula. Then,* $\varphi \in E$ *for some constrained extension* (E, C) *of* (D, W) *iff there is a spanning mating* Π *for the matrix* M *of* $W \cup W_D \cup \{\neg\varphi\}$ *such that* (M, Π) *is admissible and compatible.*

As defined above, we have that $W_D = \left\{ \alpha_\delta \to \gamma_\delta \ \middle|\ \frac{\alpha_\delta : \beta_\delta}{\gamma_\delta} \in D \right\}$.

As regards the concept of a default proof given in Definition 9.2.1, it is easy to see that the default rules D_φ used for proving φ may be extracted from the δ-clauses in the core of M wrt Π, or formally $\{\delta \mid \{\neg\alpha_\delta, \gamma_\delta\} \in \kappa(M, \Pi)\}$. Alternatively, we can extract the actual default proof from the index set used for verifying admissibility. Since by definition (M, Π) is admissible wrt some I, the default proof D_φ is also describable as a sequence $\langle \delta_i \rangle_{i \in I}$ of default rules. This corresponds to the conception of default proofs conceived in Definition 9.5.1.

Finally, let us summarize our approach in the remainder of this section by means of a coherent example. Consider the statements "students are typically adults", "adults are typically employed", and "students are typically not employed" along with the corresponding default theory dealing with a student:

$$\left(\left\{ \frac{S : \neg E}{\neg E}, \frac{S : A}{A}, \frac{A : E}{E} \right\}, \{S\} \right) \tag{9.9}$$

The encoding of the set of default rules yields the following set of implications:

$$W_D = \{S_{\delta_1} \to \neg E_{\delta_1}, S_{\delta_2} \to A_{\delta_2}, A_{\delta_3} \to E_{\delta_3}\}$$

As before, the indexes denote the respective default rules in Default theory (9.9) from left to right. Let us consider the query E, asking whether a student is employed. Transforming the fact S, the implications in W_D, and the negated query $\neg E$ into clausal form yields the matrix in (9.10).

$$\begin{bmatrix} & \neg S_{\delta_1} & \neg S_{\delta_2} & \neg A_{\delta_3} & \neg E \\ S & \neg E_{\delta_1} & A_{\delta_2} & E_{\delta_3} & \end{bmatrix} \tag{9.10}$$

This matrix has spanning mating $\{\{S, \neg S_{\delta_2}\}, \{A_{\delta_2}, \neg A_{\delta_3}\}, \{E_{\delta_3}, \neg E\}\}$, whose connections are indicated as arcs linking the respective literals. This default proof yields the following enumeration:

$$\langle\{\neg S_{\delta_2}, A_{\delta_2}\}, \{\neg A_{\delta_3}, E_{\delta_3}\}\rangle,$$

For admissibility, we have to consider the following submatrices of Matrix (9.10):

$$\begin{bmatrix} & \neg S_{\delta_2} \\ S & \end{bmatrix} \qquad \begin{bmatrix} & \neg S_{\delta_2} & \neg A_{\delta_3} \\ S & A_{\delta_2} & \end{bmatrix} \qquad (9.11)$$

Observe that each of these submatrices has a spanning mating, so that the original matrix and its mating, given in (9.10), constitute an admissible proof.

For compatibility, we have to verify that the following matrix has no spanning mating.

$$\begin{bmatrix} & \neg S_{\delta_2} & \neg A_{\delta_3} \\ S & A_{\delta_2} & E_{\delta_3} \end{bmatrix}$$

Obviously this is the case since there is a non-complementary path, $\{S, A_{\delta_2}, E_{\delta_3}\}$. We thus obtain an admissible and compatible proof for the original query, E, asking whether a student is employed. Note that we employed Theorem 9.3.2 for verifying compatibility.

Observe that there is yet another spanning mating for the matrix in (9.10), namely

$$\{\{S, \neg S_{\delta_1}\}, \{S, \neg S_{\delta_2}\}, \{\neg E_{\delta_1}, E_{\delta_3}\}, \{A_{\delta_2}, \neg A_{\delta_3}\}\}. \qquad (9.12)$$

This mating discards the negated query $\neg E$. The cause for this is that we deal with conflicting defaults. That is, from S we can derive $\neg E$ via the first default rule in Default theory (9.10) as well as E via the second and third default rule. Although the resulting proof can be shown to be admissible, it is however not compatible:

$$\begin{bmatrix} & \neg S_{\delta_1} & \neg S_{\delta_2} & \neg A_{\delta_3} \\ S & \neg E_{\delta_1} & A_{\delta_2} & E_{\delta_3} \end{bmatrix}$$

This matrix has the spanning mating given in (9.12). This shows that the corresponding proof is not compatible.

The last part of the example stresses the importance of the concept of compatibility. In particular, it seems advantageous to prune incompatible proofs as early as possible, since defaults might conflict with each other.

9.4 Implementing the approach

In this section, we pursue our initial goal of providing a simple method for query-answering in default logics that needs few modifications to existing implementations of automated theorem provers.

There are several ways of implementing our approach by using existing automated theorem provers. An extreme way would be to prove each query conventionally and to leave the verification of admissibility and compatibility to special-purpose algorithms. This is rather expensive, since one might have to generate numerous proofs before our qualifying conditions are confirmed or even denied. The other extreme yet opposite approach is to modify an existing automated theorem prover in order to incorporate both the verification of admissibility and compatibility. To this end, however, one has to put consistency-checks into the "inner-loop" of a theorem prover, which is a difficult and (sometimes) expensive undertaking, too.

Even though we argue later that the integration of consistency-checks into the "inner-loop" of a theorem prover is often worthwhile, provided one may rely on techniques as introduced in Section 9.8.2 and used in Section 10.2 that allow us to restrict our attention to ultimately necessary consistency checks, this section provides nonetheless a meritorious minimalist's approach that needs the *fewest* modifications to an underlying automated theorem prover.

9.4.1 An algorithm

The two aforementioned extreme approaches do not fully concur with our initial desire for a simple and feasible approach to default theorem proving that is *easily* adaptable by existing implementations of the connection method, like SETHEO [LBSB92] or PPP [NS91]. We address this problem in this section by separating the verification of compatibility (or consistency) from that of complementarity and admissibility. This is motivated by the incongruity between the "global" notion of consistency employed in default logics (by referring to the final extension or constraints) and the stepwise execution of inference-steps encountered in existing theorem provers. In order to avoid the resulting difficulties, we rather pursue for the time being an "off-line" approach by compiling compatibility; thereby taking advantage of the compliant conception of consistency in constrained default logic. This approach is justified by the following corollary to Theorem 3.3.2.

Corollary 9.4.1. Let (D,W) be a default theory and let E and C be sets of formulas. Then, (E,C) is a constrained extension of (D,W) iff (E,C) is a constrained extension of (D',W) for a maximal $D' \subseteq D$ such that $W \cup Justif(D') \cup Conseq(D')$ is consistent.

We say that a default theory (D,W) is compatible iff $W \cup Justif(D) \cup Conseq(D)$ is consistent. Accordingly, we compile a given default theory (D,W) into several compatible default theories (D',W). Compiling a default theory (D,W) amounts to computing the generating default rules[8] D' of each extensions of default theory

$$\left(\left\{ \frac{:\beta \wedge \gamma}{\beta \wedge \gamma} \ \middle| \ \frac{\alpha:\beta}{\gamma} \in D \right\}, W \right).$$

Observe that any compatible default theory has a unique constrained extension.

---

[8] See Definition 3.3.1 for a formal definition.

For example, we can turn Default theory (9.2) into a single compatible default theory by removing the last default rule, $\frac{A : \neg S}{E}$. This usually costly computation should be done "off-line" by special-purpose algorithms, as for instance described in [BH92] or even [Sla93]. Once this has been done, we can verify whether a query is in the *unique* extension of a compatible default theory *without* any consistency checks. An effective way of querying multiple compatible default theories is described in [Rot93]. The pre-computation of compatible default theories has the advantage that we are able prune computations with incompatible defaults in advance. Thus, for instance, the approach avoids the difficulties with incompatible default theories sketched at the end of Section 9.3.

On the other hand, the approach is problematic if there is a large number of compatible default theories. In fact, there may be an exponential number of such theories in the worst case.[9] As usual, such a compilation is favorable whenever its computational cost can be amortized over the total set of subsequent queries.

The purpose of this compilation approach is to minimize modifications to existing automated theorem provers. In fact, it turns out that admissibility is more integrative than compatibility as regards such modifications. We discuss alternative approaches in brief at the end of this section and in more detail in Section 9.5.

Let us now turn to the verification of admissibility and complementarity. In fact, we confirm admissibility while systematically checking the complementarity of each path through a matrix. Following [Ede92], we use $compl(p, M)$ for defining a declarative algorithm for deciding whether a matrix is complementary and admissible. With it, Eder shows in [Ede92] that a matrix M consisting of ω-clauses only is complementary iff $compl(\emptyset, M)$ is true wrt the first two conditions of the following definition.

Definition 9.4.1. *Let C_W be a set of ω-clauses and C_D be a set of δ-clauses. Let p be a set of literals and let $M = C_{W'} \cup C_{D'}$ for $C_{W'} \subseteq C_W$ and $C_{D'} \subseteq C_D$. Then, we define $compl(p, M)$ relative to C_W as follows.[10]*

1. *If $M = \emptyset$ then $compl(p, M)$ is false.*
2. *If $M \neq \emptyset$ and $c \in M$ is an ω-clause then $compl(p, M)$ is true iff for all $L \in c$ at least one of the following two conditions holds.*
   a) *L is complementary to some literal of p.*
   b) *$compl(p \cup \{L\}, M \setminus \{c\})$ is true.*
3. *If $M \neq \emptyset$ and $c \in M$ is a δ-clause then $compl(p, M)$ is true iff the following two conditions hold, where $c = \{\neg \alpha_\delta, \gamma_\delta\}$.*
   a) *γ_δ is complementary to some literal of p.*
   b) *$compl(\{\neg \alpha_\delta\}, (M \setminus \{c\}) \cup C_W)$ is true.*

As mentioned above, the first two conditions provide a sound and complete algorithmic characterization of the standard connection method (see [Ede92] for details). In fact, the original characterization given in [Ede92] differs only in two ex-

---

[9] This is so because there may be an exponential number of extensions in the worst case.

[10] For simplicity, we assume in what follows that $compl(p, M)$ is always relative to the original set of ω-clauses C_W.

tremely minor points from the one obtained by deleting Condition *3* above. First, there is no case-analysis in Condition *2* for distinguishing ω- from δ-clauses. Second, $compl(p, M)$ is independent of C_W in [Ede92]. The latter set represents in Definition 9.4.1 the original set of ω-clauses, whereas $C_{W'}$ and $C_{D'}$ function as parameters. This distinction is necessary because Condition *(3b)* makes reference to the original set of ω-clauses, given by C_W. We will come back to this below.

Now, let us discuss Definition 9.4.1 in some detail. Condition *1* accounts for the limiting case where the matrix is empty. Condition *2* deals with ω-clauses. Each literal L in the ω-clause at hand has either to be complementary to some literal on the active path p or all path through p extended by L and the remaining clauses have to be complementary. The choice of the ω-clause from M is a *"don't care"*-choice. That is, the result is independent of what ω-clause is taken. In the literature, one often refers to Condition *(2a)* as an inference called *reduction*, while *(2b)* is called an *extension*.

Condition *3* deals with δ-clauses. Condition *(3a)* corresponds to Condition *(2a)* and says that the consequent of a default rule γ_δ can be used for query-answering as any other proposition—provided Condition *(3b)* is satisfied. In fact, *(3b)* "implements" Statement (9.5) in Definition 9.3.2 and ensures that the prerequisite α_δ of a default rule is derivable in a non-circular way. Observe that we do not provide two alternatives for resolving γ_δ in *(3b)*, as done in *2*. In fact, we can restrict ourselves to one of the alternatives in *(2a)* and *(2b)* for solving a single literal.[11] The purpose of resolving γ_δ in analogy to *(2a)* rather than *(2b)* is to minimize the "application of default rules" in the course of a proof search. This minimization is advantageous since the choice of δ-clauses in *3* is a *"don't know"*-choice. That is, one has to find the right one, which means that—in the worst case—all possibilities have to be tested. The choice is *"don't know"* because a selected δ-clause may not lead to an admissible proof so that Condition *(3b)* will be falsified.

Another interesting point in Condition *(3b)* is the addition of the initial set of ω-clauses C_W to $(M \setminus \{c\})$. The need for this is obvious since admissibility has to be verified wrt the given set of facts represented by C_W. Some of these ω-clauses however might have been "consumed" at an earlier stage. This is so because Eder's formulation deletes in Condition *(2b)* ω-clauses after their "usage".[12] So on the one hand, our approach avoids verifying admissibility by ever-increasing submatrices, as stipulated in Definition 9.3.2. In this way, it compromises the query-oriented and thus "top-down"-search for a proof with the "bottom-up" verification of admissibility. On the other hand, an ω-clause may contribute to the derivation of several "prerequisites". Thus in the worst case this yields a proof length bounded by $O(|C_W| \times (|C_D| + 1))$, where $|M|$ stands for the number of clauses in a matrix M.

We observe how easily complementarity and admissibility can be verified simultaneously by adding a single condition to the original definition of $compl(p, M)$ in

---

[11] That is, for any non-empty path p and any (unit-)clause containing a single literal L we can restrict ourselves either to testing *(2a)* or *(2b)*. This however renders the choice in *2* a *"don't know"*-choice (see below).

[12] Recall that we want to stick as close as possible to existing technologies, so that we refrain from making additional changes.

[Ede92]—provided that M represents a compatible default theory. Let us illustrate this along with our algorithm by investigating the "compatible" matrix

$$\{\{S\}, \{\neg S_{\delta_1}, A_{\delta_1}\}, \{\neg A_{\delta_2}, C_{\delta_2}\}, \{\neg C\}\}$$

obtained by removing clause $\{\neg A_{\delta_3}, E_{\delta_3}\}$ from Matrix (9.3). In order to proceed in a query-oriented way, we "push" the negated query $\neg \varphi$ on the initial path, and use the ω- and δ-clauses, $C_W \cup C_D$ representing the underlying default theory as the initial matrix. That is, we verify whether $compl(\{\neg \varphi\}, C_W \cup C_D)$ is true. Selecting the query clause $\{\neg C\}$ makes us confirm

$$compl(\{\neg C\}, \{\{S\}, \{\neg S_{\delta_1}, A_{\delta_1}\}, \{\neg A_{\delta_2}, C_{\delta_2}\}\}). \qquad (9.13)$$

This can be done by choosing clause $\{\neg A_{\delta_2}, C_{\delta_2}\}$ in Condition 3. This choice is not arbitrary, it rather reflects the connection-driven search used in the connection method. That is, C_{δ_2} is complementary to $\neg C$ so that *(3a)* is satisfied. In addition, we have to establish

$$compl(\{\neg A_{\delta_2}\}, \{\{S\}, \{\neg S_{\delta_1}, A_{\delta_1}\}\}) \qquad (9.14)$$

according to *(3b)*. It is instructive to verify that the latter corresponds to invoking our algorithm on the second (sub)matrix in (9.6), after applying Condition *(2b)* to clause $\{\neg A_{\delta_2}\}$.

Applying Condition *3* to the goal in (9.14) yields

$$compl(\{\neg S_{\delta_1}\}, \{\{S\}\}) \qquad (9.15)$$

which is true by *(2a)*. Accordingly, the query C is provable from the compatible equivalent of Default theory (9.2) by means of default rules $\frac{S\,:\,A}{A}$ and $\frac{A\,:\,C}{C}$.

For a complement, let us consider the proof in (9.4) involving reasoning by contraposition. This proof is not admissible. We start with

$$compl(\{A\}, \{\{\neg E\}, \{\neg A_{\delta_3}, E_{\delta_3}\}\}).$$

We choose $\{\neg A_{\delta_3}, E_{\delta_3}\}$ in Condition 3. Since $\neg A_{\delta_3}$ is complementary to A, we have to confirm

$$compl(\{\neg A_{\delta_3}\}, \{\{\neg E\}\}).$$

Clearly, this is false since there are no complementary literals left. The same result is obtained by initially choosing $\{\neg E\}$. Hence, our initial goal is not confirmed which shows that the proof in (9.4) is not admissible.

The general relation between query-answering in constrained default logic and the above algorithm is summarized in the following theorem.[13]

---

[13] Recall that $W_{D'} = \{\alpha_\delta \rightarrow \gamma_\delta \mid \frac{\alpha_\delta\,:\,\beta_\delta}{\gamma_\delta} \in D'\}$ for any subset D' of D.

Theorem 9.4.1. *Let* (D, W) *be a default theory in atomic format and let* φ *an atomic formula. Then, we have that* $\varphi \in E$ *for some constrained extension* (E, C) *of* (D, W) *iff* $compl(\{\neg\varphi\}, M)$ *is true for the matrix* M *of* $W \cup W_{D'}$ *for some* $W_{D'} \subseteq W_D$ *such that* $W \cup Justif(D') \cup Conseq(D')$ *is consistent.*

Observe that merely the choice of the compatible set of default rules D' is specific to constrained default logic. Hence this result and with it the underlying algorithm apply to "compatible" default theories in any (semi-monotonic) default logic—provided that an appropriate notion of compatibility is provided (cf. Section 9.8).

The previous exposition is dominated by the view that the integration of consistency into existing implementations of automated theorem provers is difficult. In particular, we have argued in favor of special purpose algorithms for compilation into compatible default theories. Without any question, these algorithms show a better performance than a theorem prover whose failure indicates that the underlying formula is satisfiable. For coherence, actually, notice that we can also compile default theories into compatible ones by means of $compl(p, M)$. That is, a default theory (D, W) is compatible iff $compl(p, M)$ is false for the matrix of $W \cup Justif(D) \cup Conseq(D)$.

Also, recall that the compilation of default theories leads to difficulties whenever there is a large number of compatible default theories. Then, an "on-line" approach is definitely preferable over an "off-line" approach. In fact, this is also accomplishable by means of what we have developed so far. For this, let $(C_D)^\omega$ be the set of ω-clauses obtained by turning each δ-clause in C_D into an ω-clause. This leads us to the following corollary to Theorem 9.4.1, which allows us to reason from arbitrary and thus also non-compatible default theories.

Corollary 9.4.2. *Let* (D, W) *be a default theory in atomic format and let* φ *an atomic formula. Then, we have that* $\varphi \in E$ *for some constrained extension* (E, C) *of* (D, W) *iff* $compl(\{\neg\varphi\}, M)$ *is true and* $compl(Justif(D'), M^\omega)$ *is false for the matrix* M *of* $W \cup W_{D'}$ *for some* $W_{D'} \subseteq W_D$.

Observe that this corollary relies on Theorem 9.3.2 which shows that compatibility is verifiable on the same matrix M as used in $compl(\{\neg\varphi\}, M)$. Also, we used the fact that for any (unit-)clause $\{L\}$ containing a single literal L, we have that $compl(p, M \cup \{\{L\}\})$ is true iff $compl(p \cup \{L\}, M)$ is true. Hence, we shifted all justifications on the initial path. In this way, the actual matrix M remained the same in $compl(\{\neg\varphi\}, M)$ and $compl(Justif(D'), M)$.

9.4.2 A preliminary case-study

Aaron Rothschild has implemented the approach in [Rot93] by slightly extending PPP, a PROLOG implementation of a (first-order) theorem prover carrying out the pool-based connection calculus [NS91]. The purpose this implementation was to provide an initial case-study in how far an existing theorem prover for the connection method has to be modified for incorporating admissibility.

We briefly describe the main idea underlying the implementation while assuming some basic familiarity with the connection method: We prove in a goal-oriented fashion, starting from the goal and attempting to find complementary paths through the matrix. As soon as a path cannot be complemented using facts only, we call in δ-clauses to achieve complementarity. As in Definition 9.4.1, we do not attempt to use ever-increasing submatrices, as stipulated in Definition 9.3.2 for verifying admissibility. Rather we enforce the admissible application of defaults by two extra conditions resembling the ones in Condition 3 in Definition 9.4.1: The first condition (corresponding to *(3a)*) says that only connections "into" γ_δ-literals of δ-clauses $\{\neg\alpha_\delta, \gamma_\delta\}$ are permissible in the course of the backward chained search. In this way, a subgoal is never resolvable by the prerequisite α_δ of a default rule. Once an inference step with a δ-clause is performed, the second condition restricts the resolution of subgoals with literals of the current path to literals that entered the path *after* the aforementioned "default step". This amounts to discarding the literals of the path p in *(3b)* in order to avoid circular chains of inference.

Importantly these two conditions are implemented by simply adding another PROLOG clause (along with some case-analysis distinguishing δ- and ω-clauses) to the PROLOG implementation of PPP. That is, apart from a *single* PROLOG clause the rest of our implementation corresponds to the original implementation given in [NS91]. Hence, it was possible to minimize modifications by utilizing as much of the original implementation as possible.

In practice, however, the length of the proofs had to be limited by a parameter in the size of $O(|C_W| \times (|C_D| + 1))$ in order to guarantee completeness in the propositional case. Otherwise the implementation ran into infinite branches since PPP is a first-order theorem prover that deals with clause instances. A much simpler yet similar PROLOG implementation that relies on the characterization in Definition 9.4.1 is given in Figure 9.5 on Page 124.

Chapter 10 purses the mapping of our approach onto existing automated theorem provers. There, we show how we can build a compiler for query-answering by transposing our method onto a high-performance theorem-prover, namely PTTP [Sti90].

9.5 An incremental approach

In the previous section, we have developed an algorithm for our method while aiming at implementing the approach by using existing automated theorem provers. For this purpose, we concentrated on minimizing the modifications to existing implementations. This has led to a pragmatic solution separating the verification of compatibility (or consistency) from that of complementarity and admissibility. In this section, we investigate an alternative approach that requires more modifications to an automated theorem prover but which allows for integrating the verification of compatibility.

9.5.1 An alternative characterization of extensions

The fundamental basis for the approach developed in the previous sections was provided by Theorem 3.3.2. In particular, we have stressed the fact that semi-monotonicity allows for focusing on the default rules needed for proving a query, while developing the corresponding characterization of query-answering in Corollary 9.2.1.

In fact, semi-monotonicity offers yet another but conceptionally different characterization of extensions. Observe that the specification given in Theorem 3.3.2 employs a rather "global" notion of consistency. Yet, semi-monotonicity implies also that extensions are constructible in a truly iterative way by applying one applicable default rule after another. This involves an incremental and thus rather local notion of consistency. To this end, semi-monotonicity leads us to the following corollary to Theorem 3.3.2 that provides an alternative characterization of constrained extensions:

Corollary 9.5.1. *Let (D, W) be a default theory and let E and C be sets of formulas. Then, (E, C) is a constrained extension of (D, W) iff*

$$
\begin{aligned}
E &= \mathit{Th}(W \cup \mathit{Conseq}(D')) \\
C &= \mathit{Th}(W \cup \mathit{Justif}(D') \cup \mathit{Conseq}(D'))
\end{aligned}
$$

for a maximal $D' \subseteq D$ such that there exists an enumeration $\langle \delta_i \rangle_{i \in I}$ of D', where for $i \in I$ we have that

1. $W \cup \mathit{Conseq}(\{\delta_0, \ldots, \delta_{i-1}\}) \vdash \mathit{Prereq}(\delta_i)$,
2. $W \cup \mathit{Conseq}(\{\delta_0, \ldots, \delta_{i-1}\}) \cup \mathit{Justif}(\{\delta_0, \ldots, \delta_{i-1}\})$
   $\nvdash \neg(\mathit{Justif}(\delta_i) \wedge \mathit{Conseq}(\delta_i))$.

This specification explicates the formation of sequences of default rules that remained implicit in Theorem 3.3.2. In fact, Condition *1* spells out that D' has to be grounded in W. So the conceptional difference between the two alternative characterizations rests on the second condition. Condition *2* expresses the aforementioned notion of *incremental consistency*. Here, the "consistent" application of a default rule is checked at each step, whereas this is done jointly for all default rules in D' in Theorem 3.3.2.

Indeed, Corollary 9.5.1 provides the conceptual basis for the approach to query-answering, which we develop in this section. Even though the characterization of query-answering is analogous to the one given in Corollary 9.2.1, we give below a refined yet equivalent notion of a default proof (cf. Definition 9.2.1):

Definition 9.5.1. *Let (D, W) be a default theory and φ a formula. A default proof for φ from (D, W) is a finite sequence of default rules $\langle \delta_i \rangle_{i \in I}$ with $\delta_i \in D$ for all $i \in I$ such that $W \cup \{\mathit{Conseq}(\delta_i) \mid i \in I\} \vdash \varphi$ and Condition 1 and 2 in Corollary 9.5.1 are satisfied for all $i \in I$.*

Observe that in Theorem 3.3.2 groundedness and consistency constitute rather separate constraints on the "generating default rules" in D'. We strongly relied on the possibility of separating these concepts in Section 9.4. In contrast to this, the concepts of groundedness and consistency are meshed together in Corollary 9.5.1. Hence, both concepts jointly direct the *formation of sequences of default rules*. This is also reflected by the above notion of a default proof. This is the salient feature of the approach developed in the sequel. Moreover, we have seen in [Sch94a] that the combination of both concepts is very useful for implementing priorities.

9.5.2 Incremental compatibility

Clearly, the "global" notion of compatibility given in Definition 9.3.3 is inappropriate in order to account for the above characterization. Rather Condition 2 in Corollary 9.5.1 requires an incremental approach in which compatibility is gradually verified each time a δ-clause is considered. This motivates the following definition.

Definition 9.5.2 (Incremental compatibility). *Let C_W be a set of ω-clauses and C_D be a set of δ-clauses and let Π be a mating for $C_W \cup C_D$. Let $\langle\{\neg\alpha_{\delta_i}, \gamma_{\delta_i}\}\rangle_{i \in I}$ be an enumeration of $\kappa(C_D, \Pi)$. Then, $(C_W \cup C_D, \Pi)$ is incrementally compatible wrt I iff for all $i \in I$, there is no spanning mating for*

$$C_W \cup \left(\bigcup_{j=0}^{i-1}\{\{\beta_{\delta_j}\}, \{\gamma_{\delta_j}\}\}\right) \cup \{\{\beta_{\delta_i}\}\} \cup \{\{\gamma_{\delta_i}\}\}, \qquad (9.16)$$

where $\beta_{\delta_i} = Justif(\delta_i)$.

We say that $(C_W \cup C_D, \Pi)$ is compatible at i in an index set I, if (9.16) holds for $i \in I$. Moreover, we say that $(C_W \cup C_D, \Pi)$ is incrementally compatible wrt an index set I, if it is compatible at all $i \in I$.

The next theorem tells us that "global" and incremental compatibility are in fact equivalent.

Theorem 9.5.1. *Let C_W be a set of ω-clauses and C_D be a set of δ-clauses and let Π be a mating for $C_W \cup C_D$. Let $\langle\{\neg\alpha_{\delta_i}, \gamma_{\delta_i}\}\rangle_{i \in I}$ be an enumeration of $\kappa(C_D, \Pi)$. Then, $(C_W \cup C_D, \Pi)$ is compatible iff $(C_W \cup C_D, \Pi)$ is incrementally compatible wrt I.*

Consider our initial student example. Instead of checking whether the matrix in (9.7) has no spanning mating, we can stepwise verify whether this holds for the following matrices.

$$\begin{bmatrix} \mathsf{S} & \mathsf{A}_{\delta_1} \end{bmatrix} \qquad \begin{bmatrix} \mathsf{S} & \mathsf{A}_{\delta_1} & \mathsf{C}_{\delta_2} \end{bmatrix} \qquad (9.17)$$

In this way, we check first the compatibility of the facts $\{\mathsf{S}\}$ and the consequent of δ_1. Then, the same test is performed on the matrix extended by the consequent of δ_2. Note that at each step, it is sufficient to consider only the non-complementary paths obtained in the previous step.

We obtain the following corollary to Theorem 9.3.3 and Theorem 9.5.1. This result shows that our incremental method is correct and complete for query-answering in constrained default logic.

Corollary 9.5.2. *Let (D, W) be a default theory in atomic format and φ an atomic formula. Then, $\varphi \in E$ for some constrained extension (E, C) of (D, W) iff there is a spanning mating Π for Matrix $M = C_W \cup C_D \cup \{\{\neg\varphi\}\}$ of $W \cup W_D \cup \{\neg\varphi\}$ and an enumeration $\langle c_i \rangle_{i \in I}$ of $\kappa(C_D, \Pi)$ such that (M, Π) is admissible wrt I and incrementally compatible wrt I.*

Now, recall that by Theorem 9.3.2 compatibility and hence also incremental compatibility can be verified by using δ-clauses, like $\{\neg\alpha_\delta, \gamma_\delta\}$, instead of clauses containing merely the consequent of a default, like $\{\gamma_\delta\}$, in the case of "admissible matrices". Consequently, incremental compatibility can be equivalently verified by replacing the matrices in (9.16) by matrices of the following form:

$$C_W \cup \left(\bigcup_{j=0}^{i-1}\{\{\neg\alpha_{\delta_j}, \gamma_{\delta_j}\}\}\right) \cup \{\{\neg\alpha_{\delta_i}, \gamma_{\delta_i}\}\} \cup \left(\bigcup_{j=0}^{i-1}\{\{\beta_{\delta_j}\}\}\right) \cup \{\{\beta_{\delta_i}\}\},$$

This offers the computational advantage that we can verify incremental compatibility on (almost) the same matrices as used for verifying admissibility. In fact, admissibility is checked on matrices of the form given in (9.5):

$$C_W \cup \left(\bigcup_{j=0}^{i-1}\{\{\neg\alpha_{\delta_j}, \gamma_{\delta_j}\}\}\right) \cup \{\{\neg\alpha_{\delta_i}\}\}$$

For admissibility, all path through the latter matrix have to be complementary. For compatibility, there has to emerge an open path if we replace the clause $\{\{\neg\alpha_{\delta_i}\}\}$ by the clause $\{\{\neg\alpha_{\delta_i}, \gamma_{\delta_i}\}\}$; simply by adding the consequent of the default δ_i. In addition, each such open path must not contain a literal complementary to any justification in $\left(\bigcup_{j=0}^{i-1}\{\{\beta_{\delta_j}\}\}\right) \cup \{\{\beta_{\delta_i}\}\}$. This additional requirement is obsolete in the case of normal default theories. On the whole, Theorem 9.3.2 provides a valuable refinement that allows for structure and information sharing while *jointly* verifying admissibility and compatibility.

In order to illustrate this let us look at our initial default proof in (9.3). For verifying its admissibility, we used the submatrices in (9.11). These are repeated as M_1 and M_3 below. In fact, we can share the use of these matrices for testing compatibility. This amounts to considering in turn the following submatrices of (9.3):

$$M_1 = \begin{bmatrix} & \neg S_{\delta_1} \\ S & \end{bmatrix} \qquad M_2 = \begin{bmatrix} & \neg S_{\delta_1} \\ S & A_{\delta_1} \end{bmatrix}$$

$$M_3 = \begin{bmatrix} & \neg S_{\delta_1} & \neg A_{\delta_2} \\ S & A_{\delta_1} \end{bmatrix} \qquad M_4 = \begin{bmatrix} & \neg S_{\delta_1} & \neg A_{\delta_2} \\ S & A_{\delta_1} & C_{\delta_2} \end{bmatrix}$$

We start by verifying whether all paths through Matrix M_1 are complementary. Since this is the case, M_1 is admissible. For checking the compatibility of M_2, we merely have to look for a non-complementary path through the facts, here $\{\{S\}\}$

and the consequent of δ_1, A_{δ_1}. All other path are complementary by admissibility. In fact, the path $\{S, A_{\delta_1}\}$ is not complementary and so the Matrix M_2 is compatible.

For verifying admissibility in the case of Matrix M_3, we can make use of the information gathered on M_2. In this example, it is enough to check whether adding the negated prerequisite of δ_2, $\neg A_{\delta_2}$ closes all open path in Matrix M_2. In fact, this is the case since $\{S, A_{\delta_1}\}$ is the only open path in Matrix M_2 and $\{S, A_{\delta_1}\} \cup \{\neg A_{\delta_2}\}$ is complementary. The compatibility of Matrix M_4 is established in analogy to that of M_2; again by reusing the information gathered while verifying admissibility for M_3. The final proof of query C in (9.3) is obtained by adding the query clause $\{\neg C\}$ to Matrix M_4. Clearly, the resulting matrix is complementary so that the proof is completed.

9.5.3 An incremental algorithm

The general idea of our algorithmic approach is to proceed in a query-oriented manner. For this, we extend the definition of $compl(p, M)$ as given in Definition 9.4.1 in the following way. We use a predicate $compl(p, C_W, C_D)$ for defining a declarative algorithm for deciding whether a matrix is complementary, admissible *and* compatible. The first argument is a set of literals describing a partial path, the second argument represents a set of ω-clauses, and the last argument accounts for δ-clauses.

Definition 9.5.3. *Let C_W be a set of ω-clauses and C_D be a set of δ-clauses. Let p be a set of literals and let $C_{W'} \subseteq C_W$ and $C_{D'} \subseteq C_D$. Then, we define $compl(p, C_{W'}, C_{D'})$ relative to C_W as follows.*[14]

1. *If $C_{W'} \cup C_{D'} = \emptyset$ then $compl(p, C_{W'}, C_{D'})$ is false.*
2. *If $C_{W'} \neq \emptyset$ and $c \in C_{W'}$ then $compl(p, C_{W'}, C_{D'})$ is true iff the following two conditions hold for $c = c_1 \cup c_2$.*
    a) *for all $L \in c_1$, L is complementary to some literal of p.*
    b) *for all $L \in c_2$, there is a set of δ-clauses $C_{D'_L} \subseteq C_{D'}$ such that following two conditions hold.*
        i. *$compl(p \cup \{L\}, C_{W'} \setminus \{c\}, C_{D'_L})$ is true.*
        ii. *$compl(Justif(\bigcup_{L \in c_2} D'_L), C_W \cup \bigcup_{L \in c_2} C_{D'_L}, \emptyset)$ is false.*
3. *If $C_{D'} \neq \emptyset$ and $c \in C_{D'}$ then $compl(p, C_{W'}, C_{D'})$ is true iff the following two conditions hold for $c = \{\neg \alpha_\delta, \gamma_\delta\}$.*
    a) *γ_δ is complementary to some literal of p.*
    b) *There is a set of δ-clauses $C_{D''} \subseteq C_{D'}$ such that $\{\neg \alpha_\delta, \gamma_\delta\} \in C_{D'} \setminus C_{D''}$ and the following two conditions hold.*
        i. *$compl(\{\neg \alpha_\delta\}, C_W, C_{D''})$ is true.*
        ii. *$compl(Justif(D'' \cup \{\delta\}), C_W \cup C_{D''} \cup \{\{\neg \alpha_\delta, \gamma_\delta\}\}, \emptyset)$ is false.*

As in Definition 9.4.1, C_W and C_D represent the original set of ω- and δ-clauses, whereas $C_{W'}$ and $C_{D'}$ function as parameters. Condition *1* and *2* correspond to the ones in Definition 9.4.1. There are two differences. First, we have separated ω- and

---

[14] As above, we assume in what follows that $compl(p, C_{W'}, C_{D'})$ is relative to C_W.

δ-clauses. This separation allows for an easier formulation of Condition *3*. Second, we have added Condition *(2bii)* in order to guarantee the compatibility of multiple subproofs found in *(2bi)*. We explain the treatment of compatibility in *(2bii)* in the context of Condition *(3bii)* below. Anyway, we have that a matrix M consisting of ω-clauses only is complementary iff $compl(\emptyset, M, \emptyset)$ is true wrt the first two conditions of Definition 9.5.3.

As in Definition 9.4.1, Condition *(3a)* corresponds to Condition *(2a)* and allows for solving subgoals on the actual path by the consequent of a default rule γ_δ— provided Condition *(3b)* is satisfied. Condition *3* combines the verification of admissibility with that of incremental compatibility. For that, a set of δ-clauses $C_{D''}$ is selected from the available set of δ-clauses $C_{D'}$. $C_{D''}$ is meant to represent a compatible subset of δ-clauses that allows for deriving the "prerequisite" α_δ. Condition *(3bi)* corresponds to Condition *(3b)* in Definition 9.4.1; here it is restricted to the δ-clauses in $C_{D''}$. Condition *(3bii)* "implements" incremental compatibility. For coherence, the compatibility of δ-clauses in $C_{D''}$ is verified by the part of $compl(p, C_W, C_D)$ accounting for ω-clauses only. For this, we turn all δ-clauses in $C_{D''} \cup \{\{\neg\alpha_\delta, \gamma_\delta\}\}$ into ω-clauses and add the latter ones to the original set of ω-clauses in C_W. In this way, we make use of Theorem 9.3.2 and pass Matrix $C_W \cup C_{D''} \cup \{\{\neg\alpha_\delta\}\}$— whose admissibility is verified Condition *(3bi)*—to the compatibility check in *(3bii)*. There, the clause $\{\neg\alpha_\delta\}$ is extended by γ_δ. Moreover, we push the justifications of the default rules in D'' along with the justification of the considered default rule δ on the path. This additional requirement is obsolete in the case of normal default theories. The failure of $compl(Justif(D'' \cup \{\delta\}), C_W \cup C_{D''} \cup \{\{\neg\alpha_\delta, \gamma_\delta\}\}, \emptyset)$ indicates that $W \cup Conseq(D'' \cup \{\delta\}) \cup Justif(D'' \cup \{\delta\})$ is consistent (by completeness of the standard connection method). Since Condition *(3bi)* and *(3bii)* are verified separately neither of them benefits from the information gathered in the other one. A minimal condition that is equivalent to Condition *(3bii)* is the following one:

$$ii.'\ \ compl(Conseq(D'' \cup \{\delta\}) \cup Justif(D'' \cup \{\delta\}), C_W, \emptyset) \text{ is false}$$

The incoherence of this condition to Condition *(3bi)* however is not favorable for an efficient algorithm meshing conditions *(3bi)* and *(3bii)*.

In order to illustrate the definition of $compl(p, C_W, C_D)$ let us reconsider the derivation given in (9.13) to (9.15). There, we have shown that C is a default conclusion of our initial Default theory (9.2). For this, we have shown that $compl(\{\neg\mathsf{C}\}, M)$ evaluates to true for the "compatible" Matrix given by $M = \{\{\mathsf{S}\}, \{\neg\mathsf{S}_{\delta_1}, \mathsf{A}_{\delta_1}\}, \{\neg\mathsf{A}_{\delta_2}, \mathsf{C}_{\delta_2}\}\}$. Now, the restriction to "compatible" matrices is obsolete. Rather we show that

$$compl(\{\neg\mathsf{C}\}, \{\{\mathsf{S}\}\}, \{\{\neg\mathsf{S}_{\delta_1}, \mathsf{A}_{\delta_1}\}, \{\neg\mathsf{A}_{\delta_2}, \mathsf{C}_{\delta_2}\}, \{\neg\mathsf{A}_{\delta_3}, \mathsf{E}_{\delta_3}\}\}) \text{ is true.}$$

Observe that together, the query clause $\{\neg\mathsf{C}\}$, the ω-clause in $\{\{\mathsf{S}\}\}$, and the δ-clauses in $\{\{\neg\mathsf{S}_{\delta_1}, \mathsf{A}_{\delta_1}\}, \{\neg\mathsf{A}_{\delta_2}, \mathsf{C}_{\delta_2}\}, \{\neg\mathsf{A}_{\delta_3}, \mathsf{E}_{\delta_3}\}\}$ form the matrix given in (9.3).

As in Section 9.4, we select clauses in a connection-driven way. Thus, we select the clause $\{\neg\mathsf{A}_{\delta_2}, \mathsf{C}_{\delta_2}\}$ since C_{δ_2} is complementary to the literal $\neg\mathsf{C}$ on the active path. This establishes Condition *(3a)*. Next, we have to verify Condition *(3b)*. For this, we have to find a subset $C_{D''}$ of the remaining δ-clauses in $\{\{\neg S_{\delta_1}, A_{\delta_1}\}, \{\neg A_{\delta_3}, E_{\delta_3}\}\}$ that satisfies Condition *(3bi)* and *(3bii)*. For illustration, we direct our subsequent choices along the line sketched by the derivation in (9.13) to (9.15). Accordingly, we choose $C_{D''} = \{\{\neg S_{\delta_1}, A_{\delta_1}\}\}$. This choice along with the previously chosen δ-clause $c = \{\neg A_{\delta_2}, C_{\delta_2}\}$ yields in turn the following evaluations.[15]

1. $compl(\{\neg A_{\delta_2}\}, \{\{S\}\}, \{\{\neg S_{\delta_1}, A_{\delta_1}\}\})$ is true,
   since by Condition *3*, where $c = \{\neg S_{\delta_1}, A_{\delta_1}\}$ and $C_{D''} = \emptyset$,
   a) $compl(\{\neg S_{\delta_1}\}, \{\{S\}\}, \emptyset)$ is true by *(2a)*.
   b) $compl(\emptyset, \{\{S\}, \{\neg S_{\delta_1}, A_{\delta_1}\}\}, \emptyset)$ is false by *(2b)* and *1*.
2. $compl(\{C_{\delta_2}\}, \{\{S\}, \{\neg S, A\}, \{\neg A, C\}\}, \emptyset)$ is false,
   since by repeated applications of *2*
   a) $compl(\{C_{\delta_2}, S, A, C\}, \emptyset, \emptyset)$ is false.

Items 1. and 2. confirm Condition *(3bi)* and *(3bii)* so that our proof of C is completed.

Observe that choosing $C_{D''} = \{\{\neg S_{\delta_1}, A_{\delta_1}\}, \{\neg A_{\delta_3}, E_{\delta_3}\}\}$ yields the same result, while the choices $C_{D''} = \emptyset$ or $C_{D''} = \{\{\neg A_{\delta_3}, E_{\delta_3}\}\}$ lead to a failure. One possibility for choosing $C_{D''}$ is to consider ever-increasing subsets of the given set of δ-clauses $C_{D'}$. Another—more promising–possibility is to leave the choice of $C_{D''}$ to the admissibility check in *(3bi)*. In concrete terms, this can be accomplished by passing all δ-clauses in $C_{D'}$ to Condition *(3bi)* and adding an additional argument to $compl(p, C_W, C_D)$ in order to account for the δ-rules that are actually used for establishing admissibility in *(3bi)*. Then, the returned set of δ-clauses is checked for compatibility in *(3bi)*. Such an approach is described in [Sch95b].

For a complement, consider default rules $\frac{S : A}{A}$ and $\frac{A : \neg S}{E}$ along with fact S. For answering query E, we have to check whether

$$compl(\{\neg E\}, \{\{S\}\}, \{\{\neg S_{\delta_1}, A_{\delta_1}\}, \{\neg A_{\delta_3}, E_{\delta_3}\}\}) \text{ is true.}$$

For solving the negated query $\neg E$, we have to select clause $\{\neg A_{\delta_3}, E_{\delta_3}\}$ in Condition *3*. This however requires by Condition *(3bii)*, where the active path $\{\neg S\}$ is formed by the justification of the default rule $\frac{A : \neg S}{E}$, that

$$compl(\{\neg S\}, \{\{S\} \cup C_{D''} \cup \{\{\neg A_{\delta_3}, E_{\delta_3}\}\}\}, \emptyset) \text{ is false}$$

for some δ-clauses $C_{D''}$. This is however impossible since any path through the underlying matrix contains the connection $\{S, \neg S\}$. That is, the justification $\neg S$ is inconsistent with the set of facts $\{S\}$.

Finally, we obtain the following result showing that our incremental algorithm is correct and complete for query-answering in constrained default logic:

---

[15] Recall that we do not have to add the justification to the path in the case of normal default rules.

Theorem 9.5.2. *Let* (D, W) *be a default theory in atomic format and let* φ *an atomic formula. Then, we have that* $\varphi \in E$ *for some constrained extension* (E, C) *of* (D, W) *iff* $compl(\{\neg\varphi\}, C_W, C_D)$ *is true, where* C_W *is the matrix of* W *and* C_D *is the matrix of* W_D.

9.6 Discussion

This section summarizes the different mouldings of our approach developed in the previous sections. The presented approach integrates the distinguishing features of default logics into a classical deduction method. This allows for a homogeneous characterization and treatment of default proofs at the level of the calculus. In this way, there are no limits for interactions between the three notions of complementarity, admissibility, and compatibility—corresponding to classical deduction and the concepts of groundedness and consistency in default logic. The basic method, say M, relies on Theorem 3.3.2 and provides with admissibility and compatibility two independent concepts restricting default proofs to classical proofs confirming the two previous properties. To a turn, we refined our approach by meshing together the concepts of admissibility and (incremental) compatibility. While the resulting method, say M^i, leaves admissibility unaffected, it offers an incremental approach to compatibility in which the consistent usage of δ-clauses is gradually verified. Hence, the conceptional difference between the two methods M and M^i rests on the treatment of consistency. While M relies on a rather global notion of consistency, M^i employs an incremental and thus rather local notion of consistency.

Apart from the encoding of default rules as implication, a distinguishing feature of our approach is the formation of sequences of δ-clauses. In M, this formation is mainly affected by the notion of groundedness, while consistency plays more or less the role of a global constraint. In contrast to this, groundedness and consistency are meshed together in M^i and hence jointly direct the formation of sequences of δ-clauses. In both mouldings, groundedness and consistency are integrated into the underlying logical calculus. This is another feature distinguishing our methods from others found in the literature.

We have seen that both methods result in algorithms supporting an easy concurrent verification of complementarity and admissibility. In other words, groundedness is enforced while query-answering. The concurrent verification of consistency is added to the algorithm derived from M^i. Moreover, we have shown in Section 9.5 that M^i allows for structure and information sharing while jointly verifying admissibility and (incremental) compatibility. All of the presented algorithms are query-oriented. This reflects the idea that the theorem prover is in charge of finding a proof that is gradually confirmed by the concepts of admissibility and compatibility in the course of the proof search. In this way, the proof search is directed by the notions of groundedness and consistency. A summary of the derived algorithms along with their features is given in Figure 9.1.

We have proposed an "off-line" integration of compatibility in order to minimize modifications while using existing automated theorem provers for implement-

Method	Algorithm	Prototype	Pruning by	
			admissibility	compatibility
M (Sect. 9.3)	A (p. 108)	I (p. 124)	incremental	compilation
	A' (p. 111)	I' (p. 125)	incremental	additional test
M^i(Sect. 9.5)	A^i (p. 116)	I^i (p. 126)	incremental	incremental

Table 9.1. A summary of the algorithmic approaches.

ing our method. This has resulted in the algorithm given in Definition 9.4.1, say A, which allows for simultaneously verifying complementarity and admissibility. This approach is derived from our basic method M that allows for separating the concepts of admissibility and compatibility. Algorithm A expects matrices stemming from compatible default theories. In this way, it never runs into redundant computations with incompatible defaults. This approach is advantageous over all others whenever there are few compatible default theories. In such a case, the derivation of a query is not "detracted" by any consistency checking, since all conflicts have been "compiled away". In fact, we can verify whether a query is in the unique extension of a compatible default theory without any consistency checks. In the worst case, however, there may be an exponential number of compatible default theories.

A simple alternative to compiling default theories is described in Corollary 9.4.2. This variant, say A', uses algorithm A but refrains from compiling consistency and rather verifies compatibility for each completed, admissible proof. This approach shares with A the advantage of minimizing changes to existing automated theorem provers. Also, it avoids representing a possibly exponential number of compatible default theories. However, it is a "generate and test" approach in principle, in which we generate admissible proofs and verify their compatibility afterwards. In the worst case, however, this belated compatibility check may have to be performed exponentially many times. Consequently, A' may cause a lot of redundancy, since incompatible proofs are not avoided in the course of the proof.

Algorithm A^i is derived from M^i and hence integrates the verification of compatibility (cf. Definition 9.5.3). As A', this approach is not restricted to matrices stemming from compatible default theories. Rather each δ-clause has to confirm admissibility and compatibility when entering a proof. In this way, redundant computations with incompatible defaults are avoided. In general, this approach is advantageous over the other ones whenever a default theory contains many conflicting default rules. Then, the additional costs of repeated consistency checks can be amortized by pruning many incompatible subproofs. The disadvantage of this approach is however that it requires more modifications to existing automated theorem provers. This renders algorithm A^i orthogonal to A (and A'). Also, the successive consistency checks may slow down the performance of the prover. This applies in particular to domains where proofs are usually built from compatible default rules only. A promising way of avoiding this is to use model checking techniques as described in Section 9.8 and 10.3.

In all, we argue that the concurrent verification of admissibility while query-answering is indispensable. In particular, we have demonstrated that this can be done with few modifications to an automated theorem prover. The treatment of compatibility is more subtle. Here, a lot depends on the underlying theory. That is, if a default theory comprises a feasible number of compatible default theories, then a pre-compilation of compatibility is favorable. Otherwise, that is, if a default theory comprises too many compatible default theories, an integration of compatibility is preferable, as done in $\mathbf{A}^i$. This has been confirmed by our experimental studies, detailed in [Sch94b]. On the whole, the common general idea of all mouldings of our approach is to employ a goal-directed search for a proof while minimizing redundancy.

9.7 Experiments

In this section, we present prototypical implementations of the algorithms described in the previous sections. The purpose of this is two-fold. First, we want to show how easily these approaches can be implemented. Second, we want to provide some experimental analysis.

We have seen how easily admissibility and compatibility are simultaneously verifiable. Hence, it will be interesting to investigate whether this is a feasible process. Moreover, we explore the issue of compatibility by comparing the results obtained in the diverse approaches. In all, we want know which modifications to an existing automated theorem provers are worthwhile under which circumstances.

We have refrained from using any advanced implementation techniques in order to keep the exposition transparent. Thus, the prototypes are intended to provide transparent case-studies for certain default reasoning architectures rather than efficient implementations. For instance, none of the given programs makes use of structure sharing, as suggested in Section 9.5. Moreover, such enhancements would influence the different settings in different ways so that the corresponding results would be hardly comparable. Rather we use in each implementation the same classical inference mechanism and the same way of consistency checking. This allows for a simple common implementation platform. For simplicity, we restrict ourselves to normal default theories.

9.7.1 A straightforward implementation

We start by giving an extremely simple and straightforward PROLOG implementation of Eder's algorithm for the standard connection method [Ede92]. This implementation serves two purposes. First, it provides the basic theorem proving techniques that we will use for our prototypical implementations. Second, it supplies us with a simple way for consistency checking.

The implementation given in Figure 9.1 corresponds to the first two conditions given in Definition 9.4.1. Matrices are represented by lists of lists of literals. A literal is of the form a or -a. The first program clause of compl/2 implements Condition *1* in Definition 9.4.1, while the second one selects clauses out of the matrix M and initiates their treatment in complC(Path,Clause,MatrixRest) according to Condition *2* in Definition 9.4.1. complC/3 verifies that each literal in a considered clause satisfies either Condition *(2a)* or *(2b)*. That is, while the first program clause of complC/3 captures the limiting case, the second one accounts for Condition *(2a)* and the third one accounts for Condition *(2b)*. Finally, complL/2 checks whether the negation of the literal Literal is a member of the path Path. Auxiliary program

```
compl(_Path, []      ) :- !,fail.
compl( Path, Matrix ) :-
        select(Clause,Matrix,MatrixRest),!,
        complC(Path,Clause,MatrixRest).

complC(_Path, []                          ,_Matrix ) .
complC( Path, [Literal|ClauseRest], Matrix ) :-
        complL(Path,Literal),!,
        complC(Path,ClauseRest,Matrix).
complC( Path, [Literal|ClauseRest], Matrix ) :-
        compl([Literal|Path],Matrix),
        complC(Path,ClauseRest,Matrix).

complL( Path, Literal ) :-
        neg(Literal,NegLiteral),!,
        member(NegLiteral,Path).
```

Fig. 9.1. An implementation of Eder's algorithm.

clauses, like neg/2 are given in Figure 9.2. The predicates member/2, select/3,

```
neg( -Literal, Literal ) :- !.
neg( Literal, -Literal ) .

split( [],                       [],              []          ) .
split( [Clause|MatrixRest], CW          , [Clause|CD] ) :-
        d_clause(Clause),!,
        split(MatrixRest,CW,CD).
split( [Clause|MatrixRest], [Clause|CW], CD          ) :-
        w_clause(Clause),!,
        split(MatrixRest,CW,CD).

d_clause( [ _AlphaLiteral > _GammaLiteral ] ).
w_clause( Clause                           ) :-
        not(d_clause(Clause)).

omega( []                        , []              ) .
omega( [[_Alpha>Gamma]|CDRest], [[Gamma]|CWRest] ) :-
        omega(CDRest,CWRest).
```

Fig. 9.2. Auxiliary program clauses.

etc. have their obvious meaning and belong to the underlying PROLOG-system.

As mentioned above, we refrain from using any advanced implementation techniques in order to provide a simple common implementation platform. For this purpose, we verify the compatibility of a set of δ-clauses relative to a set of ω-clauses by appeal to `compl/2`. This results is the predicate `compatible/2` given in Figure 9.3. `compatible/2` takes a list of ω-clauses `CW` and a list of δ-clauses `CD`, unions `CW` with the consequents of the δ-clauses in `CD` and checks whether the result satisfies `not(compl([],M))`. This amounts to a classical satisfiability test.

```
compatible( CW, CD ) :-
        omega(CD,CDOmega),
        union(CW,CDOmega,M),
        not(compl([],M)).
```

Fig. 9.3. A simple way of checking compatibility.

9.7.2 Implementations separating compatibility

In this section, we give implementations that simultaneously verify admissibility and complementarity but separate the verification of compatibility. That is, we discuss implementations of the algorithm given in Definition 9.4.1.

For illustration, let us start by introducing the underlying representation. Consider Default theory

$$\left(\left\{\frac{S : A}{A}, \frac{S : \neg E}{\neg E}, \frac{A : C}{C}, \frac{A : E}{E}\right\}, \{S\}\right).$$

The representation of this default theory is given in the left column of Figure 9.4. As mentioned above, ω-clauses are lists of literals. δ-clauses like $\{\neg S, A\}$ are represented as `[s>a]`. This allows for an easy distinction between ω- and δ-clauses; and moreover between "prerequisites" and "consequents" of δ-clauses. The compatible

```
sample(students,[              sample(studentsC,[
       [s],                           [s],
       [s>a],                         [s>a],
       [s> -e],                       [s> -e],
       [a>c],                         [a>c]
       [a>e]                          ]).
       ]).                     sample(studentsC,[
                                      [s],
                                      [s>a],
                                      [a>c],
                                      [a>e]
                                      ]).
```

Fig. 9.4. The representation of our example.

counterpart of the default theory is given in the right column of Figure 9.4. For transparency, we have chosen this naive representation rather than a more efficient one where each δ-clause in represented only once. Such a representation is used in [Rot93].

The implementation, I say, of the algorithm in Definition 9.4.1 is given in Figure 9.5. As in Definition 9.5.3, we have separated ω- and δ-clauses. Moreover, we

```
compl( Path, M, Proof ) :-
        split(M,CW,CD),
        compl(Path,CW,CD,CW,Proof).

compl(_Path, [], [], _,_Proof ) :- !,fail.
compl( Path, CW, CD, M, Proof ) :-
        select(OmegaClause,CW,CWRest),
        select(Literal,OmegaClause,OmegaClauseRest),
        complL(Path,Literal),
        complW(Path,OmegaClauseRest,CWRest,CD,M,Proof).
compl( Path, CW, CD, M, Proof ) :-
        select([Alpha>Gamma],CD,CDRest),
        complL(Path,Gamma),!,
        complD(Path,[Alpha>Gamma],CW,CDRest,M,Proof).

complW(_Path, []                      ,_CW,_CD,_M, []     ) .
complW( Path, [Literal|ClauseRest], CW, CD, M, Proof ) :-
        complL(Path,Literal),
        complW(Path,ClauseRest,CW,CD,M,Proof).
complW( Path, [Literal|ClauseRest], CW, CD, M, Proof ) :-
        compl([Literal|Path],CW,CD,M,Proof1),
        complW(Path,ClauseRest,CW,CD,M,Proof2),
        append(Proof1,Proof2,Proof).

complD(_Path, [Alpha>Gamma],_CW, CD, M,
                            [[Alpha>Gamma]|Proof] ) :-
        neg(Alpha,NegAlpha),
        compl([NegAlpha],M,CD,M,Proof).
```

Fig. 9.5. l: An implementation of algorithm A.

have extended each predicate by two additional arguments. One containing the original set of ω-clauses and another one accumulating the proof of the query. Observe that the counterpart of compl/2 in Figure 9.1 is given by compl/5. The principal difference is that compl/5 selects ω- as well as δ-clauses in a connection-driven way. That is, a clause is only selected if one of its literals is complementary to a literal on the active path. The counterpart of complC/3 in Figure 9.1 is given by complW/6 and complD/6. complW/6 treats ω-clauses and is identical to complC/3 in Figure 9.1. δ-clauses are processed by complD/6. Since the complementarity of the consequent Gamma to one of the literals on the active path is checked in compl/5, merely Condition *(3b)* in Definition 9.4.1 remains to be verified by complD/6. This is done by compl([NegAlpha],M,CD,M,Proof). Observe that this is the point where the original set of ω-clauses M "reenters" the proof. This is necessary for checking admissibility. If the last subgoal in complD/6 succeeds, the δ-clause [Alpha>Gamma] is added to the proof in Proof.

A query like e is posed to the "knowledge base" studentsC[16] in Figure 9.4 by evaluating the following PROLOG query:

```
?- sample(studentsC,M),compl([-e],M,P).
```

This yields the answer:

```
P = [[a>e],[s>a]]
```

We have tested the various implementations in [Sch94b] on numerous examples. In what follows, we report on the major insights obtained from those experiments, without repeating the respective test-series.

For comparison, we have also implemented algorithm A'. Its implementation, say I', is obtained by replacing the definition of compl/3 in Figure 9.5 by the one given in Figure 9.6.

```
compl( Path, M, Proof ) :-
        split(M,CW,CD),
        compl(Path,CW,CD,CW,Proof),
        compatible(CW,Proof).
```

Fig. 9.6. I': The change for algorithm A'.

A first major question is whether the integration of admissibility slows down the underlying theorem prover. For this purpose, we contrasted in [Sch94b] "default knowledge bases" with their classical counterparts obtained by replacing each δ-clause by the corresponding Hornclause. In turn, we queried both the "default knowledge bases" and their classical counterparts with the same query. The results given in [Sch94b] spoke for themselves: In fact, we observed that the "default proofs" needed in all respects less calls to predicates than their classical counterparts. This is a strong argument in favor of our approach to "on-line" admissibility (or groundedness) checking.

9.7.3 Implementations integrating compatibility

This section gives an implementation that integrates the verification of compatibility. Figure 9.7 contains an implementation of algorithm A^i, as described in Definition 9.5.3. This implementation is obtained from the one given in Figure 9.5 by modifying the definitions of complW/6 and complD/6. As stipulated in Condition *(2bii)* in Definition 9.5.3, we extended complW/6 in order to check the compatibility of all accomplished subproofs. This modification is given by the last two lines of complW/6 in Figure 9.7. Analogously, we have added a single line of code to complD/6 in order to check the compatibility of the considered δ-clause with the accomplished subproof.

It is interesting to observe that the implementation avoids the selection of the sets of δ-clauses $C_{D'_L}$ and $C_{D''}$ in conditions *(2bii)* and *(3bii)*, respectively. As suggested in Section 9.5, we leave the selection of these sets to the theorem prover along with

---

[16] This is the compatible version of the "knowledge base" students.

```
compl( Path, M, Proof ) :-
       split(M,CW,CD),
       compl(Path,CW,CD,CW,Proof).

compl(_Path, [], [], _,_Proof ) :- !,fail.
compl( Path, CW, CD, M, Proof ) :-
       select(OmegaClause,CW,CWRest),
       select(Literal,OmegaClause,OmegaClauseRest),
       complL(Path,Literal),
       complW(Path,OmegaClauseRest,CWRest,CD,M,Proof).
compl( Path, CW, CD, M, Proof ) :-
       select([Alpha>Gamma],CD,CDRest),
       complL(Path,Gamma),!,
       complD(Path,[Alpha>Gamma],CW,CDRest,M,Proof).

complW(_Path, []                          ,_CW,_CD,_M, []     ) .
complW( Path, [Literal|ClauseRest], CW, CD, M, Proof ) :-
       complL(Path,Literal),
       complW(Path,ClauseRest,CW,CD,M,Proof).
complW( Path, [Literal|ClauseRest], CW, CD, M, Proof ) :-
       compl([Literal|Path],CW,CD,M,Proof1),
       complW(Path,ClauseRest,CW,CD,M,Proof2),
       append(Proof1,Proof2,Proof),
       compatible(M,Proof).

complD(_Path, [Alpha>Gamma],_CW, CD, M,
                             [[Alpha>Gamma]|Proof] ) :-
       neg(Alpha,NegAlpha),
       compl([NegAlpha],M,CD,M,Proof),
       compatible(M,[[Alpha>Gamma]|Proof]).
```

Fig. 9.7. I^i: An implementation of algorithm A^i.

the admissibility check by taking the δ-clauses obtained from the subproof in `Proof` in `complW/6` and `complD/6`. In this way, compatibility acts as a local constraint on subproofs. In fact, we often observed that default proofs in non-artificial examples were quite rarely corrected by the compatibility check. Hence, the resulting default proofs contained only few occasions for distracting the theorem prover by choosing incompatible δ-clauses.

For comparison, we have also implemented in [Sch94b] a "generate-and-test" version in which arbitrary subsets are generated and afterwards treated by admissibility and compatibility. Even in the simplest examples this yields a drastic increase of calls to all predicates.

Finally, we want to discuss briefly the influence of the compatibility check. For this purpose, we have primarily studied examples involving failing queries due to incompatibilities, since this case embodies a worst-case scenario for compatibility checking. An important observation was that an incremantal compatibility check does not necessarily lead to a worse performance. Rather we have observed in many cases that even a large number of incremantal compatibility checks does not result in a large deceleration. In one example, having an incompatibility near the bottom of the search space, it was interesting to observe that our implementation I^i (integrating compatibility) invokes fewer times the predicate "establishing a connection" than I' (using a posterior compatibility check)—even though I^i performs almost twice as much compatibility checks. This is insofar remarkable since the predicate "establishing connections" is one of the innermost predicates of the theorem proving loop. The least number of calls to this predicate is done by program I that deals with "compatible matrices". In another example, having an incompatibility near the top of the search space, we made a similar observation: Here, the number of compatibility checks in I^i is nine times larger than in I'. This has to be contrasted with the number of calls to the predicate "establishing connections" that is in I^i only 1.2 times larger than in I'. As above, the least number of calls to this predicate is obtained in program I. More examples and a more detailed discussion can be found in [Sch94b].

In all, we observed in [Sch94b] that program I performs best on the given examples due to the lack of consistency checking. However, we have already discussed that this approach has its difficulties in the presence of many conflicting default rules. In such a case, our experiments suggest that it is worthwhile to integrate compatibility checks in order to prune redundant incompatible subproofs, rather than to check compatibility separated from the actual proof procedure.

9.8 Extensions

This sections summarizes some enhancements and extensions of our approach and gives hints for further reading.

9.8.1 Integration of lemma handling

The integration of lemma handling it is of great practical relevance in automated theorem proving. This is so because the use of lemmas is often needed for reducing computational efforts. In Chapter 8, we described a theoretical framework for lemma handling by example of classical and constrained default logic.

Lemma handling as such must be decomposed in two phases: Generation and usage. These tasks are detailed in sequel.

Generation.. At the methodical level, we can generate lemma default rules or "lemma δ-clauses" for any proven (sub)query φ. In such a case, we have a spanning mating Π for some matrix M of $W \cup W_D \cup \{\neg\varphi\}$ such that (M, Π) is admissible and compatible. The default proof is then given by

$$D_\varphi = \{\delta \mid \{\neg\alpha_\delta, \gamma_\delta\} \in \kappa(M, \Pi)\}.$$

Things become however more complicated, if default lemmas are taken from an "inner" part of a proof: In theorem provers for classical logic, a lemma ℓ is a set of literals such that each path containing ℓ is complementary. Given two matrices M and M' with $M' \subseteq M$, and a lemma ℓ (wrt M'), then each path p through M containing ℓ as a subset is complementary.

In default theorem proving, the proof of ℓ (ie. the proof that a path containing ℓ is complementary) might additionally depend on a set of δ-clauses C_{DL}. The use of ℓ during a derivation employing defaults not consistent with C_{DL} would be incorrect. In the context of default theorem proving, we therefore have to extend the concept of lemmas:

Definition 9.8.1. [BS96b] *Let C_W be a set of ω-clauses and C_D be a set of δ-clauses and let M_1 and M_2 be subsets of $C_W \cup C_D$, where $M_2 = \{c_1 \cup \{L_1\}, \ldots, c_n \cup \{L_n\}\}$. Let Π be a mating such that $(M_1 \cup M_2, \Pi)$ is admissible and compatible. If Π spans $M' = M_1 \cup \{L_1\} \cup \cdots \cup \{L_n\}$, and $\kappa(\Pi, M') = M'$ then we call $\{L_1, \ldots, L_n\}$ a default lemma wrt M_1 and the set of default rules $\{\delta \mid \{\neg\alpha_\delta, \gamma_\delta\} \in (C_D \cap M_1)\}$.*

The usage of such lemmas is detailed in [BS96b].

As regards the algorithm given in Definition 9.5.3, we can generate lemma default rules for each obtained subproof as follows. Consider Condition *(3b)*. A "lemma δ-clause" for γ_δ can be generate from the default proof

$$D_\varphi = \{\delta \mid \{\neg\alpha_\delta, \gamma_\delta\} \in C_{D''}\}.$$

Otherwise, it suffices to find a subset D_φ of D such that $compl(\{\neg\varphi\}, C_W, C_{D_\varphi})$ is true. This technique generates lemmas for unit clauses only, that is $\ell = \{\varphi\}$.

Usage.. The usage of lemma default rules is obvious at the "logical" level, since they constitute ordinary albeit prerequisite-free default rules.

As above, things become more interesting, when considering default lemmas taken from an "inner" part of a proof (in the connection method):

Theorem 9.8.1. *Let C_W be a set of ω-clauses and C_D be a set of δ-clauses such that $W \cup Justif(D) \cup Conseq(D)$ is consistent. Let $M' \subseteq C_W \cup C_D$ be a matrix and let $\{L_1, \ldots, L_n\}$ be a default lemma wrt M' and some set of default rules $D' \subseteq D$. Then, each path p through $C_W \cup C_D$ is complementary if $\{L_1, \ldots, L_n\} \subseteq p$.*

The above definition presupposes a "compatible context" for using ℓ. In practice, the interesting part in this definition is however the verification of $W \cup Justif(D) \cup Conseq(D)$ being consistent. In other words, is lemma ℓ, relying on D', usable in the context given by D?

For instance, [LS95] distinguishes between *static* and *dynamic default lemmas*: A static lemma may be kept along with its underlying consistency assumptions, comprised in D', throughout a whole deduction; this requires verifying compatibility of D' each time such a lemma is used. Instead, the validity of dynamic lemmas expires as soon as one of the default rules used in their proof, that is D', is withdrawn from the overall default proof. Thus, they are usable without any consistency checks. The latter form of lemmas may result in a significant speed-up, while they practically never harm the proof search due to their restricted viability.

Let us return the algorithm given in Definition 9.5.3. For using "lemma δ-clauses", we can adapt Condition *3* as follows:

4. *If $C_{D'} \neq \emptyset$ and $c \in C_{D'}$ is a lemma δ-clause then $compl(p, C_{W'}, C_{D'})$ is true iff γ_δ is complementary to some literal of p for $c = \{\neg\alpha_\delta, \gamma_\delta\}$.*

This drastic simplification is possible since neither admissibility nor compatibility have to be verified for "lemma δ-clauses". The former is obsolete since lemma default rules are prerequisite-free default rules, while the latter is redundant because the compatibility with C_W has been checked while generating the lemma. The compatibility with the remaining δ-clauses in the proof is checked at a higher level of the recursion. This is therefore a very simple example of dynamic lemma handling.

A full account of the modifications to Definition 9.5.3 that are needed for lemma handling is given in [LS95].

9.8.2 Model-based consistency-checking

In Section 9.5 a consistency check is envisaged each time a default rule is taken into account. Such a consistency-driven search for a default proof has the advantage that "inconsistent" applications of default rules are pruned right away. On the other hand, such successive checks can be very expensive.

The interesting question is then whether we can find a way to full-fledged pruning of "inconsistent subproofs" while restricting our attention to ultimately necessary consistency checks. For this, we observe that a formula is consistent (or satisfiable) iff it has a model. In fact, checking whether a model satisfies a formula can be done in linear time in propositional logic. This led us in [BS96b] to the following approach to incremental consistency checking:

For reducing computational efforts one clearly should avoid exhaustive general purpose mechanisms for consistency checking. Our goal is rather to furnish an approach that allows for full-fledged pruning of "inconsistent subproofs" while restricting our attention to ultimately necessary consistency checks. We address this problem by means of a *model-based approach*: We use a model as a compact representation of the compatibility of a default proof at hand. The aim is then to reuse such a model for as many subsequent compatibility checks as possible. Of course, this reusability depends strongly on the chosen model. Hence, we sometimes encounter situations in which we have to look for a "better" model. We support this search by a synergistic treatment of theorem proving and model handling: This treatment is based on so-called *model matrices* which represent in a compact way all models of the initial set of facts that satisfy the justifications and consequents of the applied default rules.

First of all, let us make precise how we treat consistency checks via model handling:[17] For a set of formulas W and a sequence of *normal* default rules $\langle \delta_j \rangle_{j<i}$ (representing the default proof at hand), let m be a model for $W \cup Conseq(\{\delta_0, \ldots, \delta_{i-1}\})$. Function ∇ checks whether

$$W \cup Conseq(\{\delta_0, \ldots, \delta_{i-1}\}) \nvdash \neg Conseq(\delta_i) ,$$

as stipulated in Condition 2 in Corollary 9.5.1:

$$\nabla(\delta_i, \langle m, W, \langle \delta_j \rangle_{j<i} \rangle) = \begin{cases} \langle m, W, \langle \delta_j \rangle_{j \leq i} \rangle & \text{if } m \models Conseq(\delta_i) \\ \langle m', W, \langle \delta_j \rangle_{j \leq i} \rangle & \text{if } m \nvDash Conseq(\delta_i) \text{ and} \\ & \quad \text{for some } m' \neq m \\ & \quad m' \models W \cup \{Conseq(\delta_j) \mid j \leq i\} \\ \bot & \text{if there is no } m'' \text{ such that} \\ & \quad m'' \models W \cup \{Conseq(\delta_j) \mid j \leq i\} \end{cases}$$

Function ∇ gives a general description of our approach while making precise the intuition given above. We refine this specification in the sequel.

At the start of a derivation, m is set to an arbitrary model of C_W[18], as provided by an open path through the matrix of C_W. Note that such models are actually partial models that only fix the truth-values of certain literals; hence, they are refineable along their degrees of freedom. In fact, whenever a δ-clause $\{\neg\alpha_\delta, \gamma_\delta\}$ is selected as input clause, we check whether γ_δ is satisfied by m; that is, due to the nature of m, we check whether $\neg\gamma_\delta \notin m$.[19] If this is the case, γ_δ is added to the partial model m. In this way, we enforce that $m \cup \{\gamma_\delta\}$ is a model for

$$C_W \cup \{\{\gamma_{\delta_1}\}, \ldots, \{\gamma_{\delta_i}\}\} \cup \{\{\gamma_\delta\}\}, \tag{9.18}$$

where $\gamma_{\delta_1}, \ldots, \gamma_{\delta_i}$ stand for the (justifications and) consequents of the previously used defaults. This amounts to the criterion given in Definition 9.5.2, since Matrix (9.18) equals the one in (9.16). Otherwise, a new model for (9.18) has to be generated for carrying on with the current derivation (by searching another open path

---

[17] For readability, we illustrate the approach by means of normal default rules. The extension to general default rules in constrained default logic is straightforward by replacing each occurrence of $Conseq(\cdot)$ by $Conseq(\cdot) \wedge Justif(\cdot)$.

[18] Such a model exists since we assume W to be consistent.

[19] In constrained default logic, this requires testing $\beta \wedge \gamma$ when regarding $\frac{\alpha : \beta}{\gamma}$.

through Matrix (9.18)). If no such model can be found, δ-clause $\{\neg\alpha_\delta, \gamma_\delta\}$ cannot be used in the current situation.

For reducing computational efforts of searching new models, we consider so-called *model matrices* $M^\star$ that are simplified yet equivalent variants of (9.18). At the start of a derivation this model matrix equals C_W; during a proof it is extended by the justifications (and consequents) of the used defaults and by certain lemmas provided by the theorem prover. The key idea is then to *simplify* $M^\star$ after each such addition; hence, in case a new model has to be generated, one does not have to start with the full matrix in (9.16) but rather a matrix which is already simplified as much as possible.[20,21] Each such simplification, has to be model-preserving, ie. a simplified matrix has to have the same *open paths* as the original one. To this end, simplifications reduce the search space by eliminating closed paths. When restricting ourselves to Unit-reductions and subsumptions, we may proceed as follows. In the former case, we replace a clause $\{L\} \cup c$ by c in the presence of the unit-clause $\{\neg L\}$, while in the latter, we delete a clause c in the presence of one of its proper subsets (cf. [Bib87]).

Another interesting question is then whether a simultaneous treatment of theorem proving and satisfiability checking allows for synergistic procedures by means of structure and information sharing. The idea is to communicate information from the theorem prover to a model generator. This communication is accomplished by lemma handling, as already sketched above. We show in [BS96b] that this allows for a drastic reduction of the search space in case a new model has to be generated.

9.8.3 Skeptical query-answering

A major extension of our query-answering approach, namely the treatment of skeptical reasoning, is discussed in [ST95]. This work builds on [TS95], where a general framework to skeptical reasoning in (semi-monotonic) default logics was proposed. There, we have given a high-level description of skeptical query-answering that abstracts from an underlying credulous reasoner. [ST95] make the aforementioned meta-algorithm precise and employ it to extend the credulous approach described in this chapter to skeptical query-answering.

In fact, [TS95] follow an approach whose underlying principle was originally applied by Poole [Poo91] to a restricted version of his nonmonotonic Theorist formalism [Poo88, Poo89a], and which was extended to the entire Theorist framework by [Thi93]. Informally, the approach is based on the notion of a discourse in which two protagonists alternately raise arguments and counterarguments. Specifically, to prove skeptical entailment the first protagonist tries to find a single default proof of the formula under consideration, then his antagonist replies by giving a counterargument which "annuls" this proof. Afterwards, it is again the first protagonist who searches for another default proof in view of the restriction determined by the

---

[20] In fact, such simplification are doable in an anytime manner.

[21] Note, however, that in case derivation steps have to be withdrawn, the corresponding modifications of the respective model matrices have to be withdrawn, too.

preceding counterargument, and so on. This procedure ends if it is impossible to find either a default proof or a counterargument at some state. In the former case, the formula is not skeptically entailed while it is in the latter. (This approach relies heavily on the technique of supplying pre-constraints, introduced in Section 3.5, for reasoning in the presence of counter-arguments; see [TS95] for details.)

[ST95] keep this fundamental idea and base their connection calculus for skeptical reasoning on the one for credulous reasoning: The idea is to start with an arbitrary credulous default proof of a given query, as described in Section 9.5. Then, we determine in some way a representative selection of other credulous default proofs that are incompatible with our initial credulous default proof. These incompatible proofs indicate extensions in which our initial default proof is invalid. Intuitively, these are the aforementioned putative counterarguments challenging our initial credulous default proof. Next, we verify in turn whether our query is derivable "in the presence" of each these default proofs representing a counterargument. If this is indeed the case, then our initial query is skeptically derivable. Technically, this was accomplished by employing a further (yet recursive) restriction on credulous default proofs, expressed by what [ST95] call a *stability* criterion. This has led to a homogeneous characterization of skeptical default proofs at the level of the connection method.

For brevity, we refer the reader to [TS95] and [ST95] for details.

9.9 Conclusion

We have presented an approach to query-answering in default logics by treating default rules as classical implications along with some qualifying conditions restricting the use of such rules in the course of the proof search. This has resulted in a novel methodology taking advantage of the conception of structure-oriented theorem proving provided by the connection method. To this end, we have decomposed default theorem proving (in the connection method) into the verification of complementarity, admissibility, and compatibility—corresponding to classical deduction and the concepts of groundedness and consistency in default logic.

We introduced in Section 9.3 our basic method that provides with admissibility and compatibility two independent concepts restricting default proofs to classical proofs confirming the two previous properties. To a turn, we refined the approach in Section 9.5 by meshing together the concepts of admissibility and (incremental) compatibility. While the former relies on a rather global notion of consistency, the latter employs an incremental and thus rather local notion of consistency.

Apart from the encoding of default rules as implication, a distinguishing feature of the approach is the formation of sequences of default rules or δ-clauses, respectively. In our basic method, this formation is primarily directed by the notion of groundedness, while consistency plays more or less the role of a global constraint. In contrast to this, groundedness and consistency jointly direct the formation of sequences of δ-clauses in our refined method.

We have discussed in detail the different mouldings of our approach and their differences to other approaches found in the literature in Section 9.6. To summarize, the distinguishing methodical features of our approach are

- the treatment of default rules as classical implications,
- the formation of sequences of default rules or δ-clauses, respectively, and
- the integration of the concepts of groundedness *and* consistency into a classical deduction method.

These qualities allow for a homogeneous characterization and treatment of default proofs at the level of the logical calculus. This makes the approach extraordinarily qualified for implementations by means of existing automated theorem proving techniques. We have substantiated this claim by implementing the resulting algorithms in diverse prototypical settings, and we show how this extends to state-of-the-art automated theorem provers in the next chapter.

At first, we derived in Section 9.4 from our basic method an algorithm that supports the joint verification of complementarity and admissibility in very natural way. Notably, the algorithm is obtained by slightly extending an existing algorithm for the standard connection method due to [Ede92]. However, we have proposed an "off-line" integration of compatibility by compiling default theories into compatible default theories. This separation is supported by the independence of admissibility and compatibility in our basic method. The advantages of this approach are the following. First, the algorithm never runs into redundant computations with incompatible defaults. Second, it is implementable with very few modifications to an existing automated theorem prover. This is underpinned by an initial case-study due to Aaron Rothschild [Rot93]. That is, Rothschild was able to implement our algorithm by slightly extending an existing automated theorem prover for the connection method. The disadvantage however is that one might obtain an exponential number of compatible default theories in the worst-case. So in general, such an approach is favorable whenever the computational cost of the compilation can be amortized over the total set of subsequent queries.

Second, we have presented an alternative algorithm based on the refinement of our basic method. This algorithm fully integrates the concepts of complementarity, admissibility, and compatibility and accordingly supports their joint verification. Hence, it works with arbitrary default theories and thus avoids the pre-compilation of default theories into compatible fragments. At the same time, it also avoids redundant computations with incompatible defaults. On the other hand, this approach requires more changes to existing automated theorem provers. Also, successive consistency checking may slow down the performance of the prover. A promising way of avoiding this is to use model checking techniques as sketched in Section 9.8, and notably applied in Chapter 10.

However, our experiments in [Sch94b] have shown that the latter approach is still favorable over a belated consistency check that verifies the compatibility of completed, admissible proofs. Moreover, our experiments have demonstrated that enforcing groundedness while query-answering poses no additional burden on the theorem prover. Hence, we argue that the concurrent verification of admissibility and complementarity is indispensable for query-answering in default logic. As discussed in Section 9.6, the treatment of compatibility is more subtle. Here, a lot depends on the underlying theory. That is, if a default theory comprises a feasible number of compatible default theories, then our former approach along with its precompilation of compatibility is favorable. Otherwise, that is, if a default theory comprises many conflicting defaults, an integration of compatibility as accomplished in our latter approach is preferable.

All of the presented algorithms along with their implementations are query-oriented. This reflects the idea that the theorem prover is in charge of finding a proof while being directed by the concepts of admissibility and compatibility. On the other hand, our method leaves plenty of room for other algorithmic approaches, which have not yet been pursued. For instance, Section 9.5 provides another valuable refinement that allows for structure and information sharing while jointly verifying admissibility and compatibility.

Even though our approach has been presented from the perspective of constrained default logic, it has a general nature that principally allows for query-answering in any (semi-monotonic) default logic. To this end, one merely has to adjust the concept of compatibility in order to account for the respective notion of consistency. For a complement, we have applied the approach in [Sch94a] to a prioritized version of default logic. This has been accomplished by stepwisely refining the concepts developed for prioritized default logic and by mapping them in turn onto the techniques developed in the preceding sections. This extension of our method has served two purposes. First, it has shown that the presented method is flexible enough to be adapted to other conceptions of default logic. Second, it has shown how priorities can be integrated.

In all, the approach bridges the gap between default logics and classical theorem proving by providing a simple yet powerful method for default theorem proving that is easily adaptable by existing implementations of automated theorem provers. In particular, the approach should be easily extensible to a (decidable) first-order language since it relies on standard theorem proving techniques. This claim is substantiated in the following chapter, where we show how an existing automated theorem prover can be turned into an efficient inference engine for default reasoning.

10. A Prolog-technology compiler for query-answering

In many AI applications default reasoning plays an important role since many sub-tasks involve reasoning from incomplete information. This is why there is a great need for systematic methods that allow us to integrate default reasoning capabilities. In fact, the last 15 years have provided us with a profound understanding of the underlying problems and have resulted in well-understood formal approaches to default reasoning. Therefore, we are now ready to build advanced default reasoning systems. For this undertaking, we have chosen the method for query-answering introduced in the previous chapter as a point of departure: We show how Prolog technology can be used for efficient implementation of query answering in default logics. The idea is to translate a default theory along with query into a Prolog program and a Prolog query such that the original query belongs to an extension of the default theory iff the Prolog query is derivable from the Prolog program.

10.1 Motivation

We are interested in implementing the basic approach to query-answering that allows for determining whether a formula is in *some* extension of a given default theory.[1] Unlike other approaches that address this problem by encapsulating the underlying theorem prover as a separate module, we are proposing a radically different approach that integrates default reasoning into existing automated theorem provers. For this endeavor, we follow the incremental approach to query-answering developed in Section 9.5. This approach integrates the notion of a default proof into a calculus for classical logic, which renders it especially qualified for implementations by means of existing theorem provers. In fact, Chapter 9 furnishes a connection calculus for query-answering in semi-monotonic default logics. The advantage of these default systems is that they allow for local proof procedures, as we detailed in Section 9.2.

On the other hand, there are various implementations of the connection method. Most of them, like the high performance theorem prover SETHEO [LBSB92, GLMS94], are based on model elimination [Lov78] which can be regarded as a member of the family of connection calculi. We draw on this relationship in this

---

[1] Membership in *all* extensions is efficiently computable by appeal to a procedure testing membership in *some* extension (see [TS95]).

chapter and show how an implementation technique for model elimination, namely Prolog Technology Theorem Proving (PTTP) [Sti89, Sti90], can be used for default reasoning. This contribution can be looked at from different perspectives: First, we provide implementations for (semi-monotonic) default logics. Second, we extend an existing automated theorem prover by means for handling default information. And finally, one can view our contribution as a logic programming system integrating disjunction, classical as well as default negation.

While our current implementation deals with full-fledged default logics, namely at once justified and constrained default logic,[2] we restrict our exposition in what follows to normal default theories over a propositional language, even though our implementation treats variables over a finite universe. [3]

10.2 Implementing query-answering

The key observation that led to the results reported in this chapter is that the approach for query answering presented in the previous section allows to apply Prolog technology in a rather straightforward manner. This is due to the fact that the corresponding connection calculus can be mapped onto model elimination [Lov78] which itself is implementable by means of so-called Prolog Technology Theorem Provers (PTTPs) [Sti89, Sti90]. This is because model elimination is closely related to Prologs linear input resolution [Lov78]. As regards classical theorem proving, this approach has already resulted in quite impressive high-performance proof systems, like [BF94, GLMS94]. The main reason for their convincing performance is their ability to take advantage of highly efficient underlying Prolog systems.

In what follows, we describe how Prolog technology can be used for implementing default reasoning systems. For this, we follow by and large the approach by Stickel's PTTP [Sti89, Sti90] as regards classical theorem proving. PTTP can be seen as an extension of Prolog that provides a proof system for full first-order predicate calculus. In order to attain this, one has to enhance Prolog via measures guaranteeing (i) sound unification, (ii) complete search, and (iii) complete inference. In what follows, we concentrate on the last item, since we have restricted our exposition to the propositional case. In fact, there is no need for modifying the classical methods addressing the first two items when dealing with default reasoning, so that we refer the reader for details to [Sti89].

The overall approach is based on the idea to transform a formula W along with a query φ into a Prolog program P_W and a Prolog query Q_φ such that Q_φ is derivable from P_W iff $W \wedge \neg\varphi$ is unsatisfiable. In this way, the Prolog inference mechanism remains unchanged, while the transformation has to guarantee the implementation of item (i) to (iii). Although this approach is conceptually very simple it has proven to be very successful.

---

[2] More precisely, we deal with fragments of contextual default logic that allow for E- and C-justifications and rely on the translations given in Section 5.3.

[3] Although this boils down to propositional logic, too, it allows for expressing things more concisely.

As an example, consider the statements "students are adults", "adults usually have a driving license", and "having a driving license usually implies being able to drive a car". The corresponding default theory along with fact S (for students) is the following one:

$$\left(\left\{ \frac{A : L}{L}, \frac{L : C}{C} \right\}, \{S, S \rightarrow A\} \right) \tag{10.1}$$

For instance, we can prove C (or, given S, that students drive cars) by means of default proof: $\langle \frac{A:L}{L}, \frac{L:C}{C} \rangle$.

On the proof-theoretic side, we obtain from Default theory 10.1 and query C the following matrix:

$$\{\{S\}, \{\neg S, A\}, \{\neg A_{\delta_1}, L_{\delta_1}\}, \{\neg L_{\delta_2}, C_{\delta_2}\}, \{\neg C\}\} \tag{10.2}$$

This matrix has the spanning mating $\{\{S, \neg S\}, \{A, \neg A_{\delta_1}\}, \{L_{\delta_1}, \neg L_{\delta_2}\}, \{C_{\delta_2}, \neg C\}\}$. As can be easily verified, Matrix (10.2) and its spanning Mating enjoy admissibility and compatibility, which renders it a default proof of C.

Let us now turn to the issue of compilation. The first step of the transformation is to generate all contrapositives of all clauses of a given matrix. For illustration, consider the classical formulas in Theory (10.1). While S is turned into a single contrapositive S $\leftarrow$, we obtain two contrapositives from $\neg S \lor A$, namely $A \leftarrow S$ and $\neg S \leftarrow \neg A$. A clause consisting of n literals yields thus n contrapositives that take care of reasoning by contraposition. Following PTTP's translation schema [Sti89], this amounts to the following Prolog rules:[4]

```
s.
a :- s.
not_s :- not_a.
```

For complete inference, one has to provide moreover means for reasoning by cases. For this purpose, let us detail the inference operations in model elimination that are called *extension* and *reduction* step. An extension step amounts to Prolog's use of input resolution; it is expressed in Definition 9.4.1 by Condition *(2b)*. That is, a subgoal is resolved with an input clause if the subgoal is complementary to one of the literals in the input clause. For illustration, let us consider the clauses in (10.2): There, we can resolve the goal $\neg C$ with clause $\{C_{\delta_2}, \neg L_{\delta_2}\}$ ("along" connection $\{\neg C, C_{\delta_2}\}$). The resulting subgoal $\neg L_{\delta_2}$ can then be resolved ("along" connection $\{\neg L_{\delta_2}, L_{\delta_1}\}$) with clause $\{L_{\delta_1}, \neg A_{\delta_1}\}$ and so on.

The reduction step renders model elimination complete for (full) propositional clause logic: It allows to solve a subgoal by simply resolving it with one of its ancestor subgoals. Note that given a subgoal, its ancestors subgoals correspond to a partial path through the matrix at hand. In Definition 9.4.1 this inference rule is expressed by Condition *(2a)*. In our example, we thus obtain path $\{\neg C, \neg L_{\delta_2}\}$ after the two aforementioned extension steps; this allows for applying reduction steps to putative subgoals C and L.

---

[4] Following PTTP's syntax, a and not_a stand for A and $\neg A$ etc.

Following PTTP's translation schema [Sti89], reduction steps can be added as follows. First, we must memorize ancestors goals by adding another argument (a list Anc) to each literal (see left column below). Second, we must add for each literal, which is added in some rule to the ancestor list, a further rule that allows for testing whether a subgoal is complementary to this (memorized) literal (see right column). In our example, we get the following rules.

```
s(Anc).
a(Anc) :-                          not_a(Anc) :-
    NewAnc = [a|Anc],                  member(a,Anc).
    s(NewAnc).
not_s(Anc) :-                      s(Anc) :-
    NewAnc = [not_s|Anc],              member(not_s,Anc).
    not_a(NewAnc).
```

Let us now turn to the transformations needed for integrating default rules. We have seen in Chapter 9, how this is achievable via the proof-theoretic conditions imposed by admissibility and compatibility. In fact, admissibility is integratable via an adaption of model elimination's extension step: Whenever a δ-clause $\{\neg\alpha_i, \gamma_i\}$ is used as input clause, one has to guarantee (i) that only γ_i is resolved upon, and (ii) that after such an "extension step" the ancestor goals of the resulting subgoal $\neg\alpha_i$ must not be used for later reduction steps. In Theorem 9.4.1, it was shown that these conditions correspond to the conditions imposed on matrices used for verifying admissibility. This amounts to the following changes when transforming δ-clauses as opposed to conventional clauses:

First, we add for each δ-clause $\{\neg\alpha_i, \gamma_i\}$ a *single* Prolog rule γ_i :- α_i, corresponding to contrapositive $\gamma_i \leftarrow \alpha_i$. We refer to such rules as δ-*rules* and sometimes abbreviate a δ-rule stemming from a default ζ by r_ζ. In our example, we thus obtain for the default rules in (10.1) Prolog rules l :- a. and c :- l. Note that adding only a single Prolog rule for δ-clauses makes it impossible to reason by contraposition. Second, as with ordinary clauses, we have to add an additional argument memorizing ancestor subgoals. But instead of extending the resulting list by the head γ_i of the δ-rule, it is set to the empty list in order to avoid reduction steps using γ_i or any ancestor subgoals of γ_i. In this way, our transformation encodes groundedness/admissibility into the resulting Prolog program. For the δ-clauses in our example, we thus get:

```
l(Anc) :-                          c(Anc) :-
    a([]).                             l([]).
```

(In fact, another such ancestor list for tracing δ-rules must be added for the regularity check, detailed in Section 10.3.)

The next step in our transformation provides means for checking compatibility. Recall from Section 9.8.2 that this task can be mapped onto the generation of propositional models. For this purpose, many approaches known for classical propositional logic can be applied. We take advantage of this and implement the verification of compatibility relative to a δ-clause $\{\neg\alpha_i, \gamma_i\}$ by means of testing whether there is a model for[5]

$$C_W \cup \{\{\gamma_j\} \mid j < i\} \cup \{\gamma_i\}. \tag{10.3}$$

This amounts to verifying compatibility for the matrices of the form (9.16) in Section 9.5 (here, stemming from a normal default theory). Observe that $\delta_1, \ldots, \delta_{i-1}$ gives the list of defaults used so far in the overall derivation of the initial query.

For implementing compatibility, we finally add a further argument to each literal which *by and large*[6] contains a model for $C_W \cup \{\{\gamma_j\} \mid j < i\}$ provided that δ-rules $r_{\delta_1}, \ldots, r_{\delta_{i-1}}$ have been successfully applied in the accomplished derivation. When testing compatibility at δ-rule r_{δ_i}, we check (via run-time predicate model/3, detailed in Section 10.3) whether the actual model M satisfies γ_i. If this is the case, we continue proving with M. If not, we try to generate a new model NewM satisfying Matrix (10.3). If this succeeds, we continue proving with NewM. Otherwise, we know that δ-rule r_{δ_i} cannot be applied in a consistent way, given our current default proof. In this case, predicate model/3 fails and backtracking is engaged.

We actually need two physical variables for propagating models throughout the derivations. This yields the following δ-rules in our example:

```
l(Anc,(M,NewM))  :-          c(Anc,(M,NewM))  :-
    a([],(M,M1)),                l([],(M,M1)),
    model(l,M1,NewM).            model(c,M1,NewM).
```

In fact, our implementation allows us to decide at compile-time whether we check compatibility *before* or *after* finding an admissible proof of α_i. In the former case, our first δ-rule is then replaced by:

```
l(Anc,(M,NewM))  :-
    model(l,M,M1),
    a([],(M1,NewM)).
```

(An empirical analysis of both options showed that changing the order of compatibility and admissibility checking may lead to improvements by orders of magnitude, depending on the test-cases' topologies.)

The propagation of models affects also the Prolog rules stemming from "classical" clauses, which completes the resulting Prolog program:

```
s(Anc,(M,M)).
a(Anc,(MI,MO))  :-           not_a(Anc,(M,M))  :-
    NewAnc = [a|Anc],            member(a,Anc).
    s(NewAnc,(MI,MO)).
not_s(Anc,(MI,MO))  :-       s(Anc,(M,M))  :-
    NewAnc = [not_s|Anc],        member(not_s,Anc).
    not_a(NewAnc,(MI,MO)).
```

---

[5] This is the first place referring specifically to normal default rules. Eg. in constrained default logic one has to add justifications $\{\{\beta_j\} \mid j < i\} \cup \{\beta_i\}$.

[6] This approach will be detailed in Section 10.3.

The above material provides a recipe for transforming a default theory (D, W) into a Prolog program $P_{D,W}$. For query-answering, however, we have to provide a further transformation for queries, like φ. Following PTTP, we use for this purpose a special predicate query along with a Prolog rule query $\colon - \varphi$. In our example, we thus obtain initially a Prolog rule of the form query $\colon - c(\ldots)$., which allows us to pose our initial query C via Prolog query ?-query. Without entering details, rule query $\colon - \varphi$ is then enriched by further run-time predicates providing means for finding an initial model of C_W and proof printing.

In all, we thus compile a default theory (D, W) along with a query φ into a Prolog program $P_{D,W,\varphi} = P_{D,W} \cup \{$query $\colon - \varphi\}$ along with a Prolog query query. The resulting program is compilable using a standard Prolog compiler which leads to its impressive performance. Subsequent queries are easily posed by replacing and recompiling the single query rule *only*.

10.3 Extensions and implementation

The previous section has presented our basic approach to implementing default reasoning by taking advantage of the power provided by PTTP. Our current implementation refines this basic approach in several ways in order to improve its flexibility and efficiency. This section summarizes the most important improvements.

Compatibility: As sketched above, we pursue a model-based approach for reducing computational efforts of successive consistency checks. As detailed in Section 9.8.2, a model provides us with a compact representation of the consistency of a (partial) default proof at hand. We start with an initial model m of C_W, given by a non-complementary path through the matrix of C_W. Notably, m is a partial model fixing truth-values of certain literals only. Whenever a δ-rule $\gamma_\delta \colon - \alpha_\delta$ is used, we check whether m satisfies γ_δ by $\neg\gamma_\delta \notin m$. If this easy test succeeds, we continue while adding γ_δ to m. If not, a new (partial) model is generated or, if this fails too, backtracking is engaged. For finding new models, we use an adapted variant of the Davis-Putnam procedure [DP60], which is currently one of the fastest complete procedures for finding propositional models. Further improvements are detailed in [BS96b]. Among them, we rely on a so-called model-matrix representing all possible partial models. Importantly, this matrix can be significantly reduced during a derivation by using information gathered during the proof search by means of lemma techniques. This leads to a drastic reduction of the search space for finding new models.

Lemma handling is an important means for eliminating redundancy in automated theorem proving. This task is however more difficult in our context, since proofs may depend on default rules. Therefore, we distinguish between *static* and *dynamic lemmas* (cf. Section 9.8.1). A static lemma may be kept along with its underlying consistency assumptions throughout a whole deduction; this requires verifying compatibility each time such a lemma is used. As opposed to this, the validity of dynamic lemmas expires as soon as one of the default rules used for deriving the lemma is withdrawn. Thus, valid dynamic lemmas are usable without any consistency checks. The latter form of lemma handling may result in a significant speed-up, while it practically never harms the proof search due to the restricted viability of dynamic lemmas.

Regularity provides a highly efficient means for discarding subgoals identical to one of their ancestor subgoals in proof systems based on model elimination (eg. see [LBSB92]). As above, however, this tool has to be adapted for default reasoning. This leads us to what we call *blockwise regularity*, which requires (i) that no subgoal is equal to one of its ancestors unless a δ-rule is used in between, and (ii) that after using a δ-rule $\gamma_\delta :- \alpha_\delta$, no δ-rule with head γ_δ must be used to prove α_δ; this is verified via the ancestor list tracing δ-rules, mentioned in Section 10.2. Besides pruning large parts of the search space, blockwise regularity also guarantees completeness since it is necessarily violated by infinite branches.

Expressiveness: For simplicity, our presentation was so far dominated by default rules having atomic components only. As PTTP, however, we deal with formulas in negation normal form. Let us illustrate this by sketching the transformation of default rule $\frac{A\wedge(\neg B\vee C) : \neg D\vee E}{\neg D\vee E}$. As detailed in Section 9.2, this rule is first translated into three implications, namely $(\neg D \vee E \leftarrow \gamma_\delta), (\gamma_\delta \leftarrow \alpha_\delta)$, and $(\alpha_\delta \leftarrow A \wedge (\neg B \vee C))$, where α_δ and γ_δ are new atoms. The second implication can now be translated into a δ-rule as described above, while the two other implications are treated in the classical way.

Finally, we mention that our implementation deals with full-fledged (semi-monotonic) default logics, namely fragments of contextual default logic allowing for E- and C-justifications; thus encompassing at once justified and constrained default logic. Notably, this necessitates changes to the compatibility check only. Current work includes also benchmark generators tailored to *query-answering* in *semi-monotonic* default logics, since existing ones for computing entire extensions in Reiter's (non-semi-monotonic) default logic are hardly applicable.

10.4 Conclusion

We showed how Prolog technology can be used for implementing efficient default reasoning systems. This was accomplished by appeal to the approach taken by Stickel's PTTP. We described how a default theory (D, W) along with a query φ has to be transformed into a Prolog program $P_{D,W,\varphi}$ along with a Prolog query query such that query is derivable from $P_{D,W,\varphi}$ iff φ has a finite default proof from (D, W). For brevity, we have restricted our exposition to normal default theories, even though the approach applies to any semi-monotonic default logic. To see this, note that the treatment of full-fledged semi-monotonic default logics is identical to that of normal default theories, except for the compatibility check. In this way, our approach can be regarded as a general methodology for implementing semi-monotonic default logics. From another perspective, we have shown how an existing (high-performance) automated theorem prover, namely PTTP, can be enhanced by means for handling default information. And finally, one can view our contribution as a logic programming system integrating disjunction, classical as well as default negation.

Our approach is quite different from other approaches found in the literature: Apart from [SR94], all other approaches, like [Rei80, JK90, BH92, Nie95], abstract from an underlying theorem prover. We integrate both groundedness and consistency into an existing standard theorem prover which uses a standard sub-prover for generating models. In [Poo91], Poole proposes an approach dealing with the fragment of prerequisite-free normal default rules that is also based on PTTP. The restriction to prerequisite-free default rules however renders an implementation of groundedness obsolete, so that PTTP serves mainly as an underlying theorem prover.

The methods described in [SR94, JK90, Nie95] aim at computing entire extensions in Reiter's default logic; queries are then answerable from such an extension. This is somehow unavoidable in Reiter's default logic, since it lacks semi-monotonicity and it does thus not allow for local proof procedures. This is why we concentrate on query-answering from semi-monotonic default logics, which is much more apt to the standard query-answering process of PTTP. As already advocated in Section 9.5, consistency checking is treated differently: [Rei80] puts forward a belated consistency check; [SR94] computes first entire sets of "consistent default rules" and verifies groundedness separately. We integrate both groundedness and consistency. Finally, our approach differs from all of the aforementioned ones in proposing a model-based treatment of consistency checking. This novel approach aims at minimizing computational efforts by reusing models as compact representations of former consistency checks.

First experiments have shown that the pursued avenue is quite promising. On different families of examples, our current implementation outperforms previous ones that do not rely on PTTP by an order of magnitude. In fact, credulous reasoning in propositional default logic is Σ_2^P-complete [Got92], whose two sources of exponentiality are reflected by an extended PTTP inference engine along with model handling capacities.

11. Conclusions and perspectives

The everlasting aim of this book was the automation of reasoning from incomplete information. For this endeavor, we have chosen default logic as our formal starting point. This was motivated by the great expressiveness and the proof-theoretic character of default logic. Even though, the resulting approaches range from semantic foundations to practical implementations, they all aim primarily at bridging the gap between theory and practice in default reasoning. For this purpose, it was necessary to provide alternative conceptualizations and to conceive novel reasoning techniques in default logics. The overall undertaking has resulted in a new methodology for query-answering in the absence of complete information. This approach provides us with a simple yet powerful method for default theorem proving that is easily adaptable by existing implementations of automated theorem provers, as demonstrated in the last chapter.

On the other hand, this monograph furnishes semantical and syntactical instruments for comparing existing default logics in a simple yet very substantial manner. The semantical framework may give rise to a semantical discipline in the field of default logics due to its generality. Complementary to this, the context-based framework for default logics offers a system for default reasoning that goes well beyond existing default logics. Due to this expressive power, this system constitutes a prime candidate for formalizing further unexampled reasoning patterns (by identifying the corresponding contextual default theories) instead of proposing yet other variations of default logic.

In all, the previous chapters have laid a first basis for reasoning from incomplete information in intelligent software system. However, there remain still some important issues unaddressed before such systems are available off-the-shelf. The previous chapters have mainly addressed the question how to draw conclusions from a given incomplete knowledge-base. In our view, this leaves open the following questions: (1) How do we model incomplete information? That is, how do we acquire, formulate, and employ the corresponding default rules? (2) How do we deal with changing knowledge-bases? That is, how do we incorporate new items of information or even new default rules? (3) How do we treat inconsistent knowledge-bases? (4) How will a final system look like? What will be its prospective applications? And will the additional expressiveness of default logic outweigh its additional complexity when dealing with these applications?

For us, this set of questions is hardly answerable from a purely theoretic point of view. Rather we have to perform experiments and model first applications indicating putative solutions or even more intricating unsettled questions. So, as one of the next major practical steps on this research avenue we envisage the conception of a *default logic programming language*. This will provide us with a first experimental setting for modeling incomplete information. For this purpose, it will be necessary to consolidate the theoretically and practically developed concepts in an appropriate programming language. This involves moreover the conception of a corresponding programming paradigm that accounts for the expressive power supplied by default logic. This is of great practical relevance since the expressiveness of default logic surpasses that of other knowledge representation languages, like standard logic or even DATALOG-like languages with negation [CEG94]. Consequently, there is a need for an appropriate programming discipline. The necessity for such an advanced programming discipline is also motivated from the experience gained in the TASSO project [dP95], while modeling configuration tasks in a restricted default logic setting (see [JP92, BS95b] for details).

A first realistic implementation platform was presented in Chapter 10 based on the automated theorem-prover PTTP [Sti89]. Another prospective implementation platform may be obtainable by regarding the field of logic programming [Llo87, LMR92]. In fact, a considerable amount of research aimed at a better understanding of the relationships existing between logic programming and formalisms for nonmonotonic reasoning, which was mutually beneficial to both areas. The field of nonmonotonic reasoning—and in particular default logic—helped to determine suitable semantics for logic programming. Conversely, we can also take advantage of the wide body of knowledge already gathered in the field of logic programming and apply existing implementations from this area. In any case, a resulting default reasoning system will help us to answer question (1). That is, it will provide us with an experimental yet effective environment for elucidating the principles involved in formulating and using default rules for modeling incomplete information.

So far, question (2) has been paid only little attention in the area of nonmonotonic reasoning, even though the problem of changing information states has been studied in the field of theory revision and updates (cf. [KM91]) as well as in database theory (cf. [FUV83]). The problem of updating theories with information contradicting either factual or derived information is however common to all these subareas of computer science. In fact, it is the change of information that renders default reasoning nonmonotonic. Hence, there is a need of analyzing the dynamic behavior of incomplete knowledge-bases. Links between theory revision and nonmonotonic reasoning were established in [MG90]. Hence, studying the problems stemming from updating incomplete knowledge-bases should also be mutually beneficial for all concerned subareas.

Question (3) is somehow related to (2) in the sense that an inconsistent knowledge-base can be regarded as the result of a careless update with contradictory information. Such a situation constitutes a severe problem for any logical reasoning system, since contradictions trivialize the set of drawable conclusions: A contradictory theory allows for concluding anything one wants. From a practical point of view, such a total collapse of information in the presence of a contradiction is clearly unacceptable. In fact, the treatment of contradictory information is in some way orthogonal to that of incomplete information, since a contradictory knowledge-base somehow comprises "too much" information. In practice, however, both phenomena are intimately related and arise hand in hand due to the inherent heterogeneity of knowledge. Accordingly, we need intelligent software systems that are versatile enough to overcome both contradictory and incomplete information. A major goal for future research is thus the development of a homogeneous approach jointly addressing both aforementioned problems.

A full answer to question (4) on the applicability of default reasoning techniques in intelligent software systems will have to be given by the final outcome of this research programme. Of course, we have already outlined first architectures for resulting systems. These architectures however will have to evolve along the requirements of challenging applications. A list of corresponding domains, in which default reasoning has already been put to use, was given on Page 4 in Chapter 1. In fact, some first real-world applications, as for instance the configuration of office furniture in the TASSO project (see [BS95b]), already indicate that the utilization of advanced default reasoning methods offers a powerful and effective way of modeling complex domains. Hence, we are optimistic that this technology furnishes new ways of computer programming.

A. Appendix

A.1 Original definition of rational extensions

We repeat here the original definition of a rational extension from [MT95]. In order to distinguish the original notion of a rational extension from that used in Section 4.1.4, we refer in what follows to rational extensions as defined in Definition 4.1.2 as *modified constrained extensions*.

Let D be a set of default rules and define

$$Mon(D) = \left\{ \frac{Prereq(\delta)}{Conseq(\delta)} \;\middle|\; \delta \in D \right\}.$$

Given a set of inference rules A, by $Th^A(\cdot)$ we mean the consequence operator of the formal proof system $PC + A$, consisting of the propositional calculus and the rules in A.

Definition A.1.1. [MT95] *A set A of default rules is active wrt sets of formulas W and S iff it satisfies the following conditions*

    AS1 *Justif$(A) = \emptyset$ or Justif$(A) \cup S$ is consistent,*
    AS2 *Prereq$(A) \subseteq Th^{Mon(A)}(W)$.*

The set of all subsets of a set of default rules D which are active wrt W and S will be denoted by $\mathcal{A}(D, W, S)$.

We define $\mathcal{MA}(D, W, S)$ to be the set of all maximal elements in $\mathcal{A}(D, W, S)$.

Definition A.1.2. [MT95] *Let (D, W) be a default theory. A set of formulas S is called a rational extension for (D, W) if $S = Th^{Mon(A)}(W)$ for some $A \in \mathcal{MA}(D, W, S)$.*

The first half of the equivalence between rational and modified constrained default logic is given in the next theorem.

Theorem A.1.1. [LS96] *Let E be a rational extension for a default theory (D, W) and let $A \in \mathcal{MA}(D, W, E)$ be such that $E = Th^{Mon(A)}(W)$.*

*   If $C = Th(E \cup Justif(A))$ then (E, C) is a modified constrained extension of (D, W).*

The second half is the following one.

Theorem A.1.2. [LS96] *Let (E, C) be a modified constrained extension of default theory (D, W). Then E is a rational extension of (D, W).*

A.2 Modal logic

We follow the definitions in [Bow79] of a Kripke structure (called K–model in the sequel) as a quadruple $\langle \omega_0, \Omega, \mathcal{R}, i \rangle$, where Ω is a non–empty set (also called a set of worlds), $\omega_0 \in \Omega$ a distinguished world, $\mathcal{R}$ a binary relation on Ω (also called the accessibility relation) and i is a function that defines a first order interpretation i_ω for each $\omega \in \Omega$. As usual, a K–model $\langle \omega_0, \Omega, \mathcal{R}, i \rangle$ is such that the domain of i_ω is a subset of the domain of $i_{\omega'}$ whenever $(\omega, \omega') \in \mathcal{R}$.

Formulas in K–models are interpreted using a language enriched in the following way: In a K–model $\langle \omega_0, \Omega, \mathcal{R}, i \rangle$, for each $\omega \in \Omega$, the first order interpretation i_ω is extended so that for each $e \in D_\omega$ (the domain of i_ω), a constant $\bar{e}$ is introduced, letting $i_\omega(\bar{e}) = e$. In every world ω, each term is mapped into an element of D_ω as follows:

$$i_\omega(f(t_1, \ldots, t_n)) = (i_\omega(f))(i_\omega(t_1), \ldots, i_\omega(t_n)), \ n \geq 0.$$

Given a K–model $\mathfrak{k} = \langle \omega_0, \Omega, \mathcal{R}, i \rangle$, the modal entailment relation $\omega \models \alpha$ (in $\mathfrak{k}$) is defined by recursion on the structure of α:

$$
\begin{array}{lll}
\omega \models P(t_1, \ldots, t_n) & \text{iff} & (i_\omega(t_1), \ldots, i_\omega(t_n)) \in i_\omega(P) \\
\omega \models \neg\alpha & \text{iff} & \omega \not\models \alpha \\
\omega \models \alpha \vee \beta & \text{iff} & \omega \models \alpha \text{ or } \omega \models \beta \\
\omega \models \forall x \, \alpha[x] & \text{iff} & \omega \models \alpha[\bar{e}] \text{ for all } e \in D_\omega \\
\omega \models \Box\alpha & \text{iff} & \omega' \models \alpha \text{ whenever } (\omega, \omega') \in \mathcal{R}
\end{array}
$$

We write $\mathfrak{k} \models \alpha$ if $\omega_0 \models \alpha$ (in $\mathfrak{k}$). This means that $\mathfrak{k}$ is a model of α. We denote classes of K–models by $\mathfrak{K}$. We extend the modal entailment relation $\models$ to classes of K–models $\mathfrak{K}$ and write $\mathfrak{K} \models \alpha$ to mean that each element in $\mathfrak{K}$ (that is, a K–model) entails α.

References

[BED92] R. Ben-Eliyahu and R. Dechter. Propositional semantics for default logic. In D. Etherington and H. Kautz, editors, *Working Notes of the 4th International Workshop on Nonmonotonic Reasoning*, pages 13–27, 1992.

[Bes88] P. Besnard. Axiomatizations in the metatheory of nonmonotonic inference systems. In R. Goebel, editor, *Proceedings of Canadian Society for Computational Studies of Intelligence Conference*, pages 117–124, 1988.

[Bes89] P. Besnard. *An Introduction to Default Logic*. Symbolic Computation — Artifical Intelligence. Springer Verlag, 1989.

[BF91] N. Bidoit and C. Froidevaux. General logical databases and programs: Default logic semantics and stratification. *Information and Computation*, 91(1):15–54, 1991.

[BF94] P. Baumgartner and U. Furbach. PROTEIN: A PROver with a Theory Extension INterface. In A. Bundy, editor, *Proceedings of the Conference on Automated Deduction*, volume 814 of *Lecture Notes in Artificial Intelligence*, pages 769–773. Springer Verlag, 1994. System description.

[BH92] F. Baader and B. Hollunder. Embedding defaults into terminological knowledge representation formalisms. In B. Nebel, C. Rich, and W. Swartout, editors, *Proceedings of the Third International Conference on the Principles of Knowledge Representation and Reasoning*, pages 306–317, Cambridge, MA, October 1992.

[BH93] F. Baader and B. Hollunder. How to prefer more specific defaults in terminological default logic. In *Proceedings of the International Joint Conference on Artificial Intelligence*, pages 669–674, 1993.

[BHS93] W. Bibel, S. Hölldobler, and T. Schaub. *Wissensrepräsentation und Inferenz*. Vieweg Verlag, Braunschweig, 1993.

[Bib87] W. Bibel. *Automated Theorem Proving*. Vieweg Verlag, Braunschweig, second edition, 1987.

[BMS91] G. Brewka, D. Makinson, and K. Schlechta. JTMS and logic programming. In W. Marek, A. Nerode, and V. Subrahmanian, editors, *Proceedings of the First International Workshop on Logic Programming and Nonmonotonic Reasoning*, pages 199–210. The MIT Press, 1991.

[Bob80] D. Bobrow, editor. *Special issue on nonmonotonic logic*, volume 13. Artificial Intelligence, 1980.

[Bou91] C. Boutilier. *Conditional Logics for Default Reasoning and Belief Revision*. PhD thesis, University of Toronto, 1991.

[Bou92] C. Boutilier. What is a default priority? In J. Glasgow and B. Hadley, editors, *Proceedings of the Canadian Artificial Intelligence Conference*, pages 148–155. Morgan Kaufmann Publishers, 1992.

[Bow79] K. Bowen. *Model Theory for Modal Logics*. Synthese Library. Reidel, Dordrecht, 1979.

[BQQ83]   P. Besnard, R. Quiniou, and P. Quinton. A theorem-prover for a decidable subset of default logic. In *Proceedings of the AAAI National Conference on Artificial Intelligence*, pages 27–30, 1983.

[Bra93]   S. Brass. On the semantics of supernormal defaults. In Ruzena Bajcsy, editor, *Proceedings of the International Joint Conference on Artificial Intelligence*, pages 578–583. Morgan Kaufmann Publishers, 1993.

[Bre89a]   G. Brewka. *Nonmonotonic Reasoning: From Theoretical Foundation to Efficient Computation*. PhD thesis, Universität Hamburg, Schloß Birlinghoven, Postfach 1240, D-5205 St. Augustin 1, 1989. Revised Version appeared as: Cambridge Tracts in Theoretical Computer Science, Cambridge University Press, 1990.

[Bre89b]   G. Brewka. Preferred subtheories: An extended logical framework for default reasoning. In *Proceedings of the International Joint Conference on Artificial Intelligence*, pages 1043–1048, 1989.

[Bre91a]   G. Brewka. Assertional default theories. In R. Kruse, editor, *Proceedings of European Conference on Symbolic and Quantitative Approaches to Uncertainty*, pages 120–124. Springer Verlag, 1991.

[Bre91b]   G. Brewka. Cumulative default logic: In defense of nonmonotonic inference rules. *Artificial Intelligence*, 50(2):183–205, 1991.

[Bre91c]   G. Brewka. *Nonmonotonic Reasoning: Logical Foundations of Commonsense*. Cambridge University Press, Cambridge, 1991.

[Bre92]   G. Brewka. Exploiting dependency information in nonmonotonic reasoning: A framework for cumulative default logics. Technical report, International Computer Science Institute, 1992.

[Bre94a]   G. Brewka. Adding priorities and specificity to default logic. In L. Pereira and D. Pearce, editors, *European Workshop on Logics in Artificial Intelligence (JELIA'94)*, Lecture Notes in Artificial Intelligence, pages 247–260. Springer Verlag, 1994.

[Bre94b]   G. Brewka. A reconstruction of rescher's theory of formal disputation based on default logic. In A. Cohn, editor, *Proceedings of the European Conference on Artificial Intelligence*, pages 366–370. John Wiley & sons, 1994.

[BS85]   G. Bossu and P. Siegel. Saturation, nonmonotonic reasoning and the closed world assumption. *Artificial Intelligence*, 25:13–63, 1985.

[BS88]   P. Besnard and P. Siegel. The preferential-models approach to non-monotonic logics. In P. Smets, E. Mamdani, D. Dubois, and H. Prade, editors, *Non-Standard Logics for Automated Reasoning*, pages 137–161. Academic Press, 1988.

[BS92]   P. Besnard and T. Schaub. Possible worlds semantics for default logics. In J. Glasgow and B. Hadley, editors, *Proceedings of the Canadian Artificial Intelligence Conference*, pages 148–155. Morgan Kaufmann Publishers, 1992. Also in: D. Etherington and H. Kautz, editors. Proceedings of the Fourth International Workshop on Nonmonotonic Reasoning, AAAI.

[BS93]   P. Besnard and T. Schaub. A context-based framework for default logics. In *Proceedings of the AAAI National Conference on Artificial Intelligence*, pages 406–411. AAAI Press/The MIT Press, 1993.

[BS94]   P. Besnard and T. Schaub. Possible worlds semantics for default logics. *Fundamenta Informaticae*, 21(1-2):39–66, 1994.

[BS95a]   P. Besnard and T. Schaub. An approach to context-based default reasoning. *Fundamenta Informaticae*, 23(2-4):175–223, 1995.

[BS95b]   G. Brewka and T. Schaub. Zur Verwendung nichtmonotoner Inferenztechniken bei der Konfiguration. In F. di Primio, editor, *Methoden der Künstlichen Intelligenz für Grafikanwendungen*, chapter 3, pages 45–60. Addison-Wesley, 1995. In German.

[BS96a]   P. Besnard and T. Schaub. A simple signed system for paraconsistent reasoning. In J.J. Alferes, L.M. Pereira, and E. Orlowska, editors, *Fifth European Workshop* on Logics in Artificial Intelligence (JELIA'96), volume 1126 of Lecture Notes in Artificial Intelligence, pages 404–416. Springer Verlag, 1996.

[BS96b]   S. Brüning and T. Schaub. A model-based approach to consistency-checking. In Z. Ras and M. Michalewicz, editors, Proceedings of the Ninth International Symposium on Methodologies for Intelligent Systems, volume 1079 of Lecture Notes in Artificial Intelligence, pages 315–324. Springer Verlag, 1996.

[CDS94]   M. Cadoli, F. Donini, and M. Schaerf. Is intractability of nonmonotonic reasoning a real drawback. In Proceedings of the AAAI National Conference on Artificial Intelligence, pages 946–951. AAAI Press/The MIT Press, 1994.

[CEG94]   M. Cadoli, T. Eiter, and G. Gottlob. Default logic as a query language. In J. Doyle, P. Torasso, and E. Sandewall, editors, Proceedings of the Fourth International Conference on the Principles of Knowledge Representation and Reasoning, pages 99–108. Morgan Kaufmann Publishers, 1994.

[CF91]   P. Chatalic and C. Froidevaux. Graded logics: A framework for uncertain and defeasible knowledge. In Z. Ras and M. Zemankova, editors, Fifth International Symposium on Methodologies for Intelligent Systems (ISMIS'91), volume 542 of Lecture Notes in Artificial Intelligence, pages 479–489. Springer Verlag, 1991.

[Che80]   B. Chellas. Modal logic: an introduction. Cambridge University Press, 1980.

[Cla78]   K. Clark. Negation as failure. In H. Gallaire and J. Minker, editors, Logic and Data Bases, pages 293–322. Plenum Press, 1978.

[Del87]   J. Delgrande. A first-order conditional logic for prototypical properties. Artificial Intelligence, 33:105–130, 1987.

[Del88]   J. Delgrande. An approach to default reasoning based on a first order conditional logic. Artificial Intelligence, 36:63–90, 1988.

[dGC90]   R. de Guerreiro and M. Casanova. An alternative semantics for default logic. In K. Konolige, editor, Third International Workshop on Nonmonotonic Reasoning, pages 141–157, 1990.

[dGCH90] R. de Guerreiro, M. Casanova, and A. Hermerly. Contributions to a proof theory for generic defaults. In Proceedings of the European Conference on Artificial Intelligence, pages 213–218, 1990.

[Dim93]   Y. Dimopoulos. The computational value of joint consistency. In G. Brewka and C. Witteveen, editors, Dutch/German Workshop on Non-Monotonic Reasoning Techniques and Their Applications, 1993.

[Dix92]   J. Dix. On cumulativity in default logic and its relation to Poole's approach. In B. Neumann, editor, Proceedings of the European Conference on Artificial Intelligence, pages 289–293. John Wiley & sons, 1992.

[DJ91]   J. Delgrande and W. Jackson. Default logic revisited. In J. Allen, R. Fikes, and E. Sandewall, editors, Proceedings of the Second International Conference on the Principles of Knowledge Representation and Reasoning, pages 118–127, San Mateo, CA, April 1991. Morgan Kaufmann Publishers.

[DP60]   M. Davis and H. Putnam. A computing procedure for quantification theory. Journal of the ACM, 7:201–215, 1960.

[dP95]   F. di Primio, editor. Methoden der Künstlichen Intelligenz für Grafikanwendungen. Addison-Wesley, 1995. In German.

[DS93]   J. Delgrande and T. Schaub. On using system Z to generate prioritised default theories. In G. Brewka and C. Witteveen, editors, Dutch/German Workshop on Non-Monotonic Reasoning Techniques and Their Applications, volume 1, 1993.

[DS94a]   J. Delgrande and T. Schaub. A general approach to specificity in default reasoning. In J. Doyle, P. Torasso, and E. Sandewall, editors, Proceedings of the Fourth International Conference on the Principles of Knowledge Representation and Reasoning, pages 146–157. Morgan Kaufmann Publishers, 1994.

[DS94b]   J. Delgrande and T. Schaub. Incorporating specificity into circumscriptive theories. In B. Nebel and L. Dreschler-Fischer, editors, KI'94: Advances in Artificial

Intelligence, Proceedings of the Eighteenth Annual German Conference on Artificial Intelligence, volume 861 of *Lecture Notes in Artificial Intelligence*, pages 272–283. Springer Verlag, 1994.

[DSJ94]   J. Delgrande, T. Schaub, and W. Jackson. Alternative approaches to default logic. *Artificial Intelligence*, 70(1-2):167–237, 1994.

[Ede92]   E. Eder. *Relative Complexities of First Order Calculi*. Vieweg Verlag, Braunschweig, 1992.

[End72]   H. Enderton. *A Mathematical Introduction to Logic*. Academic Press, 1972.

[ER83]   D. Etherington and R. Reiter. On inheritance hierarchies with exceptions. In *Proceedings of the AAAI National Conference on Artificial Intelligence*, pages 104–108, 1983.

[Eth86]   D. Etherington. *Reasoning with Incomplete Information: Investigations of Non-Monotonic Reasoning*. PhD thesis, Department of Computer Science, University of British Columbia, Vancouver, BC, 1986. Revised Version appeared as: Research Notes in AI, Pitman.

[Eth87]   D. Etherington. A semantics for default logic. In *Proceedings of the International Joint Conference on Artificial Intelligence*, pages 495–498, 1987.

[Eth88]   D. Etherington. *Reasoning with Incomplete Information*. Research Notes in Artificial Intelligence. Pitman / Morgan Kaufmann, London, 1988.

[Fah79]   S. Fahlman. *NETL: A system for Representing and Using Real-World Knowledge*. The MIT Press, Cambridge MA, 1979.

[FG90]   C. Froidevaux and C. Grossetête. Graded default theories for uncertainty. In L. Aiello, editor, *Proceedings of the European Conference on Artificial Intelligence*, pages 283–288. Pitman / Morgan Kaufmann, 1990.

[FM94]   C. Froidevaux and J. Mengin. Default logic: A unified view. *Computational Intelligence*, 10(3):331–369, 1994.

[Fro90]   C. Froidevaux. Taxonomic default theories. In *Proceedings of the European Conference on Artificial Intelligence*, pages 123–129, 1990.

[Fro92]   C. Froidevaux. Default logic for action rule-based systems. In B. Neumann, editor, *Proceedings of the European Conference on Artificial Intelligence*, pages 413–417. John Wiley & sons, 1992.

[FUV83]   R. Fagin, J. Ullman, and M. Vardi. On the semantics of updates in databases. preliminary report. In *Proceedings of the Second ACM Conference SIGACT-SIGMOD*, pages 352–365, 1983.

[Gab85]   D. Gabbay. Theoretical foundations for non-monotonic reasoning in expert systems. In K. Apt, editor, *Logics and Models of Concurrent Systems*, pages 439–457. Springer Verlag, Berlin, 1985.

[Gal86]   J. Gallier. *Logic for Computer Science: Foundations of Automated Theorem Proving*. Harper and Row, New York, 1986.

[Gen35]   G. Gentzen. Untersuchungen über das logische Schließen. *Mathematische Zeitschrift*, 39:176–210 and 405–431, 1935. English translation in [Sza69].

[Gin87]   M. Ginsberg, editor. *Readings in Nonmonotonic Reasoning*. Morgan Kaufman, Los Altos, 1987.

[Gin89]   M. Ginsberg. A circumscriprive theorem prover. *Artificial Intelligence*, 39:209–230, 1989.

[Gio93]   L. Giordano. Defining variants of default logic: A modal approach. In *Seventh International Symposium on Methodologies for Intelligent Systems (ISMIS'93)*, pages 59–68. Springer Verlag, 1993.

[Gir87]   J.-Y. Girard. Linear logic. *Theoretical Computer Science*, 50:1–102, 1987.

[GL88]   M. Gelfond and V. Lifschitz. Compiling circumscriptive theories into logic programs: Preliminary report. In *Proceedings of the AAAI National Conference on Artificial Intelligence*, pages 455–459. Morgan Kaufmann Publishers, 1988.

[GL90]   M. Gelfond and V. Lifschitz. Logic programs with classical negation. In *Proceedings of the International Conference on Logic Programming*, pages 579–597, 1990.

[GLMS94] C. Goller, R. Letz, K. Mayr, and J. Schumann. SETHEO V3.2: Recent Developments. In A. Bundy, editor, *Proceedings of the Conference on Automated Deduction*, volume 814 of *Lecture Notes in Artificial Intelligence*, pages 778–782. Springer Verlag, 1994. System abstract.

[GLPT91] M. Gelfond, V. Lifschitz, H. Przymusinska, and M. Truszczyński. Disjunctive defaults. In J. Allen, R. Fikes, and E. Sandewall, editors, *Proceedings of the Second International Conference on the Principles of Knowledge Representation and Reasoning*, pages 230–237, San Mateo, CA, April 1991. Morgan Kaufmann Publishers.

[GM94]   L. Giordano and A. Martinelli. On cumulative default logics. *Artificial Intelligence*, 66(1):161–179, 1994.

[Got92]   G. Gottlob. Complexity results for nonmonotonic logics. *Journal of Logic and Computation*, 2(3):397–425, June 1992.

[GP90]   M. Goldszmith and J. Pearl. On the relation between rational closure and system-z^*. In K. Konolige, editor, *Third International Workshop on Nonmonotonic Reasoning*, pages 130–140, 1990.

[Gro91]   B. Grosof. Generalizing prioritization. In J. Allen, R. Fikes, and E. Sandewall, editors, *Proceedings of the Second International Conference on the Principles of Knowledge Representation and Reasoning*, San Mateo, CA, April 1991. Morgan Kaufmann Publishers.

[Hew72]   C. Hewitt. *Description and theoretical analysis (using schemata) of PLANNER: A language for proving theorems and manipulating models in a robot*. PhD thesis, MIT, Department of Mathematics, 1972. AI Lab Report AI-TR-258.

[Hun95]   A. Hunter. Using default logic in information retrieval. In C. Froidevaux and J. Kohlas, editors, *Proceedings of European Conference on Symbolic and Quantitative Approaches to Reasoning and Uncertainty*, volume 946 of *Lecture Notes in Artificial Intelligence*, pages 235–242. Springer Verlag, 1995.

[Hun96]   A. Hunter. Reasoning about 'aboutness' using default logic. In *International Conference on Tools with Artificial Intelligence*. IEEE Computer Society Press, 1996. To appear.

[IH89]   K. Inoue and N. Helft. On theorem provers for circumscription. ICOT Research Center, 1-4-28 Mita, Minato-ku, Tokyo 108, Japan, December 1989. Forthcoming: ICOT Technical Report No. 527.

[JB91]   U. Junker and G. Brewka. Handling partially ordered defaults in TMS. In *Proceedings of the First European Conference on Symbolic and Quantitative Aspects for Uncertainty*, Marseille, France, 1991.

[JK90]   U. Junker and K. Konolige. Computing the extensions of autoepistemic and default logic with a TMS. In *Proceedings of the AAAI National Conference on Artificial Intelligence*, 1990.

[JP92]   U. Junker and J. Paulokat. Logic-based methods for design. Unpublished manuscript., 1992.

[KLM90] S. Kraus, D. Lehmann, and M. Magidor. Nonmonotonic reasoning, preferential models and macro generations. *Artificial Intelligence*, 44(1-2):167–208, July 1990.

[KM91]   H. Katsuno and A. Mendelzon. On the difference between updating a knowledge database and revising it. In J. Allen, R. Fikes, and E. Sandewall, editors, *Proceedings of the Second International Conference on the Principles of Knowledge Representation and Reasoning*, pages 387–394, San Mateo, CA, April 1991. Morgan Kaufmann Publishers.

[Kon88a] K. Konolige. Hierarchic autoepistemic theories for nonmonotonic reasoning. In *Proceedings of the AAAI National Conference on Artificial Intelligence*, pages 439–443. Morgan Kaufmann Publishers, 1988.

[Kon88b] K. Konolige. On the relation between default and autoepistemic logic. *Artificial Intelligence*, 35(2):343–382, 1988.

[Lé91] F. Lévy. Computing extensions of default theories. In R. Kruse and P. Siegel, editors, *Proceedings of the European Conference on Symbolic and Quantitative Approaches for Uncertainty*, volume 548 of *Lecture Notes in Computer Science*, pages 219–226. Springer Verlag, 1991.

[LBSB92] R. Letz, S. Bayerl, J. Schumann, and W. Bibel. SETHEO: A high-performance theorem prover. *Journal of Automated Reasoning*, 8(2):183–212, 1992.

[Lev90] H. Levesque. All I know: A study in autoepistemic logic. *Artificial Intelligence*, 42(2-3):213–261, 1990.

[Lif84] V. Lifschitz. Some results on circumscription. In *Proceedings of the First International Workshop on Nonmonotonic Reasoning, New Paltz, NY*. Proceedings of the AAAI National Conference on Artificial Intelligence, 1984.

[Lif85a] V. Lifschitz. Closed-world databases and circumscription. *Artificial Intelligence*, 27:229–235, 1985.

[Lif85b] V. Lifschitz. Computing circumscription. In *Proceedings of the International Joint Conference on Artificial Intelligence*, pages 121–127, 1985.

[Lif86] V. Lifschitz. On the satisfiabiltity of circumscription. *Artificial Intelligence*, 28:17–27, 1986.

[Lif87] V. Lifschitz. Pointwise circumscription. In M. Ginsberg, editor, *Readings in Nonmonotonic Reasoning*, chapter 3.3, pages 179–193. Morgan Kaufman, 1987.

[Lif89] V. Lifschitz. Between circumscription and autoepitemic logic. In R. Brachman, H. Levesque, and R. Reiter, editors, *Proceedings of the First International Conference on the Principles of Knowledge Representation and Reasoning*, pages 235–244, Los Altos, CA, May 1989. Morgan Kaufmann Publishers.

[Lif90] V. Lifschitz. On open defaults. In J. W. Lloyd, editor, *Computational Logic*, pages 80–95, Berlin, 1990. Springer Verlag.

[Lif91] V. Lifschitz. Nonmonotonic databases and epistemic queries. In J. Myopoulos and R. Reiter, editors, *Proceedings of the International Joint Conference on Artificial Intelligence*, pages 381–386, San Mateo, CA, 1991. Morgan Kaufmann Publishers.

[Llo87] J. Lloyd. *Foundations of Logic Programming*. Symbolic Computation. Springer Verlag, 2nd edition, 1987.

[LMR92] J. Lobo, J. Minker, and A. Rajasekar. *Foundations of Disjunctive Logic Programming*. The MIT Press, Cambridge, MA, 1992.

[Lov78] D. Loveland. *Automated Theorem Proving: A Logical Basis*. North-Holland, New York, 1978.

[LS95] T. Linke and T. Schaub. Lemma handling in default logic theorem provers. In C. Froidevaux and J. Kohlas, editors, *Proceedings of European Conference on Symbolic and Quantitative Approaches to Reasoning and Uncertainty*, volume 946 of *Lecture Notes in Artificial Intelligence*, pages 285–292. Springer Verlag, 1995.

[LS96] T. Linke and T. Schaub. Putting default logics in perspective. In G. Görz and S. Hölldobler, editors, *Advances in Artificial Intelligence, Proceedings of the Twentieth Annual German Conference on Artificial Intelligence*, Lecture Notes in Artificial Intelligence, pages 241–252. Springer Verlag, 1996.

[LS97] T. Linke and T. Schaub. Towards a classification of default logics. *Journal of Applied Non-Classical Logics*, 7(4):397–451, 1997.

[Łuk85] W. Łukaszewicz. Two results on default logic. In *Proceedings of the International Joint Conference on Artificial Intelligence*, pages 459–461, 1985.

[Łuk88]   W. Łukaszewicz. Considerations on default logic — an alternative approach. *Computational Intelligence*, 4:1–16, 1988.

[Łuk90]   W. Łukaszewicz. *Non-monotonic reasoning: formalizations of commonsense reasoning*. Artificial Intelligence. Ellis Horwood, 1990.

[Mac91]   C. MacNish. Hierarchical default logic. In R. Kruse and P. Siegel, editors, *Proceedings of the European Conference on Symbolic and Quantitative Approaches to Uncertainty*, volume 548 of *Lecture Notes in Computer Science*. Springer Verlag, 1991.

[Mak89]   D. Makinson. General theory of cumulative inference. In M. Reinfrank, J. de Kleer, M. Ginsberg, and E. Sandewall, editors, *Proceedings of the Second International Workshop on Non-Monotonic Reasoning*, volume 346 of *Lecture Notes in Artificial Intelligence*, pages 1–18. Springer Verlag, 1989.

[Mak94]   D. Makinson. General patterns in nonmonotonic reasoning. In D. Gabbay, C. Hogger, and J. Robinson, editors, *Handbook of Logic in Artificial Intelligence and Logic Programming*, volume 1, pages 35–110. Oxford University Press, 1994.

[McC80]   J. McCarthy. Circumscription — a form of nonmonotonic reasoning. *Artificial Intelligence*, 13(1-2):27–39, 1980.

[McC86]   J. McCarthy. Applications of circumscription to formalizing common-sense knowledge. *Artificial Intelligence*, 28:89–116, 1986.

[McD82]   D. McDermott. Nonmonotonic logic II: Nonmonotonic modal theories. *Journal of the ACM*, 29(1):33–57, 1982.

[MD80]   D. McDermott and J. Doyle. Nonmonotonic logic I. *Artificial Intelligence*, 13(1-2):41–72, 1980.

[Mer88]   R. Mercer. Using default logic to derive natural language suppositions. In *Proceedings of Canadian Society for Computational Studies of Intelligence Conference*, pages 14–21, 1988.

[MG90]   D. Makinson and P. Gärdenfors. Relations between the logic of theory change and nonmonotonic logic. In A. Fuhrmann and M. Morreau, editors, *The Logic of Theory Change*, pages 185–205. Springer Verlag, Berlin, 1990.

[Min75]   M. Minsky. A framework for representing knowledge. In P. Winston, editor, *The Psychology of Computer Vision*, pages 211–277. McGraw-Hill, New York, 1975.

[MNR90]   W. Marek, A. Nerode, and J. Remmel. A theory of nonmonotonic rule systems. *Annals of Mathematics and Artificial Intelligence*, 1:241–273, 1990.

[Moo85]   R. Moore. Semantical considerations on nonmonotonic logics. *Artificial Intelligence*, 25:75–94, 1985.

[MR94]   Y. Moinard and R. Rolland. Preferential entailments for circumscriptions. In J. Doyle, P. Torasso, and E. Sandewall, editors, *Proceedings of the Fourth International Conference on the Principles of Knowledge Representation and Reasoning*, pages 461–472. Morgan Kaufmann Publishers, 1994.

[MST91]   W. Marek, G. F. Schwarz, and M. Truszczyński. Modal nonmonotonic logic: ranges, characterization, computation. In J. Allen, R. Fikes, and E. Sandewall, editors, *Proceedings of the Second International Conference on the Principles of Knowledge Representation and Reasoning*, pages 395–404, San Mateo, CA, April 1991. Morgan Kaufmann Publishers.

[MT]   A. Mikitiuk and M. Truszczyński. Default reasoning system. http://www.cs.engr.uky.edu/ lpnmr/DeReS.html.

[MT89]   W. Marek and M. Truszczyński. Relating autoepistemic and default logics. In R. Brachman, H. Levesque, and R. Reiter, editors, *Proceedings of the First International Conference on the Principles of Knowledge Representation and Reasoning*, pages 276–288, Los Altos, CA, May 1989. Morgan Kaufmann Publishers.

[MT93a]   W. Marek and M. Truszczyński. *Nonmonotonic logic: context-dependent reasoning*. Artifical Intelligence. Springer Verlag, 1993.

[MT93b] W. Marek and M. Truszczyński. Normal form results for default logics. In G. Brewka, K. Jantke, and P. Schmitt, editors, *Nonmonotonic and Inductive Logic*, volume 659 of *Lecture Notes in Artificial Intelligence*, pages 153–174. Springer Verlag, 1993.

[MT93c] A. Mikitiuk and M. Truszczyński. Rational default logic and disjunctive logic programming. In A. Nerode and L. Pereira, editors, *Proceedings of the Second International Workshop on logic Programming and Non-monotonic Reasoning.*, pages 283–299. MIT Press, 1993.

[MT95] A. Mikitiuk and M. Truszczyński. Rational versus constrained default logic. In C. Mellish, editor, *Proceedings of the International Joint Conference on Artificial Intelligence*, pages 1509–1515. Morgan Kaufmann Publishers, 1995.

[Nie88] I. Niemelä. Decision procedure for autoepistemic logic. In *Proceedings of the Conference on Automated Deduction*, pages 675–684, Argonne, USA, 1988.

[Nie94] I. Niemelä. A decision method for nonmonotonic reasoning based on autoepistemic reasoning. In J. Doyle, P. Torasso, and E. Sandewall, editors, *Proceedings of the Fourth International Conference on the Principles of Knowledge Representation and Reasoning*, pages 473–484. Morgan Kaufmann Publishers, 1994.

[Nie95] I. Niemelä. Towards efficient default reasoning. In C. Mellish, editor, *Proceedings of the International Joint Conference on Artificial Intelligence*, pages 312–318. Morgan Kaufmann Publishers, 1995.

[Nil86] N. Nilsson. Probabilistic logic. *Artificial Intelligence*, 28:71–87, 1986.

[NS91] G. Neugebauer and T. Schaub. A pool-based connection calculus. Technical Report AIDA-91-2, FG Intellektik, FB Informatik, TH Darmstadt, Alexanderstraße 10, D-64283 Darmstadt, Germany, January 1991.

[Pea88] J. Pearl. *Probabilistic Reasoning in Intelligent Systems: Networks of Plausible Inference*. Morgan Kaufmann, Los Altos CA, 1988.

[Pea89] J. Pearl. Probabilistic semantics for nonmonotonic reasoning: A survey. In R. Brachman, H. Levesque, and R. Reiter, editors, *Proceedings of the First International Conference on the Principles of Knowledge Representation and Reasoning*, pages 505–516. Morgan Kaufmann Publishers, 1989.

[Pea90] J. Pearl. System Z: A natural ordering of defaults with tractable applications to default reasoning. In R. Parikh, editor, *Proceedings of Theoretical Aspects of Reasoning about Knowledge*, pages 121–135. Morgan Kaufmann Publishers, San Mateo, 1990.

[Pea94] D. Pearce. Default logic and constructive logic. In B. Neumann, editor, *Proceedings of the European Conference on Artificial Intelligence*, pages 309–313. John Wiley & sons, 1994.

[Per87] C. Perrault. An application of default logic to speech act theory. Technical Report CSLI-87-90, Stanford University, 1987.

[PGA87] D. Poole, R. Goebel, and R. Aleliunas. Theorist: A logical reasoning system for defaults and diagnosis. In N. Cercone and G. McCalla, editors, *The Knowledge Frontier: Essays in the Representation of Knowledge*, chapter 13, pages 331–352. Springer Verlag, New York, 1987.

[Poo88] D. Poole. A logical framework for default reasoning. *Artificial Intelligence*, 36:27–47, 1988.

[Poo89a] D. Poole. Explanation and prediction: An architecture for default and abductive reasoning. *Computational Intelligence*, 5:97–110, 1989.

[Poo89b] D. Poole. What the lottery paradox tells us about default reasoning. In R. Brachman, H. Levesque, and R. Reiter, editors, *Proceedings of the First International Conference on the Principles of Knowledge Representation and Reasoning*, pages 333–340, Los Altos, CA, May 1989. Morgan Kaufmann Publishers.

[Poo91] D. Poole. Compiling a default reasoning system into prolog. *New Generation Computing*, 9(1):3–38, 1991.

[Poo94] D. Poole. Default logic. In D. Gabbay, C. Hogger, and J. Robinson, editors, *Handbook of Logic in Artificial Intelligence and Logic Programming*, volume 1, pages 189–215. Oxford University Press, 1994.

[PP92] H. Przymusinska and T. Przymusinski. Stationary default extensions. In D. Etherington and H. Kautz, editors, *Working Notes of the 4th International Workshop on Nonmonotonic Reasoning*, pages 179–193, 1992.

[Rad96] A. Radzikowska. A three-valued approach to default logic. *Journal of Applied Non-Classical Logics*, 6(2):149–190, 1996.

[RC81] R. Reiter and G. Criscuolo. On interacting defaults. In *Proceedings of the International Joint Conference on Artificial Intelligence*, pages 270–276, 1981.

[Rei77] R. Reiter. On closed world data bases. In H. Gallaire and J.-M. Nicolas, editors, *Proceedings of Workshop on Logic and Databases*, pages 119–140. Plenum, Toulouse, France, 1977.

[Rei78] R. Reiter. On closed world data bases. In H. Gallaire and J. Minker, editors, *Logic and Databases*, pages 55–76. Plenum Press, New York, 1978.

[Rei80] R. Reiter. A logic for default reasoning. *Artificial Intelligence*, 13(1-2):81–132, 1980.

[Rei87a] R. Reiter. Nonmonotonic reasoning. *Annual Review of Computer Science*, 2:147–187, 1987.

[Rei87b] R. Reiter. A theory of diagnosis from first principles. *Artificial Intelligence*, 32(1):57–96, 1987.

[Ris93] V. Risch. *Les Tableaux Analytiques au Service des Logiques de Defauts*. PhD thesis, Universite Aix-Marseille II, G.I.A., Parc Scientifique et Technologique de Luminy, April 1993.

[Ris95a] V. Risch. On the cumulativity of justified default logic. Unpublished manuscript, 1995.

[Ris95b] V. Risch. Yet some more considerations on cumulativity in default logics. In C. Froidevaux and J. Kohlas, editors, *Proceedings of European Conference on Symbolic and Quantitative Approaches to Reasoning and Uncertainty*, volume 946 of *Lecture Notes in Artificial Intelligence*, pages 364–378. Springer Verlag, 1995.

[Rot93] A. Rothschild. Algorithmische Untersuchungen zu Defaultlogiken. Diplomarbeit, FG Intellektik, FB Informatik, TH Darmstadt, Alexanderstraße 10, D-64283 Darmstadt, Germany, 1993.

[Ryc91] P. Rychlik. Some variants of default logic. In *Proceedings of the AAAI National Conference on Artificial Intelligence*, pages 373–378, 1991.

[Sch90a] T. Schaub. Nichtmonotone Logiken und ein Default-Beweiser. Diplomarbeit, Technische Hochschule Darmstadt, Alexanderstraße 10, D-64283 Darmstadt, Germany, May 1990. In German.

[Sch90b] C. Schwind. A tableaux-based theorem prover for a decidable subset of default logic. In M. Stickel, editor, *Proceedings of the Conference on Automated Deduction*. Springer Verlag, 1990.

[Sch91a] T. Schaub. Assertional default theories: A semantical view. In J. Allen, R. Fikes, and E. Sandewall, editors, *Proceedings of the Second International Conference on the Principles of Knowledge Representation and Reasoning*, pages 496–506, San Mateo, CA, April 1991. Morgan Kaufmann Publishers.

[Sch91b] T. Schaub. On commitment and cumulativity in default logics. In R. Kruse and P. Siegel, editors, *Proceedings of European Conference on Symbolic and Quantitative Approaches to Uncertainty*, pages 304–309. Springer Verlag, 1991.

[Sch92a] T. Schaub. *Considerations on Default Logics*. Dissertation, Technische Hochschule Darmstadt, Alexanderstraße 10, D-64283 Darmstadt, Germany, November 1992.

[Sch92b] T. Schaub. On constrained default theories. In B. Neumann, editor, *Proceedings of the European Conference on Artificial Intelligence*, pages 304–308. John Wiley & sons, 1992.

[Sch93]   T. Schaub. Variations of constrained default logic. In M. Clarke, R. Kruse, and S. Moral, editors, *Proceedings of European Conference on Symbolic and Quantitative Approaches to Reasoning and Uncertainty*, pages 312–317. Springer Verlag, 1993.

[Sch94a] T. Schaub. Computing queries from prioritized default theories. In Z. Ras and M. Zemankova, editors, *Proceedings of the Eighth International Symposium on Methodologies for Intelligent Systems (ISMIS'94)*, volume 869 of *Lecture Notes in Artificial Intelligence*, pages 584–593. Springer Verlag, 1994.

[Sch94b] T. Schaub. A new methodology for query-answering in default logics via structure-oriented theorem proving. Technical report, IRISA, Campus de Beaulieu, F-35042 Rennes Cedex, France, January 1994.

[Sch95a] T. Schaub. *Automatisation de raisonnements à partir d'informations incomplètes: Des bases sémantiques à une mise en œuvre efficace.* Mémoire d'habilitation à diriger des recherches, Université de Rennes I, Campus de Beaulieu, F-35042 Rennes Cedex, January 1995. In French.

[Sch95b] T. Schaub. A new methodology for query-answering in default logics via structure-oriented theorem proving. *Journal of Automated Reasoning*, 15(1):95–165, 1995.

[Sho86]   Y. Shoham. *Reasoning About Change: Time and Causation from the Standpoint of Artificial Intelligence*. PhD thesis, Yale University, 1986.

[Shv90]   G. Shvarts. Autoepistemic modal logic. In R. Parikh, editor, *Proceedings of Theoretical Aspects of Reasoning about Knowledge*, pages 97–109, San Mateo, 1990. Morgan Kaufmann Publishers.

[Sla93]   J. Slaney. SCOTT: A model-guided theorem prover. In *Proceedings of the International Joint Conference on Artificial Intelligence*, pages 109–114, 1993.

[Som90]   Léa Sombé. *Reasoning about incomplete information in Artificial Intelligence.* John Wiley & sons, New York, 1990.

[SR91]   C. Schwind and V. Risch. A tableaux-based characterization for default logic. In R. Kruse, editor, *Proceedings of European Conference on Symbolic and Quantitative Approaches to Uncertainty*, pages 310–317. Springer Verlag, 1991.

[SR94]   C. Schwind and V. Risch. Tableau-based characterization and theorem proving for default logic. *Journal of Automated Reasoning*, 13:223–242, 1994.

[SS93]   P. Siegel and C. Schwind. Modal logic based theory for non-monotonic reasoning. *Journal of Applied Non-Classical Logics*, 3(1):73–92, 1993.

[ST95]   T. Schaub and M. Thielscher. A method for skeptical reasoning in constrained default logic. In G. Brewka and C. Witteveen, editors, *Second Dutch/German Workshop on Non-Monotonic Reasoning Techniques and Their Applications*, 1995.

[Sti89]   M. Stickel. A Prolog technology theorem prover: A new exposition and implementation in prolog. Technical Report Technical Note 464, Stanford Research Institute (SRI), 1989.

[Sti90]   M. Stickel. A Prolog technology theorem prover. In M. Stickel, editor, *Proceedings of the Conference on Automated Deduction*, volume 449 of *Lecture Notes in Artificial Intelligence*, pages 673–674. Springer Verlag, 1990.

[SWC71]   G. Sussman, T. Winograd, and E. Charniak. *Micro-PLANNER Reference Manual*, 1971. Memo no. 203A.

[Sza69]   M. Szabo, editor. *The collected papers of Gerhard Gentzen.* North-Holland, 1969.

[Tar36]   A. Tarski. Der Wahrheitsbegriff in formalisierten Sprachen. *Studia Philosophica*, 1, 1936.

[Thi93]   M. Thielscher. On prediction in Theorist. *Artificial Intelligence*, 60(2):283–292, 1993.

[Tou86] D. Touretzky. *The Mathematics of Inheritance Systems.* Morgan Kaufmann Publishers, 1986.

[Tru91a] M. Truszczyński. Embedding default logic into modal nonmonotonic logics. In W. Marek, A. Nerode, and V. Subrahmanian, editors, *Proceedings of the First International Workshop on Logic Programming and Nonmonotonic Reasoning*, pages 151–165. MIT Press, 1991.

[Tru91b] M. Truszczyński. Modal interpretations of default logic. In *Proceedings of the International Joint Conference on Artificial Intelligence*, pages 393–398. Morgan Kaufmann Publishers, 1991.

[TS95] M. Thielscher and T. Schaub. Default reasoning by deductive planning. *Journal of Automated Reasoning*, 15(1):1–40, 1995.

[TT92] Y. Tan and J. Treur. Constructive default logic and the control of defeasible reasoning. In B. Neumann, editor, *Proceedings of the European Conference on Artificial Intelligence*, pages 299–303. John Wiley & sons, 1992.

[Tur97] H. Turner. Representing actions in logic programs and default theories: A situation calculus approach,. *Journal of Logic Programming*, 1997. To appear.

[Zad75] L. Zadeh. Fuzzy logic and approximate reasoning. *Synthese*, 30:407–428, 1975.

[Zad83] L. Zadeh. Commonsense knowledge representation based on fuzzy logic. *IEEE Computer*, 16(10):61–66, 1983.

[Zav94] G. Zaverucha. A prioritized contextual default logic: Curing anomalous extensions with a simple abnormality default theory. In B. Nebel and L. Dreschler-Fischer, editors, *Proceedings of Eighteenth Annual German Conference on Artificial Intelligence (KI'94)*. Springer Verlag, 1994.

[ZM90] A. Zhang and W. Marek. On the classification and existence of structures in default logic. *Fundamenta Informaticae*, 8(4):485–499, 1990.

Springer
and the
environment

At Springer we firmly believe that an international science publisher has a special obligation to the environment, and our corporate policies consistently reflect this conviction.
We also expect our business partners – paper mills, printers, packaging manufacturers, etc. – to commit themselves to using materials and production processes that do not harm the environment. The paper in this book is made from low- or no-chlorine pulp and is acid free, in conformance with international standards for paper permanency.

Springer

Lecture Notes in Artificial Intelligence (LNAI)

Lecture Notes in Computer Science